WOOZIE
(AKA Grandmother)
WISDOM
(About Life, Sex, Love)

Woozie (AKA Grandmother) Wisdom (About Life, Sex, Love)

Lynn Hubschman

iUniverse®

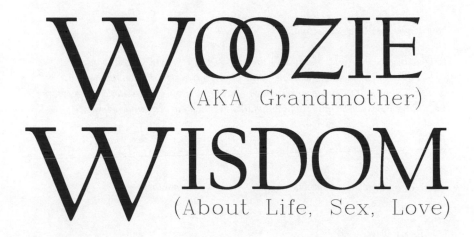

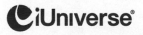

WOOZIE (AKA GRANDMOTHER)
WISDOM (ABOUT LIFE, SEX, LOVE)

iUniverse books may be ordered through booksellers or by contacting:

iUniverse
1663 Liberty Drive
Bloomington, IN 47403
www.iuniverse.com
1-800-Authors (1-800-288-4677)

ISBN: 978-1-5320-0801-6 (sc)
ISBN: 978-1-5320-0800-9 (e)

Library of Congress Control Number: 2016915759

Print information available on the last page.

iUniverse rev. date: 01/31/2017

Foreword

WHEN IT COMES TO SEX, love and relationships, Woozie Wisdom offers unique insights into the trials and tribulations of intimate relationships. As a sexuality and relationship educator and therapist, I have long described a *relationship* as one of the most joyful and one of the most painful experiences that we can choose to engage in.

Woozie Wisdom speaks to these issues and the emotions that many of us experience in our relationships. Each chapter offers heart-felt awareness, straightforward illuminations, and new insights into the relationships we live and the people we love. For example, the chapter ***Talk to Me*** speaks to the many ways in which we can communicate to create and maintain intimacy. Intimacy goes far beyond just our words. It encompasses our actions and intentions. ***Lovers are Made Not Born*** helps us understand the power of teaching our partners how to please us sexually. Communication is key to sexual satisfaction. ***Morphing of Sex*** reminds us that sex is an exploration of the senses more than it is a task to be completed. Variety truly is the spice of life. ***Get a Grip*** encourages us to be mindful of all the little complaints we have about our partners and to see how they can affect a relationship. ***A Broken Heart is Absolutely Necessary*** emphasizes that to truly love is to be vulnerable. Love opens our hearts to great pleasures and great pains and these pains only make us stronger. Each chapter in this book tells us how to be better partners, better lovers, and better people.

Lynn Hubschman is a true pioneer to the field of sex and relational intimacy. She has dedicated her life to inspiring others to have happier and healthier sexual relationships. Her positive and thoughtful energy, along with her *tell it like it is* style of writing, can be seen throughout this book. Read it, live it, and enjoy!

Chris Fariello, PhD, MA, LMFT
Founder and Director- Philadelphia Institute for Individual, Relational & Sex Therapy
Past-President of the Pennsylvania Association for Marriage and Family Therapy
AASECT Certified Sexuality Educator, Therapist & Supervisor
Adjunct Professor, Drexel University
AAMFT Approved Supervisor
Author: 99 Things Parents Wish They Knew Before Having THE Talk
And; The Lovers Guide Illustrated Encyclopedia: the definitive guide to sex and you

Preface

Yes, I am Woozie!

The name was given to me by my first grandchild, Daniel. He heard my husband call me that as an endearing name and assumed that was my name. The two granddaughters, Alina and Amelia, who followed, carried it on.

As a therapist, with a Diplomate in Social Work, I have always had a private practice in marriage and relationship counseling. In addition, I have been a sex educator for decades. My background includes a broad range of experiences with all sorts of people.

For ten years I was Director of Family Life Education at Jewish Family Service in Philadelphia and I have spoken to over two-hundred and fifty groups a year. Teaching at the graduate level and leading seminars for police, prison guards, nurses, teachers, and physicians brought me another dimension.

Writing articles, two books, one on transsexuals, and being on national TV talk shows regularly, gave me an additional perspective.

As the Director of Social Work for 15 years at Pennsylvania Hospital, America's oldest hospital in Philadelphia, I pioneered many new and innovative hospital and community services.

All of this is in addition to my 'regular' life with a wide range of people.

This vast life experience is what has offered me the 'wisdom' I now wish to share.

It started out as my blog, where the response and need for this book became clear.

My goal has always been to bring insight, and aid in preventing problems and finding solutions to life before the situations become intolerable or destructive.

We have enough proof and experience to know how to help and this book in just such an effort in that behalf.

Learn and enjoy at the same time!

Dedication

For:

Emil: Who named me

Jody and Tracy: Who made

Daniel, Alina, Amelia: For whom I will

forever be their Woozie

Contents

Section III - Love

The Art of Living

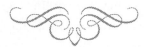

"THERE ARE FEW PEOPLE WHOM I really love, and still fewer of whom I think well. The more I see of the world, the more I am dissatisfied with it; and every day confirms my belief of the inconsistency of all human characters, and of the little dependence that can be placed on the appearance of merit or sense." - Jane Austen

Sound pessimistic? You bet! Well, I am here to tell you that it need not be that way in your own personal life.

The trick to this life, I believe, is to search for your personal joy and go after it!

Do not get me wrong I know about the mundane daily things that need attention and work, and earning money, and all the crap that can come out of the blue. The real heroes are the parents who care for sick or damaged children every day, the military who put their lives on the line for our country, and all the suffering people who through no fault of their own are damaged and struggle just to survive.

There is no perfect… anything or anyone. The rules we all live by are set by those in some sort of power and usually for their own benefit in the end so what do we do?

We have choice… ALWAYS, about how we live, what we think, and how we go about our lives. There is ALWAYS choice!

True, many people just go through as robots, do what is "expected", and never question what their lives are about. The smart ones always take a step back, look, evaluate, and change or move on.

Now there are many, many people who are afraid, insecure, dependent on others' opinions, or just not emotionally developed, and they remain unfulfilled for life. Tragic.

There is no school for life and no love expert 'on call.' There should be.

Joy can come from a variety of sources; for some it is in nature, for others it is spiritual, for many, it is in intellect and knowledge, and for a whole bunch, it comes from being productive. HOWEVER, I am here to tell you none of it will do what succumbing to love offers.

There will always be points of hesitancy or ambivalence in what we do, but to move ahead, take that leap of faith, and pull from a visceral spot in you is what will ultimately give true joy. There is always pain with loving and that is a given, but it is worth it. Truly.

Otherwise, you are merely existing and accommodating, not living in a total sense.

This is hard to deal with and harder still to do.

Love will cause you to do things you never dreamed you were capable of. It will force you to give up pride, and it is complete surrender. The beloved is the reason for being and you will do anything to please him or her.

It is the females who have the leverage by saying yes or no to intimacy. That may sound sexist and I am because we are different, for millions of years. No amount of talking or research can change what a man or woman are at the core. Bravo for the differences!!

While you cannot wind your life back you can take a deep look inside yourself and move toward loving which in turn will result in your being loved.

That is a real art!!

"We are most alive when we're in love." - John Updike

Could You Prove You're Human?

"THE GOOD LIFE IS ONE inspired by love and guided by knowledge." - Bertrand Russell

In 2009 Brian Christian, a poet with degrees in computer science and philosophy won the famous and somewhat controversial Turing test. This involves the AI, (artificial intelligence), community pitting themselves against sophisticated software programs to determine if computers can 'think.'

What is fascinating is that a computer can converse in such a way that it is difficult for a panel of judges to really know which is computer and which is a human!

Imagine… and so I began thinking how indeed do we know we are human?

Well, think about it. What makes us flesh and blood besides flesh and blood?

We are unique in that we can be self-aware, we can immerse ourselves in activities where we are like machines or animals BUT we alone are able to be self-conscious and THINK about our actions. We also like immediate feedback and are curious in a special way, and can try to improve ourselves. We have imagination and can be creative.

All of this is reviewed in Christian's book, "The Most Human, Human." While a bit difficult for me to read it offers fascinating ideas about this whole area.

Which brings me to the next question; can love be taught?

The attraction that is visceral is just there… no one teaches how to feel in that sense.

The sex drive pulls you and that's that. Yes, you can think about the person in a variety of ways but the emotional part is either there or it's not from the minute you lay eyes on one another. What you do about it and how you handle it all is what this blog is always about and the concerns never end. Thank goodness!

At any rate I have been advocating an EQ, (emotional quotient), forever, as more important than the old IQ.

Now there are a number of programs starting with small children in schools exploring this business; teaching empathy and how to handle strong feelings in constructive ways.

Just imagine a world where people could remedy grievances and hurt feelings in a caring fashion. Today problems and anger are dealt with, with guns, not even fists any more. Awful… and stupid.

Sure, we are all interested in self-preservation and maintaining our equilibrium or power or control, but could we do it better?

You bet!

Adults learn from childhood how to express or not express their feelings. Some of it is fine but a lot of it is destructive for the individual in the end.

Just watch the news, local, national, or worldwide. How is any of it being handled? Even with UN helmets on the human condition comes through many times in a negative self-defeating manner.

Even where love is coupled with passion in intimate relationships raw negative feelings can erode the positive and ruin a good thing. So, what can you expect from strangers?

Strong emotions cannot be avoided and MUST be expressed. The question is how.

This new looking at social emotional training is not easy and there are no good easy answers or curriculum to follow... yet. That the issue is on the table and being explored is a great first step. Hopefully the planet will be around long enough to make some headway!!

In an article, "Can Emotional Intelligence Be Taught?" in the New York Times September 11, 2013, by Jennifer Kahn, one of the programs reported teaching students about taking a few deep breaths before acting out angrily. One of the researchers said that for him, taking three deep breaths only made him want to think about how he might go about wringing the person's neck!!! So, see it ain't easy and it is different for each of us.

What we can learn are the many ways to deal with feelings and how to react to them. The good ones need help sometimes too, not just bad feelings.

All of this is to say we are human and can show it in many forms BUT the best is by loving that special someone and all else radiates from there.

"Love must be learned, and learned again and again; there is no end to it. Hate needs no instruction, but waits only to be provoked." - Katherine Anne Porter

Do We Have Any Role Models Today?

"WHEN YOU REACH FOR THE stars, you may not quite get them, but you won't come up with a handful of mud either." - Leo Burnett

"Trust yourself. You know more than you think you do." - Benjamin Spock

Have you ever watched Jay Leno and his bit on Jaywalking? Well, he stops people on the street and asks some usually basic questions, like who the person is in the picture... vice-president, for example. You would be amazed at how many people old and young, mostly educated who know little. It is a disgrace for our educational system and the lack of information. It is our country's most troubling problem I think.

So I thought about it and decided to ask a few people about whom they admired; some living and some dead.

A few gave me a list but surprisingly the young people from sixteen to twenty-three that I queried felt they had none and they were 'their own person' and did not look to anyone else. So, no role models? Maybe too full of themselves, or whatever. They were all probably spoiled and fairly narcissistic or too young and inexperienced in life to look at others as models. One told me the system of whom Americans value was not a good one: materialistic. Maybe he's right about a large group of people, but not all.

Another is full of herself and confident and can stand alone against the crowd and that's a good thing in many instants, but not all.

So, I thought I'd ask a few 'mature' people.

One very smart, successful man told me; Roger Federer, John Walsh, and Dwight Eisenhower.

Most young people probably never heard of some of the names!

Another mature man gave me; Ted Turner, John Kennedy, and Nelson Harris, (former head of Tastykake).

I myself thought about it and came up with a list of dead people first; Jackie O, Alma Mahler, and Marjorie Merriweather Post.

I followed that with a living list; Barbara Walters, (wish I had followed my television career), Jane Fonda and Melissa Gates. All have qualities I value and appreciate.

It would be nice if we could encapsulate all the things we admire into one person; ourselves. Not possible, but I do think some people can serve as examples that help us 'tailor' ourselves into our fantasy selves.

So, what is your list?

Do you have one?

I guess it depends on who you are and what you know.

Now in real life we probably can't achieve all that we wish for and that's why we strive or in some sad cases give up.

When one child, usually the eldest, is 'successful' others may not strive, as they feel they will never get to the heights the other sibling has reached. That is too bad. It is up to parents to differentiate each child with their talents and interests and foster them and give each one the opportunities they need to explore where their passion and goals should be. Parents are not always good at this and comparing children is never a good idea!

We all come with a clean slate and what we write on it will depend on us and at some point we have to take responsibility for our own destiny. Yes, the family and the environment can help or hinder and not all of us can cut through what we have to, in order to be the most we can be. Role models can help. They're all out there; rich, poor, talented, crippled in many forms, and we can look at what they have done. Creativity in many areas has been accomplished against all odds in many cases.

My advice is to seek out role models and look at your own life.

What I believe is difficult today is that many people who we believe to be what we aspire to, turn out to be not just merely human but in some cases false gods that let us down. In other cases, the values we think are good to go after, turn out to be hollow in the end.

Happiness can really only come from being totally fulfilled, and that can only come in the end from loving and being loved.

Studies were recently performed in France, where, by the way, the value system is different in many respects from the United States, looking at happiness.

The results, not surprisingly, were that poorer people were only seven percent happy, while the wealthy were only twenty-three percent happy! So there you have it.

My own illiterate grandmother was an inspiration for me. She was widowed very young with five small children and came here from another country. She was fabulous and became a business woman, raised her children, and was happy because she was full of love. What a lady!!

"Use what talents you possess: the woods would be very silent if no birds sang there except those that sang best." - Henry Van Dyke

Common Sense... Not So Common

"The mere intellect is perverse; it takes all sides, maintains all paradoxes, and comes to understanding only when it listens to the whisperings of common sense." - John Lancaster Spalding

So where does this magical, mythical quality come from? Remember when we had 'wise' old grandparents that knew what life was about? They taught us what we needed to learn. More important than any education, or reading a thousand books.

That's a different kind of learning. Not what you REALLY need in life. It will get you a job but NOT a life!!

It will help you spout off facts but that's not thinking and being creative.

Anyone who does not know how to be intimate, and love and be loved, is a moron, in my book. Or at the least, a limited frightened pathetic excuse for a human being.

Some of those grandparents were too busy surviving to have time for much intimacy but they knew enough to teach us.

Where does common sense come from?

Basically, it comes from experience and learning from people you trust and respect who have lived well.

Now think about it; it cannot be an instinct from birth.

As small children, we are protected and learn that fire is harmful so we don't go near it. We do not run into streets as cars can come and kill us. Our parents teach us how to physically survive.

As teenagers we experiment and test what is more important and not physical safety; the values that parents and others have shown us; not by talk but by their behavior. The most important influence at this stage is our peers. Lots of poor judgment and lack of common sense these years. But that is all good learning if we don't get too burned in the process. The scared ones follow like lemmings and don't learn to leave the nest or fly. Both parent and child can facilitate this process.

As adults, we may or may not be secure in ourselves and be independent people. If not, we look to parents still, or 'experts' for advice and approval. No matter how educated or 'smart' in those terms; many are lacking in trusting their own now warped instincts.

Have you ever seen the fools gushing over what is called 'art' when it really is the Emperor has no clothes, merely because some wealthy fool has bought it?

And then there are the other jackasses who look ridiculous wearing the latest fashion design or a 'label.' Where is the common sense… or mirrors?

Real people trust themselves, and do not have to compete or impress anyone. It is not easy to stand-alone at times.

When I was very early in my counseling practice, a mother with a young girl, about five, came into my office. When we had finished she walked to the door, and looked out to see light snow falling.

With that, she turned to the child and asked, "Susie, do you want to wear your coat?"

At that point, I intervened and said, "Just put her coat on. It's freezing outside."

She was taken aback and said children had rights. I suggested she read something else and not buy wholesale what the current experts were saying.

It is ridiculous to not have a life that teaches you how to behave automatically. That only comes from experience, both good and bad.

I am often saddened by the young people who get into trouble with really bad people because they grew up trusting and not knowing a full circle of what is 'out there.'

Common sense has little to do with grey hair or years lived. It has only to do with values and what real learning about life entails. Some people 'wake up' late in life to learn they have missed the boat to true happiness. Too bad.

To be a responsible adult you MUST be independent, make your own decisions, and stand by the results. Yes, you can consult others whom you respect who have lived well, but in the end, you can ONLY be fulfilled as a human being by doing what works for you…and not harming others intentionally. Use your own opinions that have been tested and do not worry about anyone else's judgment.

So let's bring back those illiterate grandparents who knew what was what and taught their children and grandchildren well.

If you see someone with 'bad' instincts, you know they are stupid and without common sense. In the end, that's the real education, I would mandate for all of us!!

"There is no greater panacea for every kind of folly than common sense." - William Barrett

Having It All

"APART FROM MAN, NO BEING wonders at its own existence." - Arthur Schopenhauer

Ain't it the truth!

We are all so caught up in our lives and daily rituals, and responsibilities that many of us never even look at who we are, what we are doing with our lives, or whether we are truly fulfilled.

Why are we here? What is this life about? How do we spend our time and emotional energy?

Of course we have to rule out health and mental health for ourselves and those we care about but aside from that what does having it all mean?

For me it means using whatever abilities you have to the fullest and giving and receiving true love.

Now how to get it all?

The first part may be easier than that second aspect. That's the scary one!

We can become educated and learn skills and keep developing them and using them as best we can. That takes time and talent, and getting through a lot of junk sometimes. The traits that make that area possible are often counterproductive to achieving that second goal; the love thing.

That's why there are few that do have it all, in my book.

Look around. Whom do you list?

We can never know for sure about anyone else's life; only the people living it really know. We can however speculate from what we do know and observe or learn about them.

Being a 'success' can be a number of things besides the good old American dollar accumulation.

It can be being creative. I would call Mozart, Einstein, and Monet successes although they were not 'rich' with money in their lifetimes.

I would call Madame Curie, Elizabeth Browning, and Mary Cassatt successes although they too did not pile up money.

There's a whole long list of such creative people and people who have offered fabulous things to this world that were not chasing money as their goal.

Being 'rich' has a different connotation in my book.

How you relate to the world and what you offer others of yourself is what to look at.

Having passion and pursuing it is so important.

Now true, we are not all creative at high levels, or able to 'succeed' at everything we might like, BUT we can have values that make this life worthwhile.

It is NEVER things that money buys that bring true happiness.

So, what does?

You know the answer; ONLY love!!!

Having it all means finding your path that uses your time and work well, and giving and receiving real love.

Can they be together in one person?

Yes, indeed, but not easily.

Look around again, and see who might have figured it out.

Maybe people like Bill Gates. Maybe Brian Roberts? Maybe Ruth Bader Ginsburg? Maybe Elizabeth Warren?

I think they display their qualities and talents and they seem to have real love.

An elderly woman I know recently spoke about her marriage of over 70, (yes, 70 years). The core of it was great sex she said, and I loved it!! She was also a known professional in her field and her husband was well regarded in his. How wonderful!! Not a lot of people like them around.

The average guys and women out there can have it all too. You just don't hear about them and they are not famous. They have learned what matters and have given themselves to it.

It cannot happen by dumb luck usually.

We are the only creatures that can look at our lives and we are the only ones that also know we are here for a limited time. That means ... USE YOURSELF WELL.

The days and years are not a rehearsal for life; it's the real deal... every damn day!!

"Death is not the greatest loss in life. The greatest loss is what dies inside us while we live." – Norman Cousins

Happiness Is Relative

"Happiness is the interval between periods of unhappiness." - Don Marquis

So do you have to have been unhappy to know happiness?

In some cases, the answer is yes. Having a crisis, not being able to survive, in any form, physically or emotionally, or financially, will certainly cause stress and all that comes with it.

Once the obstacle is removed, there is certainly relief and a form of happiness.

The whole business of relevancy depends on your values.

Having been to Nepal and seeing families in dirt shacks with children in threadbare clothes, smiling and being welcoming is a message. They have transcendency that allows happiness on a daily basis.

We have all seen Diana, the late Princess of Wales, in a palace, far from happy.

There have been all sorts of studies dealing with this subject.

A recent one dealing with the question about money and happiness found that money was not an answer.

Sure, a new car, a great meal, having fun with friends or family, going places, watching a gorgeous sunset, communing with nature, and doing what you enjoy with work or play, does make us feel good and indeed happy. BUT, and it is a BIG BUT, it is not the ultimate.

Now, do not get me wrong, supreme happiness, (and you all know what I mean by that), finding a deep intrinsic love, is not possible for all people. I would even venture to say, not for the majority, just as fabulous creativity, is not possible for all of us. However, the hope is there that you can learn how to truly love and be loved. People who know can teach others.

We are all victims of our times and backgrounds. We are our own worst enemy with our limitations, and often we are not even looking at any of these things.

I have had clients who were helped to be in love, say they had thought they were happy before and wasted so much of their lives. That is a sad state of affairs. It's like a blind person, who has been helped to see.

Most people get into their zone of comfort and even if it is not good, they are there, often for life. It's what they have learned to expect from this short life. It feels familiar, and therefore safe, and they can live with their compromises.

I am here to tell you this life is not a dress rehearsal!!

I advocate a Love U(niversity), where we all learn how to do IT.

The trick is to follow that initial drive, (sex), with a testing period where you reveal yourself, and experiment in many ways, (sexually, of course), and then share you, the real you, totally. For my money, intimacy has NO boundaries.

When you are complete and RISK yourself, you will know what real happiness is. That does not mean there is no pain or problem, along the way. It only means that happiness at its' height will be achieved and felt more than you can imagine. It will carry you over the bad times and get you through the depths. There is no pain or joy like being in love, and sharing it with someone who loves you.

Once your eyes and ears have been opened to it, you will never view people or the world in the same way. Love has depth and will last much longer than any other happiness, if handled well. It needs attention, nurturing, and lots of forgiveness, and it is worth it. Even small moments are special, and only need the two of you… nothing else. You don't even have to talk.

Once there, you will believe in it and never want to live without it. You will share all that life brings. That makes the ride worthwhile and whatever price is exacted, it is small compared to that feeling. Your heart will never lie… follow it!!! Only then can you die with a smile of contentment on your face.

"Not many things are certain in our own haphazard world, but there is at least one thing about which there is little doubt, that is that those who seek happiness miss it, and those who discuss it, lack it." - Holbrook Jackson

How To Grow A Person

"The greater danger for most of us lies not in setting our aim too high and falling short, but in setting our aim too low, and achieving our mark." - Michelangelo

You know when you buy most plants they come with instructions about how to care for them and how to make them bloom; not so with people. That's the problem!

To become a parent, you don't even have to get out of bed…

There are no real instructions and most of us copy what we learned in our family of origin.

Now, I'm here to tell you it makes little difference what you do as to how the child will grow into a person.

We all arrive with a personality and a potential in many areas. Whatever the parents do can assist in developing the potential or thwart it, but in the end, the outcome is within the child itself.

Yes, the young helpless child needs the basics of care, and yes stimulation of the brain is useful but carrying it too far is not really offering much in the end.

Just look at the examples throughout history or people like Oprah Winfrey, or Steve Jobs. Could they have blossomed any more if they had what we think of as great backgrounds? It would have turned out the same I believe.

While parents' values are usually emulated and the hurts of growing up can be ameliorated, that is not all that makes a person.

The culture and environment, the peers, and other adult examples, real or not, all assist in the process.

One of the biggest hurdles in becoming your own person is to say or behave in a manner that says, "I hate you" to your parents. If the parents are too controlling, or if there is only one parent, this task becomes overwhelming. If not done however, no real person can ever evolve.

Just look around at the adults who need approval; they are uncompleted people. While we all like affirmation and positive feedback, the grown up person who goes on to do their own thing and becomes accomplished has weathered the break emotionally from the parents. It is usually completed by the early twenties but some only get brave enough much later, or never. It can be done with words or deeds. The message is clear; I am my person, and not dependent on you for any type of support. Finances can also play into this and today's young people do have a difficult time standing on their own two feet in this area. But again, the real deal is the emotional one.

What is your first memory? What one word would you choose to describe how you feel about the family in which you grew up? What was the most important value they taught you? Think about it. We move from victim to self.

What we then do with who we are is the next step. How often do you hear people, quite old, still talking about their parents on a regular basis and in many cases blaming their parents for this that or the other? Being a responsible full-blown person is not easy, often not fun, and once there hard to get out of. Hence we have mental and health issues stemming from just this cause.

How many new parents know what to expect? How many are prepared with knowing the various stages and progressions an infant and child goes through?

Today children are given a great deal that money can buy, but often the emotional side is bankrupt.

We want what we want from our children. We think we or 'experts' have the answers. Well, guess what… no one has the answers.

The best any of us can do to help a child bloom is to take a step back and ask ourselves is what we are doing, for the child or us. Can we truly accept what we see that the child brings as unique and different from us? Can we even begin to move into their rapidly changing world?

I watch many of today's parents with their expensively outfitted children, with a million gadgets around them, and their push for the 'right' schools, and the 'right' friends, and the lessons every day, and I wonder where does this person end up?

My true feeling is that by providing the basics, and being there, and offering an opportunity for quiet time, fantasy, just good fun, and friends, the child will become a person and one that can be comfortable in the world. This world will always teach what a parent cannot, so relax, and just enjoy the role and watch the blooming of a person.

And it's ok to hate your kids at times too. Also do not expect thanks from them as whatever you do is taken as their 'due.'

"The real question isn't whether or not you love your kids, but how well you are able to demonstrate your love and caring so that your children really feel loved." - Stephanie Marston

Let's teach the Three P's!

So what kind of education did you have?

A good one? A college degree? Advanced degrees?

My bet is you were never really prepared for what life is about and what really matters.

I have an advanced degree from a prestigious Ivy League college and when I graduated, I thought I was ready for my life and the world. Check wrong!

That's why I do what I do. Today as a family, marriage counselor and sex educator for well over thirty years I can tell you most people know little about what it takes to be comfortable with himself or herself, in the world, with a partner, and as a parent.

So let's teach the three P's...being a person, partner and parent! It's not rocket science and after all these years we do know a bit about what it takes to avoid some of life's most intense emotional problems and learn how to deal with them.

No, there are no guarantees but it is possible to have insight and information that can help. We do little in the way of prevention but spend a fortune on crisis...both in health care and in my field, emotional health. Schools spend all sorts of money and resources on teaching things that most of us will never find valuable as we go through the years. Thoreau's, "Most men lead lives of quiet desperation."

Why not teach people how they grew up and its' impact and how to feel good about themselves no matter what they experienced when they were unknowing victims of parents. And how many had good parents for their emotional needs? And as partners what do we learn? What we saw growing up and how great was that for most people?

We can learn what to expect, how to look at a partner and how to resolve differences and grow. Yes, we in the helping professions have information to share. And parenting...we need to do more to legally drive a car than to raise the next generation! Tragic.

Let's put pressure on schools to really teach what matters, and in a fun and caring way with an opportunity for students to get their real questions answered and to help those that can be saved before tragedy occurs as it does in so many lives early or later. Just think what would you have liked to have known earlier in your life to avoid being hurt later?

Our Human Condition... Absurd

"SUCH IS THE HUMAN RACE. Often it does seem such a pity that Noah... didn't miss the boat." - Mark Twain

"The world is a botched job." - Gabriel Garcia Marquez

"In moments of great joy you know tragedy is lurking around the corner" - W. B. Yeats

Yes, it's me talking and I have been the eternal optimist all my life BUT...

This world is a mess and what really saddens me is that young twenty-somethings feel they can't get it together and that they have no role to play even the smartest of them. I hear it all the time. Life has little meaning and they look around and see what?

True many have been spoiled and were ill prepared for the real world but the values we have perpetrated are not working. Money is not enough and the pursuit is not enough and those that have a career path from families are often disappointed in what their lives turn out to be.

Having travelled all over this planet I can tell you we Americans don't appreciate what we have. Our poor are fed, housed and have cars, TV and running water for the most part. Go to the rest of this world and see what a struggle each day is. Pathetic!

What have we done? What can we do?

How much is enough for the money gluttons?

See the movie," Queen of Versailles" and you will want to throw up. Who needs all those things? George Carlin's: STUFF.

Yes, I like beautiful things and a gracious life but what does it take for some of our One Percenters? They can only end up giving it away and then they are heroes? Give me a break.

It is good to be talented and courageous and earn whatever the traffic will bear but can that be all? In a society where you can buy almost anything money is a god but why not have other gods? You cannot buy love or class!!

And live it well now for who knows if there is a heaven later on?

Man is the only living creature that is sure of how he will end. No one gets out of here alive!

It's possible that the world will go on; it survived plagues and pestilence and savagery before but this time it's different. This time we can implode or explode totally. Another difference is that you used to know who the crazy people were; now they're good looking and appear normal and often have fine educations.

Why can't we have an EQ, (emotional quotient), instead of an IQ and learn early what people need emotionally and help them develop?

Happiness is not easy to achieve and it is not a given, it is an accomplishment. Life is a chess game and we are not preparing our young people to play it well. How many are taking drugs or alcohol? Why?

So, yes, today I have sad thoughts.

Since we are all in this together and the only answer is connection with others what are we doing to connect? The internet ain't the answer!!! Human face to face is the only way.

When we had neighborhoods and family and friends around all the time laughing, singing, playing together it was different. Today who knows their neighbors… or how long are families even in one place? Different.

Why not vocational schools and apprenticeships and lessons in love?

So let's hear what you think.

"Lord, what fools these mortals be!" - William Shakespeare

Non-Sense

"Human beings cling to their delicious tyrannies, and to their exquisite nonsense… till death stares them in the face." - Sydney Smith

We are all here, well, until we're not.

What do we fill our days and nights with? What do we share? What do we talk about?

For me it seems we go the gamut from nonsense to sense and either end is not satisfying.

There are people who are thought to be 'intelligent' who live limited stupid lives according to the values that really matter… like love and passion…

There are well-educated people who have never figured out what a 'juicy' joyful life really is and live it out like 'dead carp.'

There are 'wise' people who have learned how to live and love, and may never have been what we think of as well educated.

There are also the brilliant ones who can't tie their shoelaces and cannot function.

Much can get in the way of learning how to be a fully smart person.

It means being well rounded and sensible and having the ability to relate in a genuine fashion with a variety of people. It means being secure in who you are and being fulfilled emotionally.

We all have needs that have to be met. We all have to obey the law. We all have to have money to survive in the manner we choose, hopefully. But with all of that, there is SO much nonsense.

Listen, as I do, to what people talk about and how they spend their lives.

True, we can't be into 'significant' conversation or relating every minute, however what takes the majority of our time, attention and interest?

NONSENSE for so many.

It is sickening and utterly boring NONSENSE!

In the cycle of life, there are priorities. Youth is busy with goals for the future and becoming a 'self.'

Middle age is fraught with family and work.

Older people have health issues and so on.

So what... that's life.

The really sensible people do all of that AND have developed to a point where they are constantly expanding their knowledge and experience and relationships. They become and remain significant to others. Their driving force is not nonsense but what matters.

Their conversations are fascinating. They are ALIVE!!

It does not depend on intellect. It does not depend on school degrees. Sense and wisdom are earned by living!

The most intelligent and best-educated people on this planet have often been the most miserable. There is no complete happiness to be sure but to have an acceptance and comfort within oneself and an ability to connect intensely and intimately with another is never learned in school. In fact, the best brain may inhibit the letting go of oneself emotionally. Tant pis, as the French say… too bad.

Our schools do not teach people how to be really human. Maybe soon computers will substitute for human beings. Talk about tant pis!!

So, listen to what you say and how you say it. Listen to what the people around you talk about.

If you want to throw up… move on.

We have friends who are like us, and water finds its' level in our emotional relationships. What we do not like in others is usually what we do not like in ourselves.

If your time is filled with nonsense start with changing you first. All else will follow.

When you have that joy of life it will be reflected and you will smile a lot and so will those around you.

Life will hand out many surprises, many unpleasant, or truly heartbreaking, but we can make our lives positive for the most part by being aware and working on the sense part rather than the non-part.

Try it… you won't regret it!

"Learned nonsense is nonsense still" - Benjamin Franklin

Spread Your... Wings

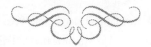

So Mr. and Mrs. Stern married young and to celebrate their fiftieth anniversary she asked to have a first class weekend in New York at the St. Regis hotel.

He readily agreed and they check into a gorgeous suite with champagne and hors d'oeuvres waiting along with a huge bouquet of roses. He knew what to do!

After a bit she asks if he would mind if she goes out shopping and he says, "Fine, have a good time. Here's the charge card."

Off she goes.

She is gone a while and he becomes bored and decides to go down to the bar for a drink.

While there a shapely good looking woman starts talking to him. She asks if he would like to have a 'good time.'

He says he is old and not sure that is possible.

With that she says," Go to your room; leave the door unlocked and I will come and do all that is necessary." He goes.

As they are engaging in intimacy with a passion Mrs. Stern opens the door with her bags and sees what is going on.

She grabs him and throws him right out of the tenth story window.

Police arrive and he is dead.

Appearing in court the judge looks at her saying," Mrs. Stern you are an intelligent woman who was married to that man so many years, why would you throw him out of a tenth floor hotel window?"

After a pause she looks at the judge and says," I figured, if he could fuck, he could fly!"

So, when do you spread your legs and then fly with wings?

Well, it's different at different ages.

Young people are learning and gaining experience. Hopefully they learn to see their bodies as their temples and allow certain people to worship there. Alcohol, while it can diminish the sex drive allows freedom of inhibition.

Today having one boyfriend may be a safety against promiscuity, and allow for emotional connection to grow. It takes time. Sex just for sex has its' benefits but it is not enough for real love over time. Passion has to be nurtured to keep it alive and interesting.

Guys learn that females have the capacity to hurt you…intentionally often. Males are not so prone to do that. So, both genders are learning stuff.

The petty concerns of youth give way over time as relationships are allowed to mature. Love never comes easily and without pain.

It is like everything else in life; the more you know the better it is. It cannot happen by magic. An architect doesn't just look at a building and say, "It's nice" He knows what goes into making it. A surgeon looks at a broken bone and knows what it will take to fix it, and so on.

So too, with sex and love. The problem here is that there is no school to teach all people what is involved and the eternal search may never get fulfilled. Pity!!

Hench the reason for my life's work and this blog. LEARN and learn early. It will be the best part of your entire life if you can do it.

Females are the gatekeepers and they are usually the ones to teach the men what to do and how to do it. Males are the weaker sex here and are dependent on the female spreading her legs willingly and lovingly. It is not easy for either one of them.

But it's like other areas of this life… if all you know is Jello for dessert you never get to know how good strawberry shortcake is!!

Experience and communication on the deepest level is what you are after. Sharing intimacy emotionally, intellectually and PHYSICALLY is the best, I promise. In this case practice does make perfect.

Avoidance and paying back for hurts, and not compartmentalizing areas of life will all get in the way but true connection will always come through and sex will make it feel good. If one person is not fulfilled, the other cannot be. All sorts of machinations go on to cover up the hole but nothing will work. It is ONLY that total human bonding that will make this short, stupid life worthwhile. Substitutes can get you through and many live their whole lives with half-assed ones but somewhere deep inside if they take that minute to reflect they know the truth. You can only avoid so long. The price paid is huge.

If you want to fly spread those legs and the wings will carry you to the sky!!

"If I told you, you have a beautiful body; you wouldn't hold it against me would you?" - David Fisher

So Why Bother To Have Children?

PROBLEM IS MOST PEOPLE DON'T really explore this question and then the children are here. Many people have told me in counseling sessions that they have wondered about this question more than once in their lives. It is a difficult thing to admit that maybe it wasn't the best idea. It is hard to express such a feeling and like it or not the children know the truth expressed verbally or not.

Children can bring you the best joy and the worst trouble in your life. And they are here for the rest of your life.

What is interesting today in America is the fact that the majority of births to women under the age of thirty are outside marriage. This is a big change and the results remain to be seen. Raising a child under the "best" of circumstances is never easy.

Why do people have children?

Some because they are mature and responsible and truly have the love to share with a child and want their genes to go on. Others because it's the thing to do or their parents or partner want a child. Others because they have nothing that is truly theirs to love. Some think it is a doll to have fun with. And others because they were drinking or not thinking clearly or did not take precaution.

We all have a fantasy child, but the real child may be quite different. They may not be the sex we preferred, or they may not look like us or someone we like, or they may in fact be quite different from us. In some cases, there may be mental or health issues to deal with.

No one tells you what you need to learn about what to expect from a child at different stages, beginning with birth. No one talks about the changes in the relationship that have to occur with the father. No one teaches about how having a child can change your lifestyle. No one gives good information about setting limits, discipline or what raising a child really involves. Most of us copy what our parents did even if we didn't like it. No one tells you that for at least eighteen years, you will be giving up part of your life to this person and they will never be as "grateful" as you would like.

How you feel about this child will be based on many factors, many of which will be covered in another article later. Who they remind you of, their place in the family, the role they assume in the family, and the joys and sorrows they bring you. When children are wanted, close, loved, and loving, the hard part is letting them grow up to be their own person and letting go of the parent role in many aspects. Never easy. This is another later topic for discussion.

So why bother to have them at all? Well if the truth be told, nature insisted on it by giving us a sex drive!

There's All Kinds Of Smart

"PEOPLE WHO ARE SENSIBLE ABOUT love are incapable of it." - Douglas Yates

We all know people who we think are 'smart.' What defines that for you?

For my money, there are all kinds of smart.

There's the book learning smart. Those people who read and can tell you all sorts of regurgitated facts or ideas from others.

There's the professorial type or school marm type who think they have mastered a subject and go on to teach it… over and over again.

There's the accomplished professional, whatever, who really knows their field and excels at it.

There's the worldly wise who may or may not be formally educated.

There's the street-smart person who has learned how to negotiate with the variety of people represented in their world.

There's the curious person who continues to expand and learn about the world at large and the people who inhabit it.

For my money IQ means nothing, BUT EQ is where it's at. That's the emotional quotient and that tells me who's truly 'smart.'

It seems that many 'smart' and accomplished people like to be in control and they are responsible, often talented, and gifted people, in a variety of fields.

They are wonderful and make this world better. They work hard at what they do and they get stuff done. No problem.

The issue is that life is full of contradictions and it is scary so the way they get through is to have a routine and not stray out of their comfort zone, with people who are different from them or areas where they are not protected emotionally. They like their 'bubble.' Fine, but limiting. They do not give in to their feelings and often bury them in other activities, or work or whatever.

Often the only real raw emotion they can feel and express is anger. This is especially true when they have leadership positions. Their tender emotions go underground, so to speak. Often they are depressed and push that way down inside themselves; sometimes getting visceral reactions or actually becoming ill.

The question then becomes, can you be successful at what you do and also learn how to love?

The really smart ones have done it. Maybe not right away but they will know how they feel and how they are living and they will search for emotional fulfillment.

Often they have to pay a big price; giving up a relationship or marriage that doesn't work, leaving children, changing jobs, disappointing family and so on.

However, ask any of them if the end was worth it and you will hear a resounding, "Yes," as then they are ALIVE!!

Being smart about all of this takes time and experience and looking at the way you relate to someone you are drawn to. It starts with that good old sex drive. Nothing good happens without that beginning.

From there it's baby steps disclosing the real you and like peeling an onion, the layers come off until you are naked in EVERY way. If you are thinking and analyzing it all, it ain't love in the end.

No one can call themselves smart as far as I'm concerned and I've been in this business a long time, until they learn and share love. All the rest is going through the motions and getting through the mundane chores of life. There can be fun, travel, dining out, dances, theater, and so on, but unless you have love with it, it is just doing stuff. When you LOVE, you can sit in a run-down coffee shop with your lover and it is magical!

Giving up control and having total surrender is indeed frightening, and not everyone will do it, but I encourage you, as that is the ONLY way to live joyously.

That is the reason for this blog and I will promise you it is worth it, so try…

"To live is like love - all reason is against it and all healthy instinct for it." - Samuel Butler

This Is Life And It Sucks

"THE EARTH... HAS A SKIN, and this skin has diseases. One of these diseases, for example, is called, man." - Friedrich Nietzsche

So, we get in these awful moods where nothing is the way we want it, and then we look at this troubled world. Was it ever different? How does it all impact us humans?

Recently I had a discussion with a bright man who was trained in astrophysics and then as a physician.

He gave me food for thought.

The universe has been around for about 14 billion years and is always in movement and changing. It is believed the planet Earth came into existence by the collapse of gases into solid materials about 4.5 billion years ago.

Earth has been through cycles of ice, jungles, deserts, and oceans, as it revolves around the sun. Today the earth still has a liquid center and a surface of solid plates of rock.

Life on earth may have begun about a billion years ago when conditions of moisture and temperature were correct.

Humans appeared about 100,000 years ago, and for the past 5000 years humans have become the dominant species adapting to changing conditions. There is little proof that humans can alter the course of the planet's changes.

Another theory is that life emerged 3.5 billion years ago and mass extinction events have occurred about five times in the course of this history. A social critic, Derrick Jensen, believes that human history may show a naturally destructive force.

Wars, nature, humans, all cause destruction. Have you visited Pompeii? We were putting people in ovens not that long ago to kill millions. Just watch any news program today to get a current state of affairs.

We only see life backward, never forward!

The human brain is now enlarged to 1400 centimeters increasing our ability to work in cooperative groups, be social, analyze intelligence, and divide labor skillfully, and so on. Has it helped? You tell me.

People looking for life to be, 'fair' are wasting their time. Wanting answers to much about life is often very limited in conclusions. Frustration!!!

Today in many parts of this world there is no shame in terrible behavior and politicians and lawyers have found ways to get what they think people will settle for, no matter what the reason. Where does that leave us?

Values that make money number one and great science can't do it.

When I talk about love and relationships, the topic seems dwarfed by the overall human condition and this planet's path. But I do it anyway, as those fleeting transitory periods are what makes this life bearable and indeed joyful.

I fluctuate between disdain and pity for most humans, and this is my professional business!!

A new book by 85-year-old E.O. Wilson from Harvard, "The Meaning of Existence" talks about who we are and who we want to be.

He thinks that after three and a half billion years of existence and evolution we are in the age of loneliness.

Those of you who follow my blog know I agree. You can see it all around you.

Young people trying to connect, and usually through a device, not direct human contact. Older people who are 'together' but have never had true intimacy. Should I go on?

He also feels that by the end of the century a half of all species we know now, will be extinct.

When are we humans on that list???

Now before you get too maudlin.... I also say, find your passion, joy, go for it, and do not let it go... no matter what.

We will get through day by day, and you have nothing to decide about it all anyway, at least not today.

My own personal solution includes a glass of wine, great music, and dancing with my own romantic ideal!

"After a year in therapy, my psychiatrist said to me, maybe life isn't for everyone." - Larry Brown

The Stupidest People on Earth

"Against stupidity the very gods Themselves contend in vain." - William Pitt

Now I talk a lot about people who for one reason or another cannot allow themselves to love.

They are limited, to be pitied, and lead empty sad lives,' making do.'

But, today I want to talk about those people who give up love.

They are just plain STUPID!

If you have been fortunate enough to have learned how to love and be loved and then find it; why on earth would anyone abandon it and give it up?

Well, let's talk about that.

When we love, we have certain needs met… emotionally. We like being desired, cherished, adored, giving of ourselves in so many varied ways. We all heard about that 'spark.'

It makes the world pleasant, gives us purpose, and makes us feel vital.

If we are reasonably mature, we share ourselves openly and without arrogance, we forgive, and then forgive again. We accept the things that won't change and occasionally try to change them or hopefully us. We are never the same when we love.

The relationship is fluid and see- saws up and down and gets refined and distilled over time. If we are smart, it is never boring but it can reach a balance that feels comfortable and steady.

We have compared lovers and have settled on this one.

We tell our secrets and feelings and believe we are in safe territory. There may be weathered crises or really tough periods but through it all we re-choose this person.

The excitement and turn on continues. Great!!

We are attached. He or she may be our own fantasy lover. They have power over us.

We find the partner we deserve and water does find its level emotionally.

Now what happens to destroy a loving relationship?

My answer is NOTHING SHOULD!

So, when it happens, instead of looking at the reasons, which we will do, let's start by saying the person who walks away from real love is just plain STUPID!!!

There is NOTHING that two people in love cannot work out or figure out to keep it going.

But, the STUPID ones can't or in many cases won't.

There is no substitute for love and once experienced you do not want to live without it. You are then the walking dead, the hollow, empty person; sleepwalking through life and making believe you are alive.

As a therapist, I have seen people end good relationships for ridiculous reasons, petty annoyances, issues that could have been talked through, behaviors that could have easily been changed to keep the partner happy, and so on.

Suffering is easy, loving is harder.

We are like onions and once peeled to the core we can never be put back again. The people, who do not look back, won't 'waste' their emotions or try to erase the dreams and memories. They cannot do it and remain dead.

Yes, they remain in control and keep their pride but have NOTHING; nothing that really matters in this life. Like I said STUPID!!!

You can only repress emotion so much. You can only substitute with so many things, and can only be so busy or drunk, but the heart's FEELINGS will creep in. No matter how hard you try and at the least expected moments, the truth will out. You need LOVE!!!

Dante's Hell is remembering happier times. You will be in Hell and wish you were actually dead.

We all use people for our purposes but when we use one another for love there is no sign that gives it a shelf life to use by a certain date.

True there are relationships and loving ones that should and do end with a mutuality and that's fine. We can outgrow someone or find that we have needs that have changed; all part of the process. It is when we are 'mature', and that is not an age, and have found a true love we had better grab on tight and hold it close, not squander or forfeit it, and nourish it and weather the tough parts to achieve the greatest happiness that is humanly possible… otherwise we are STUPID!!!

"Emotion is the chief source of all becoming conscious. There can be no transforming of darkness into light and of apathy into movement without emotion." - Carl Jung

Therapists Are People Too

"The only journey is the one within." - Rainer Maria Rilke

If you haven't really looked inside you, you are like the gerbils on the wheel; just running through the motions. Many people live out their whole lives in this way. Taking a good look at you is not easy or often pleasant. We are a combination and tapestry of wonderful and awful selves.

No angels or perfect people inhabit this earth.

True, some are 'better' than others, spread joy, and contribute to the 'good' while others bring misery, or cause harm. Just watch the news, observe people, and look at the ones you know.

Insight and wanting to develop and change certain aspects of who you are is an intelligent emotional quest. It goes on for a lifetime. Sometimes a crisis will force it. Often a love will demand it. Whatever the cause, it can be exciting, and always enlightening.

Now if you cannot get the 'job' done you may seek help. Staying uneasy or unhappy may not be your cup of tea.

There are three basic types of therapists; a psychiatrist, who is a licensed medical doctor who is able to prescribe medicine if needed, a psychologist, usually a PhD, who often uses tests to assist, and social workers or therapists in specialized fields who have a masters' or doctoral degree. All should be credentialed and licensed.

The main thing is finding someone you like and relate to and trust.

Costs will vary and are part of the equation.

What is special about therapy is that it is ALL about YOU!

What do therapists do?

Well, they:

Give advice, (common sense is sorely missing these days)

Give emotional support

Offer guidance

Force reflection and choices

Help to control acting out

Stimulate responsibility for one's actions

Release and manage appropriate feelings

Bring out the meaning of behavior and feelings

Help in understanding underlying motives

You need to know no one becomes a 'helper' without having some issues of their own. This is what brings them to their profession. Now some are severely wounded and looking to solve their own deep problems. I have known few psychiatrists that I think are free of their own searches, but that is my bias.

The really good therapists have worked through their own hurts. All therapists are required to go through a process of introspection with a qualified person. The Freudian method is rarely used today. More often cognitive therapy is the choice; dealing with the here and now.

While no living person is ever totally free of all areas of 'blockage', the good therapists are free enough to be there for you totally, and without criticism.

Being human means we have feelings too. We relate to some people easier than others, but as with your children, you have to be aware and try not to show favoritism.

We have values and we have to be open to hear and help people whose values may be vastly different from our own. And yes, we have lives.

When I was very young and beginning to work as a therapist a family came to me with a problem with a school age child. As the mother was leaving she asked if I had children and I said I did. She then asked if I ever yelled at them. All I could think of was that she should have been outside my door the night before when I was screaming like a maniac at one of them!!

It helps if the therapist has had a rich life experience. It doesn't mean you have to have a broken arm if you are a surgeon to know how to fix one, but the empathy and experience puts you closer to another's experience.

In the over three decades of practice I have had with ALL kinds of people I feel blessed to have been entrusted with secrets and issues, so that nothing, and I mean NOTHING, surprises me.

What is rewarding is the people who have moved on to happier, better relationships, and lives, and continue to stay in touch, or come back for a 'check-up' and all those that send those wonderful cards every year to tell me how they are. It is the best!!!

For people to be joyful and fulfilled they have to look inside and learn. We therapists have the privilege of helping them get there. And we get paid for it too!

"Generous people are rarely mentally ill people." - Dr. Karl Menninger

What Really Matters

"In the long run, we shape our lives, and we shape ourselves. The process never ends until we die. And the choices we make are ultimately our own responsibility." - Eleanor Roosevelt

So true, only many never take that responsibility or look at any of this; some too late in life.

We all decide what is important to us; it can be by the day, the year, the decade, the life. It can change and come and go according to our circumstances and what happens to us.

Our culture and our families, and just life experience teach us what matters. We buy into it when we are young and maybe never challenge the areas presented or perhaps we rebel just to prove we are a person in our own right. Those that are really smart take a look and evaluate as they move along.

What matters at tender years has to do with instant pleasure and satisfying basic needs. What matters as adolescents has to do with how we look, how we measure up against our peers, and how accepted we are by friends and the opposite sex or finding our particular sexual preferences.

As young adults we are ready to put our goals into action. We have to decide whether to pursue a particular course of education, a career, be creative, or if we have talent, to take the gamble and try our passion in real life.

None of this is easy and none is without difficulty and paying prices along the way. We can fail, change course or even give up. We will have to confront what REALLY matters to us. It is our choice; but some are intimidated or pushed by family or outside influences. Some never even take that silent journey and contemplate what they REALLY want.

How many people do you know who, if asked what they would change, say it would have been how they used their time with work, in some form or another.

Too bad they did not take the time for self-contemplation earlier.

We all need comfort before the known end of this life. We want to be 'happy.'

Some people can shape their future and others anticipate and deal with what befalls them.

We all stumble and have tragedy and ordinary misery. Most get up, go on and learn to repair and grow.

Some crumble.

Now, there are some things that cannot be controlled and they matter a lot. Health, mental health, crisis of one form or another; all impact our ideas of what's important at any given period in this life.

Some shoot for 'success' either in the form of earning money, being famous, or having power. All can be fine in moderation, and some of it is just plain luck, and, or, hard work. BUT, in the end nothing REALLY matters if you are not content within yourself, and loving and being loved.

You can have everything you dreamed you thought was important and you can substitute all sorts of things believing they are the MOST important things in life but guess what? It is ONLY LOVE that makes this life worthwhile.

True, money is important for all it can do; brings necessities, lack of stress about material things, makes life more gracious, pleasant, and affords many comforts for oneself and the people you care about, and allows for many areas of future legacies, such as education of children and so on.

Being 'famous' also has its' rewards. It also comes with a caveat; it ain't all it's cracked up to be and many would choose a different life in the end.

What we are left with is the human component that is ruled by the heart. This cannot be bought or demanded or fooled. It will not be denied. And this IS what matters.

How to get it?

Glad you asked.

Only one course; be ready and fulfilled as a person, and GIVE love. Not just any kind of 'love' either.

The real deal; intimacy, passion, (sex), and joyous complete vulnerability, and abandonment!! Only then will it find you.

What course it takes after that is another story and this blog deals with all of that stuff. Stay tuned!

Today what matters is finding the perfect dress for the party, tomorrow the hair has to look good, the next day the kids need dental check-ups, the next, an interview for a job, the day after, winning the tennis tournament...

Next year, a job promotion, the next five years, paying off the mortgage...

The decade...

The rest of life...

You decide and go for it!!

However, without that thing called love you have NOTHING!!!

"If you want happiness for an hour, take a nap.
If you want happiness for a day, go fishing.
If you want happiness for a year, inherit a fortune.
If you want happiness for a lifetime, help somebody."
- Chinese proverb

Will It

WHERE THERE'S A WILL...

"You never realize death until you realize love" - Katherine Butler Hathaway

We all accumulate, as the late George Carlin said," stuff."

Now some of us have money, property, and or, lots of stuff.

What happens to it at the end? There are no pockets in shrouds, the saying goes.

Hopefully, we have enjoyed the gathering of it all and hopefully we have enjoyed the fruits of our labors.

Most in the end leave everything to the last spouse whether there was love or not. Most leave it then to the 'ungrateful' children and the even more ungrateful grandchildren. They don't mean to be that way but many in this generation were given to and learned that was their due. Often you see wealthy parents living rather conservative lives based on their upbringing while their children live it up. Foolish people!

So, let's look at a few wills of some famous people.

Jackie Kennedy Onassis was a most thoughtful woman and her will shows it. She left the bulk of her large estate to her two children but she also bequeathed many personal items and money to a variety of family, friends, and employees. Her money came from both John Kennedy and more from Onassis when she and Bobby Kennedy fought for it from his daughter.

Caroline and John sold most of her memorabilia at Sotheby's for close to thirty-five million dollars! Taxes took a big chunk of their money.

Joan Crawford was made famous by one of her adopted daughters, Christina, who wrote the book, "Mommie Dearest."

She had four marriages and four adopted children: Cathy, Cynthia, Christina, and Christopher.

She lived to her late seventies and wrote that she was leaving trust funds of about $77,000 each to her two daughters but nothing to Christina and Christopher, "for reasons which are well known to them." How cruel.

The book and movie however made Christina quite wealthy. Retribution. You never win a battle with a child.

Crawford, interestingly, left money to about six charities. Wanted to look good, I suppose.

Henry Fonda was another loving parent leaving nothing to his son Peter or daughter Jane.

He left everything to his fifth wife and adopted daughter Amy, from his third marriage.

He wrote in his three page will," I have made no provision in this Will for Jane or Peter, or for their families, solely because in my opinion they are financially independent, and my decision is not in any sense a measure of my deep affection for them." Right! That leaves a sour taste in your mouth for life. But you can't let it.

It is also a delicate business if one child is better off than another. My own rule of thumb is it should always be equal, as we never know what life will bring.

Not everyone agrees with that.

Frank Sinatra left a very long will and left most of what he had to his fourth wife Barbara who was married to him for twenty-two years, when he died at age 82. His three children were from his first marriage.

He was also generous to many friends and employees.

Elvis Presley died five months after signing his Will when he was 42. He was divorced from Priscilla and left his fortune to daughter Lisa Marie to inherit when she was 25.

George Washington died one of the nation's wealthiest men.

His Will freed his many slaves and left his estate to his wife Martha. She had two children from a previous marriage. He wrote his thirty-page Will by hand.

John Kennedy wrote that his Will was written, "mindful of the uncertainty of life." Prophetic. He had a charitable foundation named for his deceased elder brother. His Will was written before he had children and never updated, interestingly, even after he was elected president.

Andy Warhol left an estate in excess of 500 million dollars. He left a small sum to two brothers but the bulk in a foundation managed by a friend, Frederick Hughes. Shortly before he died, he made a videotape and stated, "Death means a lot of money, honey."

Albert Einstein, died in his sleep at 76. From his first marriage he had two sons and then he married a second cousin, who stayed with him until his death. She was a widow with two daughters.

He, however, had a “secretary-housekeeper” named Helen Dukas, who was the top priority in his Will. His brain was kept for scientific study.

A genius and a lover!

John Jacob Astor IV one of the richest men in America in the early 1900’s had a fortune of about 200 million. On the Titanic, he made sure all the women and children were put in lifeboats before himself. As his pregnant wife left the sinking ship he lit a cigarette.

What Do You Want in Life?

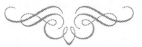

"The man who has accomplished all that he thinks worthwhile has begun to die." - E.T. Trigg

"Only the mediocre are always at their best." Jean Giraudoux

Well, what is it that you want in this life; Money, success, fame, love, contentment, health?

Whatever it is, the first question is, is it realistic and how do you set your goals. Are your desires in keeping with reality and in your control? Is it your expectation or someone else's?

Many times the problem is just a common sense one. Who's setting the goals? That takes a lot of time to decipher. Often parents force values that become our goals. Sometimes they are not possible to achieve from the get go. Only we can know and prove what we want and can obtain. Time will force the answer, and unfortunately the realization may come late in life.

Sometimes the society or peer group sets our standards and again if they are not in keeping with what is good and possible for us we are left like Sisyphus, pushing that rock up the hill only to have it immediately slide back down.

Finding out who we are and what we really can do and find happiness from is a slow and thoughtful process often fraught with trial and error and even big mistakes.

We seek perfection at times and that is impossible even for a short time, and what is perfection?

We all want happiness but do not know that happiness is an achievement and transitory, never static or constant.

We want to be content but how many people do you know who have that solidly in their lives?

We want to please parents as children and they set the standards, then we want to fit in with our peers, and then we hope to live up to what our culture says is important.

Can we do it all?

Probably not, and then the hard part… what do we really want for ourselves?

It is not uncommon for people to get caught up with just living and never even look at their lives and ask the questions. That's too bad, because it may have been different if they had.

Frequently we want partners who think like us and work on radar, but that also is not the case.

So what I think we have to do is keep looking at ourselves, and like the army, be all we can be and then be satisfied and not compare ourselves with anyone.

If we are content at our core whatever anyone else says, does, or has, will not make us discontent. Being secure inside is what it takes. That takes emotional strength.

Having to be in control, making things an issue of pride, or having to be right, will all cause a lot of wasted emotional energy and not lead to fulfillment in the end.

Communicating feelings and learning to love leads to fulfillment.

Freud said what mattered in life was work and love. Finding those areas that complete you and your capabilities will get what YOU want in this life… not much else. The other idols are false and hollow.

If you are not lazy and boring, you will celebrate life and always be expanding yourself.

The real you will always come out in the end and you cannot hide what you are and what values you live by. Do not be fooled by chasing any dream, but your own and while hard, stand up for what you believe and what you know works for you.

Go on, you can do it!

What Roles Do You Play In Life?

"All the world's a stage,

And men and women merely players:

They have their exits and their entrances;

And one man in his time plays many parts,

His acts being seven ages."

William Shakespeare; 'As You Like It'

We all grow up in some sort of family system and depending on our place in the family and our personality we play a role. The role usually stays with us for life.

So think about it. Were you the treasured first born on whom all hope rested for achievement?

The middle child is the one who gets along well with people having grown up getting "It" from both ends and maneuvering.

The baby of the family is adored just because it is the last and they are usually spoiled and often never really grow up.

If the first child messes up the hope can be transferred to the next in line, and so on.

Whether you were planned and wanted is another factor in all of this. Were you the sex child the parent preferred?

All important because you received messages about who you are from day one.

Not everyone is born into a loving wanted position with parents meeting most of their needs, emotionally.

Then your personality sets the stage for your dominant role in life.

Were you the 'intelligent' one that the family looked to for advice and opinions?

Were you the clown that was the family entertainer?

Were you the peacemaker when there was dissention?

Were you the _________ fill in the blank.

Do you still play that role today? Bet you do!

Erik Erikson outlined eight stages of life with the developmental dilemma to be resolved at each stage:

Stage of Life Dilemma To Be Reconciled Psychosocial Strength

Infancy Basic Trust vs. Mistrust Home

Early Childhood Autonomy vs. Shame and Doubt Will power

Play Age Initiative vs. Guilt Purpose

School Age Industry vs. Inferiority Competence

Adolescence Identity vs. Confusion Fidelity

Young Adult Intimacy vs. Isolation Love

Adulthood Generativeness vs. Stagnation Maturity

Old Age Integrity vs. Despair Wisdom

Whew!! Who can successfully go through all those stages and end up with wisdom? Not too many of us!!

So, we have to muddle through the best we can and learn to be satisfied and content and not too hard on ourselves making us nuts in the process!

We do the best we can with what we have to work with.

It is helpful to know a little about all of this and maybe, just maybe we can understand who we are and how we got to be that way and in a good relationship to share it with someone we can trust. That is a very difficult task. Will they still love us if they know all about us?

Often parents act out their own unresolved conflicts and the child takes it on as their problem. Don't do it, at least not when you are grown up and can examine it. Put it where it belongs, on the parent. Unfortunately, we are all 'victims' when we are young, but we don't have to be, forever.

The other extreme is what I see today with parents looking at every nuance of their behavior and how it might affect the child later. It's a delicate balance to be oneself and yet insightful.

The goal is to accept and love yourself then you can move on to others.

"To love oneself is the beginning of a life-long romance." - Oscar Wilde

When You're Having a Really Bad Day

WE ALL HAVE THEM... THAT really awful day when nothing is going your way. Now what it is, is either a crisis or something totally out of your control or something that goes against your wishes and values. The crisis we can only contend with; with whatever resources we possess materially or emotionally. Crises can actually force us to grow and be better than we were or sometimes cripple us.

The more difficult issue is when we are upset by someone who is not delivering what we want emotionally. This goes to our very core and our value system.

Let me give a few examples.

I have a bright granddaughter who was accepted at my alma mater, an Ivy League school and she was deciding between that school for college and a small western "campy" college. This truly upset me. My view of the world and my value system said her life would be better if she chose the Ivy school. Since the decision was out of my control and she had to make it, all I could do was give my opinion. So I was having a really bad day and angry at her, and at her parents for not helping her choose the 'right' place etc. In the end, all I can control is me, so I found this to write and did things I enjoyed, and friends to talk to, and a glass of wine to make the world pleasanter. I just had to say, "It's her life."

Then there's the friend who is upset at her boyfriend who hasn't called. Again her idea of what should be. If he cared, he would call when she wanted him to, on her schedule. We all want a partner like us! All she could do was be angry, hurt, or vindictive. She did all three at various times. She too relied on friends and then when he was not calling for a long time she sought therapy. Finally, he called and they talked and worked out that phase of the relationship.

There will be other phases, don't worry. Working out and hopefully communicating FEELINGS, will help when the next issue presents itself...and it will.

The husband who forgot the anniversary, or was just inconsiderate or had an argument over something you disagreed about can certainly cause a bad day How to resolve disagreements constructively is not taught in colleges.

Then there's the really bad day when the lover did not buy a nice gift for the woman he professes to love, on her birthday.

All sorts of excuses were given, none of which helped. He had no problem buying many expensive things over the years for a wife for whom there was no emotional connection for decades, let alone sex. So she was left feeling used and certainly not appreciated. When the behavior doesn't match the words always trust the behavior, not the things said. Pillow talk is easy and cheap!

Again, the value system comes into play. Is money the thing that matters? Well she decided gifts were a concrete and another way of showing love when other options were not available like taking a trip or buying a house. Ultimately, he understood that and came through with a belated birthday present. She hoped the next birthday would be different.

When other important values are challenged, it can be a bad day, month, or years. There are families that have nothing to do with children because of whom they have chosen as a marriage partner...many times over religion. This can be a big deal because if it is important in your life and the child thumbs their nose at your teaching it can really hurt.

Bad days can occur in work situations when expectations or appreciation is not given. If the boss gives you grief, some people come home and kick the cat or yell at their spouse to get the frustration out. This only exacerbates the problem, and compounds it.

Friends can be another source for a bad day when they do not understand what you are doing, saying or feeling. Strangers can also supply us with bad days by being nasty, or saying things that insult something we care about, or something personal about us. Maybe you're just moody and your hair doesn't look good so you are in a "bad" mood and touchy or vulnerable because of your self-image or ego problem. These things can cause many bad days.

All of our bad days make us unhappy. How to get over them or let them get to us is our dilemma. We all do this differently. Much of what we do is copied from what we saw our parents do. It may be good or it may not really work for our personality and us.

It is good to take a step back and see if what we are doing is making things better for us. If not maybe change the pattern, which is not easy but being aware and working on it will get you there. We see lots of people numbing themselves with drugs, alcohol, or using food as a pacifier Some take a hot bath, exercise, or jog. Others talk to themselves, friends and family, or professionals and some dance their cares away with music. Whatever works! Time will help and the bad days will be surpassed with good days and we would not know what a good day was if we never had a bad day!

You Want Grateful Children... HA

"WISDOM IS NOT THE PRODUCT of schooling but of the lifelong attempt to acquire it." - Albert Einstein

What do parents want from children? Reproducing themselves for eternity, having their accomplishments reflect back on them, having someone of their very own to love, sharing love with a partner, expanding their lives? Maybe all or some or none of that, but we have them none the less. Of course there are people who have given the matter much thoughtful attention and decided not to reproduce.

Whatever the situation, having a child is a crap shoot at best... all those genes mixed up from so many generations. Who knows how it will turn out?

But for most people they have children that they think are wonderful and they love them. Now by giving them love and whatever else, we teach them what to expect in this world.

SO, when they grow up and are expecting whatever they have learned to expect, we cannot be disappointed when we feel they are not 'grateful' to us for all we gave them.

It's the old story; a mother can take care of ten children but ten children can't take care of one mother.

There are, naturally, many examples to the contrary but there will be times when a parent, especially mothers, feel unappreciated.

We nurture from the beginning, and care for them as they grow, and go through adolescent turmoil, and then see them as independent adults.

What we really need to do is have a life of our own and find joy. It is harder as one gets older because being relevant diminishes. You can always find others who need a smile, a dollar, or time. Then you will be given gratitude. True, it is without history and deep emotion, but it can feel very nice. To not need children in a dependent way is the goal. The reverse of what a parent was earlier. Not accomplished so easily.

Here is my advice:

If I had my life to live over, I'd try to make more mistakes next time. I would relax. I would limber up. I would be sillier than I have been on this trip. I know of a very few things I would take seriously. I would be crazier. I would be less hygienic. I would take more chances. I would take more trips. I would climb more mountains, swim more rivers and watch more sunsets. I would burn more gasoline. I would eat more ice cream and less beans. I would have actual troubles and fewer imaginary ones. You see, I am one of those people who live prophylactically and sensibly and sanely, hour after hour, day after day. Oh, I have had my moments and, if I had it to do over again, I'd have more of them. In fact, I'd try to have nothing else. Just moments, one after another, instead of living so many years ahead each day. I have been one of those people who never go anywhere without a thermometer, a hot water bottle, a gargle, a raincoat and a parachute. If I had it to do over again, I would go places and do things and travel lighter than I have. If I had my life to live over, I would start barefooted earlier in the spring and stay that way later in the fall. I would play hooky more. I wouldn't make such good grades except by accident. I would ride on more merry-go-rounds. I'd pick more daisies.

This was written in 1935 by Don Herold

Think about it. What is your life and how do you like it? Start examining young so that you will be ready later.... for happiness, real happiness!

"All you teenagers out there. The big mistake you're making is that you listen to all that bad advice from kids your own age. You should listen to your parents. They're entitled to give you bad advice." - George Burns

Who Thinks So?

"Be who you are and say what you feel, because those who mind don't matter, and those who matter doesn't mind." - Dr. Seuss (Theodor Geisel)

So we all have those days when people get to us. You may not like what I say next, but it is usually true. What we don't like in others is what we really do not like in ourselves!

Recently I heard an interview with Ashley Judd and she spoke about being hurt and what criticism can do, especially to a child before they are emotionally strong enough to handle it.

It's true sticks and stones won't break your bones but words and being shunned hurt.... always.

When they say that what doesn't kill you makes you stronger doesn't always hold true.

It all depends on how you feel about yourself and when the "hurt" occurs. Before the ego is strong and independent a person can be severely damaged and feel unworthy and unloved. It's like being branded by a hot poker. Sometimes the pain lasts forever and sometimes the scars remain. It often becomes our Achilles heel for a lifetime. Sometimes it forces the pain to outweigh the pleasure. In a relationship that is when to go.

An architect just doesn't look at a building and say it's pretty. he knows how it's constructed and what went into making it.

When I see people and relationships I do the same.

There are no perfect people or angels walking the earth and we all have to overcome or deal with some aspect of ourselves that we do not like. Hopefully there is enough we do like and enough that is appreciated that gets us through. If not we can become bitter, antagonistic, unhappy, or downright mean...to pay back the hurt.

Whenever you see someone who is nasty you have to remember they are hurting and that is the way they try to feel better!

Many people lead lives of, "I should's" versus lives of "I enjoy or want." Now that does not mean you are narcissistic but if you do not like and value yourself, which comes initially from parents, you cannot be there for another.

We are but specks on the planet for a short period and taking it all too seriously is not a good thing. And yes bad things do happen to good people but that's true for all of us.

I believe that we are a part of other galaxies and this earth is the comedy channel!!

There are only rainbows after the rain, and we need to focus on that, not the rain. None of this comes automatically and so we have to train ourselves and help children deal with real life.

When we hear so much about young people bullying or being horrible or even killing other young people they don't like or understand, we have to educate them …across the board. This is what schools should be helping with, more important for life than algebra!

I had a wonderful Grandmother who came here from Russia and was basically illiterate and uneducated. But she was wise and when left a widow in her twenties with five small children, raised them and was way ahead of her time going into business and later remarrying.

Once when I was quite young and very upset after someone had said something terrible to me, I saw my Grandmother who made me tell her what had happened.

After a long pause, she looked at me and said, "Who thinks so?"

I have never forgotten that and have used it as a barometer all my life. Most if not all of the time, the "Who" turned out to be the Wizard of Oz or people I knew to be people who did not know the most important thing in life; how to love and be loved!

Women Who Work and Have Children

"I FIND THE GREAT THING in this world is not so much where we stand, as in what direction we are moving...we must sail sometimes with the wind and sometimes against it... but we must not drift nor lie at anchor." - Oliver Wendell Holmes, Jr.

Today women make up almost forty percent of full-time workers in management but the median wages are only seventy-three percent of what their male counterparts earn. Only four percent of C.E.O.'s in Fortune's top one thousand companies are women.

In the twenty-two to thirty-year old's in metropolitan areas, childless females earn less than males in every category with the same educational background.

Once married only twenty percent of wives earn half or more of the family income.

Once they have children women fall well below their husbands in earnings because they cut back their time or take off for periods of time.

So, what does all of this mean for those ladies who want to work and have children?

Not easy.

The pulls are there. The maternal instinct does not disappear and the drive to be a success using your education and talent does not evaporate.

Can you combine the two with some degree of comfort? Maybe.

It is interesting to see who has done it and how it worked out. Are there special qualities or circumstances that help?

The ability to nurture and love an infant and young child is pretty much inborn. Giving that up and leaving to pursue a career is hard. I have witnessed young children screaming, "Mommy," as a mother went off to her job.

What they don't see is that most of these children adapt rather quickly to a caretaker who is kind and loving, or a father, who remains with them. The screaming does not last.

That takes a lot for a mother… to walk away hearing her child scream for her.

The image stays however and the guilt that it produces is not easily overcome. But it can be put aside.

Now at the workplace there is another scenario.

This one is fraught with hazardous situations.

There is the need to be in control, perhaps have a superior position over others, requiring other skills, and the good parts of adult relationships; intellectual, challenging, rewarding, or sometimes leading to romantic entanglements.

The changes today in the role of father are dramatic. While many fathers are helpful in a variety of ways they do not do the full time job the way a mother does. Yes, they can help and women can go off to work knowing the child is in good and loving hands, but father is not a mother.

Watch a father when he is alone with a young child. The attention is not totally on that child as it usually is with the mother. His reactions to a fall or a problem are definitely different and less coddling than the mother's. That is not to say it is a major problem, just that it is different.

Now the bottom line.

Having worked with families all of my professional life and knowing so many people socially over the years, the histories may be very different BUT, most children will turn out the way they are whether or not they had a working mother. That should be reassuring to all you working mothers.

What children need is a sense of being loved, protected, and given opportunity to develop their talents, and interests, and that is doable with mothers who work.

What I especially like to emphasize is that the working mother using her education and drive comes home and sets a better example of a well-rounded worldly person who is not boring or shallow.

Now it is also true that a working mother may come home fatigued, annoyed at problems encountered at the workplace, or full of herself from accomplishments or appreciation from work, but given it all I believe she comes home a more satisfied person in the end and that means positive reaction to both her mate and children.

There are probably unhappier, screwed up kids from intact families or non - working mother families than anywhere else!!!

"It is not what we do, but also what we do not do, for which we are accountable." - Jean-Baptiste Moliere

You're Twenty-Four... It Ain't Easy

"YOU MAKE ME CHUCKLE WHEN you say that you are no longer young, that you have turned 24. A man is or may be young to after 60, and not old before 80." - Oliver Wendell Holmes Jr.

Lately I've been talking to a lot of young people and what has popped up is a particular age fraught with emotional issues; 24.

Both males and females seem to encounter problems at this particular age.

For girls, they are grappling with guys who don't want to say, "I love you" and can't commit. Many males don't engage in sex saying they are tied up in their careers, or doing other activities like running to the gym three times a day!

The females are frustrated and long for a relationship and they see their men all the time and really want them to come through. This can go on for a few years or longer while they hope the guy will finally settle and be with them the way they want. That happens once the guys turn 27 on.

So if you are 24, listen up. You need to look at your goals and maybe don't let a potentially great relationship wither away.

Now I'm not suggesting you have to engage and commit, or even have sex, BUT why not?

When you look throughout history what is especially interesting, (not for parents), is that very loose women have ended up with some fabulous men and great lives. Pamela Harriman is but one example.

That the men don't push for this is indeed surprising to me.

All the dating stuff that is there at every age is also part of the picture. Who calls whom, who causes fights, who makes up, where you go, who pays, and all the rest.

The physical part is the area that doesn't happen to the full extent.

While it is true many females get clutchy, demanding, and jealous and guys feel pressured and want to have their options open, there is still the possibility of having a good, and learning experience.

True, you are not at the end of the line, and marriage is not even an issue here, but you can try your wings at love and all that it involves; the great and the difficult. Love is not learned or experienced overnight or more than usually probably twice in a lifetime. That stuff that every generation copes with, writes songs and poetry about is all that it's cracked up to be, so jump in.

'Starter' boyfriends and girlfriends are wonderful. They will help you as you move along this journey. Look at your peers who have taken the gamble.

Even in the best of circumstances with much experience and maturity monogamy is not always sustainable. Forty percent of women and sixty percent of married men report affairs. Maybe they needed even more relationships in their past to know what this love thing is all about???

No matter what your age when you are attracted and long for someone the feelings are the same. You light up around them, dress for them, hang on every word and gesture and want to be SO close. That feeling that you don't want to live without them is universal. When there are problems or you feel any rejection you want to DIE! Yes, that's loving someone.

To be afraid at 24 is normal. To be afraid at any age is normal. Love is scary. Sharing thoughts, feelings, and a body is frightening, BUT, you cannot ever have it without going through the process. It is a process and you have to want it, and be brave to reap the rewards.

I am not talking about 'needy' people here, just the normal run of the mill males and females wanting to share their entire selves in an open relationship. It may take many trials to trust that you can love and be loved for yourself, but keep on trying until it happens BECAUSE there is nothing, and I mean nothing like it on this earth!!!

And do remember you are not 24 for life!

"I sometimes think we all die at twenty-five and after that we are nothing but walking corpses, with gramophones inside." - George Santayana

Zero Children... By Choice

"Children begin by loving their parents, after a time they judge them; rarely, if ever, do they forgive them." - Oscar Wilde

What do they have to forgive you ask. Nothing, but they are ALL angry at some point at something, and the parent is the easy target.

As parents we follow certain guidelines; our own parents, (not always the best examples), experts a la Dr. Spock, the new guru of the moment, friends, television personalities, fictional characters, whomever.

Whatever happened to just common sense and being the parent not the UN negotiator?

Have you watched these parents today discussing, on an equal level, whatever they want with a child? It's ludicrous!

There are cultural differences too. Have you ever even heard an Asian child's voice in a restaurant?

The most difficult thing for a parent is to really see their child as apart from them and respect whatever difference the child may have from them.

We all know the horrors the teen years bring, after the terrible twos of course, and the testing of both the limits and values of parents. Real joy there.

Then there is the dating drama and choice of a partner. All fun.

The world cannot move on or change without children doing and thinking differently from the past generation. The trick is first to come out of it alive and then to have mutual respect and love.

That's the reason many are opting not to have children today. They have looked around at all the messy lives in families.

There can be real problems in health or mental health, and there are sibling issues, and there are just a lot of problems and costs financial and emotional in raising a human being. Many want a different life; one without little ones, and it's okay today.

This generation has goals that do not include the 'sacrifices' necessary to have children. Now not everyone is included here.

There is a maternal or paternal drive that many have to fulfill. I always recommend they start with a pet, like a dog, to try it out. Dogs are like babies that never grow up and give unconditional love all the time. Easier than a baby. Or I suggest taking a baby, a family or friend's child for a weekend to try it out. Wish every teen had this experience!

Once that little being is here you have it for life with all the joy, (yes, there is much joy), and heartache. No one holds a mirror up to the real you like a child. And no one has all your dreams to fulfill like a child. Hence the rub. What if they are not that fantasy person you hoped to make? Problem!

The worrying never ceases. Ask any parent of any age child what they worry about and it's there.

With birth control, we can decide these matters today and many are opting out of the parent role. Many today also inherit other people's children when remarriage occurs. Another wonderful fun game!

Once here, the real test begins from day one. Who is in control, who will turn out the way you prefer, and who would you like to be rid of... all questions some will avoid or face.

Kahlil Gibran wrote it perfectly and artistically.

"Your children are not your children
They are the sons and daughters of Life's longing for itself."

Choose wisely!

You're Sixteen... So What Now

"A YOUTH WITH HIS FIRST cigar makes himself sick; a youth with his first girl makes everyone sick" - Mary Wilson Little

"One day Alice came to a fork in the road and saw a Cheshire cat in a tree. "Which road do I take?" She asked. "Where do you want to go" was his response. "I don't know," Alice answered. "Then," said the cat, "It doesn't matter." - Lewis Carroll.

And that's the way it is with a lot of teenagers. They are not and cannot be sure where they want to go... especially when it comes to sex.

Teen boys are driven by their hormones and teen girls want to find love and be accepted, and find and hold on to a guy.

That makes for a BIG problem.

Boys pressure and promise devotion and girls buy the line. They can really like the guy but once sex comes into the picture, whether oral, manual, or vaginal the whole story changes. Do not kid yourself the 'bad' girls still get a reputation and the boys and girls too, know who they are. Even when you convince yourself this is DIFFERENT, trust me it isn't and it will come out the same. You will have to live with it as a young woman, and maybe regret it. The boys just find relief and maybe they do 'love' the girl, but that will pass. You will not be buried in old age next to one another. There will be many more people in your love life over time.

So, what's my advice? Be cautious. You will NEVER forget your first experience, (and it is not usually terrific), and do not waste it. Starter love is great and those feelings are powerful and wonderful, BUT sex is a whole different story. When you are mature, (not an age), sex is fabulous coupled with devotion, and time and all the ups and downs that real love coupled with passion brings.

At sixteen or so you are not THERE. And yes some people never risk it but most try.

Also at sixteen or so you are still developing in many other ways. Lots of them are confusing and difficult.

You are not a young adult and no longer a child but you will waver back and forth between both ends. Act like an infant and need mommy and then act like a young adult and be independent and make your own decisions. Go back and forth and eventually you will be independent and stand on your own two feet and have ALL the responsibility for your life... not always fun. So, enjoy the process and waver back and forth and make decisions but think first.

You have a lot to do with school, career, self-image, sexual desire; perhaps friend issues, siblings, step-families, and so on. It's a lot.

Acting under the influence of others, alcohol, or drugs, or pressure of, "If you loved me you would." Or "Of course I will respect you in the morning." may not work for you in the end.

Now it doesn't mean if you do act and feel badly later or feel that you made a mistake, the world will not end and it will not be on the eleven o'clock news, but you will have work to do to learn from your behavior.

Real love takes a long time and some people never get there, and true some people just like sex for sex, so you decide what works for you. And sometimes there is room for both aspects. Again, it has to work for you, and you will KNOW what is right for you.

Sex serves many purposes. Some people need it to feel desired, or accepted. Some people need it to get back at parents. Some use it to just get it over with. And so on…

I'm not even mentioning diseases, birth control or pregnancy here but that all factors into the issue.

How you feel about yourself will determine what you DO.

Difficulty at home with parents as you struggle to emotionally separate yourself is normal but do not go too far as you are not yet finished developing or totally independent. One day you will be. And one day you will have this conversation with your own teenagers. Won't that be fun telling them about your experiences? You bet!

"I have found the best way to give advice to your children is to find out what they want and then advise them to do it." - Harry S. Truman

You MUST Hate Your Mother

THREE WORDS THAT ARE ALWAYS true - "Gam Zeh Ya Avor"

This was in King Solomon's ring from his advisor. It translates to, "This too will pass."

The tragedy in the Connecticut school can never be forgotten or excused. But we have to go on and hopefully find ways to cope, understand and ultimately prevent such horror.

For the people who loved the victims Dante's words will be in their hearts forever. "There is no greater misery then in remembering happy times."

None of us can grow up without "hating" our parents in some form, mildly or fiercely. I have a full blog on that topic, read it. It is not possible to be your own person, in your own generation, without going through the process of emotionally "killing" your parent, especially the mother. She usually holds the power, as it were, over you and tells you what is expected and how you should live and behave. At the core most mothers want the best for their children. The problem is many are acting out what they want or didn't have for themselves. They want their children to do better and make them look good. Hence, the problem. They do not really see the child as a separate individual with talents and needs of their own.

My way of dealing with it all is to write this and maybe help others.

There are no magic words but those who go on can use the feelings to make life better for others in the name of their loved one. In life every good-bye is a sort of death and when death does come and the final good-bye is there we can only hope we have said and done all that we wished to for the person that is gone. It is never complete and when a child is taken from a parent, no matter what the circumstances, the realization that they will never experience or accomplish what they might have been capable of, is tragic. The other side is that they also will not have to suffer all the hurt and disappointments that life inevitably brings, off and on.

There is no more painful loss than that of a child and John Greenleaf Whittiier wrote, "Of all the sad words of tongues or pen the saddest are these, it might have been."

Another major aspect of this whole awful incident is the young person who committed the deadly deeds.

My theory is that he was in the throes of hating his mother and trying to resolve that dilemma, albeit in a "crazy" set of circumstances.

In Greek mythology, Oedipus unwittingly killed his father and married his mother, Jocasta. She hanged herself when the truth came out and he blinded himself. They had four children, and he went into exile, although he was king of Thebes.

Freud later, (1899), named a psychological process the Oedipus complex, asserting that individuals, (sons), have a repressed desire for sexual involvement with the parent of the opposite sex while feeling rivalry with the parent of the same sex. With girls, it's the Electra complex. Usually it is worked out over adolescence and the child then identifies and copies much from the same sex parent.

This young man's parents had divorced some years ago and he may not have had a role model to work out his feelings with.

With some individuals they try but never fully resolve the issue, with a parents' divorce or not, and they spend their lives in the struggle.

My hunch is that on some level that is what was going on inside the killer, and it just got out of hand. We will never know the real facts. Why he chose the place he chose and the victims he shot will remain a mystery, except that his mother had once worked there and he saw happy children with loving families, unlike his life. We can only imagine the why and make speculations.

Freud again, said that psychoanalysis ought to be praised for its' power to convert rank misery into common everyday unhappiness. That seems to be the case for so many people these days. Just too sad.

Am I suggesting forgiveness? No. Am I suggesting something might have prevented this? Maybe, Parents seeing problems, a teacher, a friend, professional helpers? Again, who knows?

What I do know is that having guns available certainly did not help. That could be changed.

In America that freedom seems poorly given and needs addressing… NOW!!

So what can any of us do?

Just let those who mourn know we care and try to make our world better. As Dr. Spock once tried to teach; we push our children for money, and what we call success, instead of teaching caring and learning how to truly love. Can we try to start now?

"How wonderful it is that nobody need wait a single moment before starting to improve the world." - Anne Frank

Step Families Go Up and Down Like All Steps

"Parents are the last people on earth who ought to have children." - Samuel Butler

Today being in a step-family is not rare and is almost the norm. That doesn't mean it is easy or an automatic wonderful family.

There are a slew of issues associated with this arrangement.

The first, of course, is the reason for the 'step' to begin with.

If the mother or father was the decision maker that will have an impact. If the former relationship was fraught with hurt and anger that will be an area for concern. The ages of the children involved and who they belong to are another area for exploration.

It is not unusual for children to attempt to sabotage a relationship that is not their original parents.

They can do this in a variety of ways. Sometimes it is subtle and other times it is outright in your face.

Any parent that cares about their children will harbor some sort of guilt or pain about taking a child away from its' birth parent unless that parent was abusive or downright awful. Even then it is not an easy task.

The best way to handle it is to be honest, and tell the child what the circumstances are and what they can expect in the future. The most important message is that you, and hopefully the absent parent loves them, and will be there for them, and that it is not their fault.

That message may have to be delivered many times in word and deed.

Can step parents love a child as if it was their own; well, close. If they have their own be aware that there has to be competition for the love and whatever that parent delivers.

Being a child means you are dependent on your parents. You are their 'victim' so to speak.

The best thing you can do is hope for a good and open relationship with both of your birth parents. If one is deceased that may be a bit easier. Accepting the step parent, especially if they are trying to be good to you, should be a goal.

For the parent there is much work to be done. First and foremost, your love and connection to your new spouse must be so strong and tight that NOTHING can get in between. This may be tested time and again, especially in the beginning of the new family. If it is a blended family with children on both sides that too can get involved and testy.

The new family is not just that immediate one either. There are in-laws, grandparents, and all sorts of others that will impact the situation.

The dynamics of family relationships is never easy at its' best so this new configuration is not a piece of cake.

The details regarding duties, rules, where you live, how money is spent and who is in control all have to be dealt with.

When family holidays come up or specific celebrations there is cause for concern.

I cannot tell you how many events that should have been wonderful were ruined and put into that bad memory bank as a result of poor relationships within the family; especially step families.

Now don't get me wrong, every family has its' problems and roadblocks, and sometimes the step family turns out to be better than any other family could possibly be, but there are issues to be aware of at the get go.

Children need to know they are loved, protected and safe, and that they are helped to grow up and be independent

When two reasonably mature people decide to connect and create a new family they can do fabulous things. The bottom line is that when a parent is happy their children will benefit from that. They will also demonstrate through daily living what a loving relationship is and the child will emulate that as opposed to an unfulfilling one that may have existed before.

The best example for children is parents who truly love one another in the ways that make life joyous; with intimacy!

So, in the end, do not fear making a change or having children go through the pain of not living with a birth parent. Live a better life and that will make it better for all!!

"There are only two lasting bequests we can hope to give our children. One of these is roots; the other, wings." - Hodding Carter

Are You Irrelevant

"ONCE THE GAME IS OVER, the king and the pawn go back in the same box." - Latin proverb

It's true that as we age we can feel irrelevant, in many ways.

Certainly, the body and strength change. Our looks may become a source of displeasure, and our skills can diminish. All of this can make one unhappy and at times even depressed. Some of it can be altered in a variety of ways; medically, pharmacologically, plastic surgery, new learning and so on. The real test though is what I read a while ago, and that was that you are most desirable by being curious and confident. Two factors that should be nurtured throughout life. But, do we foster or teach people this? Answer; NO!

So, whether you are a king or a pawn get ready; your life may feel over while you are still breathing!

Our American society does not make it easy to grow older. We value youth, and we want old people to disappear. We do not worship at the altar of wisdom and talent or years lived well. We do not want to even hear from those who talk about the past.

Ever watch a kid's eyes glaze over when a grandparent, for example, starts to tell them a story about what they experienced over the years?

Too sad. Life is a fabulous teacher and human nature does not change. Going through this difficult path called life offers help to many who are younger. To teach is a proud ability.

Now there are ways of getting messages across too. The 'know it all' or the bullying pattern is never greeted with enthusiasm, but the apprentice or kindly helpful manner is appreciated.

Life is a chess game and those who have maneuvered well can offer good moves to make. Those who have walked the walk know the road.

All people are 'flawed' in some form, as there are no angels walking the earth. Those that have figured out how to avoid the traps, so to speak, can be very helpful.

Life is full of ambiguities and loves can be transient and frail. It takes a lot of strength and risk to live fully. Common sense seems to have diminished over the years and we turn to 'experts' as opposed to the real thing; people who have not studied or written about subjects but have gone through life with its ups and downs. You can be the CEO of life!

If you look at old men with young women or today's 'cougars', you can immediately see what getting older means and how some people try to avoid or get over it. Maybe it works... at least for some or for a while.

Look at some companies replacing older workers with young ones, or how the whole work force treats people as they age. That gold watch doesn't even happen anymore.

Where do these people go and what becomes of them? Even those in their own businesses have problems with the child who works with them or younger employees. Can they keep up? Where is the energy, excitement, and drive? What about all the new technology and ideas that conflict? Big problems.

Recently there was an article in the New York Times Style Magazine, *Laws of Attraction* by Andrew O'Hagan about the laws of attraction. It was wonderful.

The ideas included a look at the French attitude toward women as they aged.

He wrote about our youth obsessed culture and how only stupid men do not value a woman's intelligence. They are only as good as the condition of their skin, according to these men. What they have accomplished is not even taken into consideration.

On the other hand, the French feel true beauty is not built to diminish, but to mature. Sexiness is not a stroke of luck but a movable feast! There is no, 'sell by' date on being interesting.

Beauty plus time can equal deeper fascination, he writes. He goes on to say that only later can we expect women to augment that initial, guileless attractiveness with something deeper; confidence, instinct, self-knowledge, and style upon which lasting beauty depends. HOORAY!!!

So do not buy into being irrelevant. Do not let life beat you down. Do not spend your days with worry and discontent. Go out there and be like the military; be all you can be, for you have lived!

"There has been much tragedy in my life; at least half of it actually happened." - Mark Twain

Can Friends Just Be... Friends

"FRIENDSHIP IS LOVE MINUS SEX and plus reason. Love is friendship plus sex and minus reason." - Mason Cooley

There is much to be said when it comes to friendship, and we will explore some of it all here.

Friendships can consist of many multi dyads. The core of most close relationships can have friendship at the base. These can include the closest of them; mother and child, siblings, grandparents, teachers, and even lovers. But in this context, we will primarily address the relationship of males to females as friends.

The basis of any friendship is what is shared; that is both verbally, and silently, and in deed.

Often we have known the person over some period of time, observed them, and come to trust them. How far we trust is based on a multitude of factors. We test them with bits of shared parts of ourselves and gradually move the pendulum as they come through. If they betray us in any form, we retreat or may in fact back off completely. It can only be what you observe, and what goes on between the two of you, not what anyone else says.

There are friends for going out to dinner, seeing a movie, calling with daily activities on the phone or e-mail, tweeting and so on. We have friends to gossip with and there are those that we use to borrow a shoulder to cry on. There are friends to share our joy and good fortune with and those that truly have our interest at heart. Most of us cultivate a very few true friends in a lifetime and those that last with any regular connection for long periods are few and far between. Most of us have had bad experiences along the way and have been betrayed, burned, or chosen poorly at some point. Things can and often do cause close ties to change over time and circumstance.

A true friend is open and there for you, and you need have no holding back with them. They accept you for all of you. In order to have such a friend you have to be such a friend.

Acquaintances are easy to come by and they are usually there for shorter stints and for specific purposes. They come and go and appear and reappear at various intervals in our lives. That makes the 'friendship' pleasant and always welcomed. That is easy.

With family, the saying is they are not chosen but in fact the relationship that you have with any of them is indeed a chosen one.

Now when it comes to males and females… and no matter the age or circumstances, the question becomes; is it possible to 'just be friends?'

The answer I believe is, sometimes.

Today with the intermingling of the sexes at schools and work, and volunteer services, there are a myriad of possibilities to, 'come across' someone who both interests you, and 'ignites' you, in a visceral manner. Now what to do about it?

You may find yourself thinking about the person, imagining being with them under a variety of circumstances, and wishing for a closer connection, notwithstanding physically.

You can dream about them, fantasize about them, have imaginary conversations with them, and think of plots to engage them with you.

If you dress hoping to see them, do cute little gestures, make up ways to run into them and so on, you are beyond friendship.

What causes problems is if they are otherwise involved emotionally, although that need not stop you, (how many have really satisfying relationships?), if they show absolutely NO interest in you, (and that can change too), or if you do not have a drive toward them that lasts.

Initial reaction is SO important here, BUT it is only the start.

Getting to know a person takes time and most importantly, sharing oneself and TALKING. Disclosing oneself to another is a seesaw like operation and one goes and then the other feels safe and on it goes. Underneath it all is not just discovery but also a fire that is ignited and begins to burn.

In a work situation, others will notice and hiding feelings, people you see regularly is a most difficult procedure. If one of you can't keep a secret and talks, that is another issue and a dangerous one. None of this is easy.

In some cases, friendship, really just friendship, is seen by one partner as more than that, (or the hope of fostering more than that), and that can create a problem that has to be very clearly spelled out.

One of the things that always surprises me is in the great love stories of all time, how many partners did end up as lifelong friends after their love diminished or died. The earlier bond has a special hold that does not go away.

One of the real areas to be aware of is the male or female, that makes a hobby of flirting and leading people on, just for their own ego or situational needs. They have no intention of a long term or even loving connection. BEWARE! Knowing their 'love history' can help avoid hurt here. And do not EVER think you will be the one to change them. Most never leave their spouses, (women do more than men do), no matter how empty their lives are. Almost NEVER happens.

Anyway, friendship comes in all varieties, colors, and situations. Losing a friend can be painful and sometimes we never know why… so be it. Consider the source and let it be their loss and problem. You move on… ALWAYS!!!!

If you are one of the fortunate few and that 'burning' friendship moves into 'at long last love' how lucky you are. Now nurture it!!!

"Between men and women there is no friendship possible. There is passion, enmity, worship, love, but no friendship." - Oscar Wilde

Crap Happens ... Deal With It

"Nearly all the best things that came to me in life have been unexpected, unplanned by me." - Carl Sandberg

I would add that all the rotten things that happen in life, (the crap), also is unexpected and unplanned, for the most part.

Think about your life and those you know and you will see it. There is an old Yiddish expression that men plot and plan and God sits in heaven and laughs.

There was a cover article I once did for Redbook magazine about how crises can be good for you.

The premise went something like this. Crisis is one of the few ways that cause people to change and often gain insight and modify old, non-productive, patterns of behavior.

It forces it. A crisis can put you out of control. It can make you aware of feelings you defended against, and it can cause needed insight into your life. Now this is true for both upsetting things and happy events. It shakes up the complacent, the knowable, and makes you readjust. It is a quicker way; more than professional help, to look at yourself and your relationships slowly.

We don't like our comfort zones toyed with, and we like the status quo.

Crisis, no matter what kind, and no matter in what area, causes you to realize life is messy, ambiguous, and frail. It is transient, unstable, and subject to many outside factors. Often we drum up stuff ourselves and it is an internal event.

Suffering makes us compassionate to others' hardships, and great joy creates an imbalance in the 'known', which is also unsettling. Happy endings are not always available. We need to be able to be resilient and move on and GROW from experience. I always say to children; life will teach what I can't.

Now one person may perceive a crisis of a minor sort to others but to that individual it is a big deal. Another may have a huge crisis but the outside world would never know it.

Our crises are based on our value system, and our tolerance levels.

Once working with a young mother who went to pieces saying her washing machine had broken, confused me. That certainly didn't fit my definition for 'crisis.' But, what I learned in dissecting the situation was that her husband had recently left, she had a child diagnosed with an illness, and her mother was not helpful when she needed her. The washing machine was the proverbial straw that did indeed break the camel's back.

We call upon our reserves, memories, past dealings with life, family, friends, experts, and so on to get us moving along.

There are some crises that do not get worked on positively and they can do us in; severe losses, illness, change in style of life and so on. But even here many have been able to use the experience to help themselves or in many cases help others. Nice outcome!

Children who are 'protected' and do not learn how to maneuver in this world are at a distinct disadvantage. Those parents who fight their children's battles, and allegedly protect them from real life do not do them a service. Life demands a certain level of toughness to get through. Those that can't, end up 'crippled' in many ways.

When a child is sickly, weak, or not too bright a parent's natural instinct is to protect them from the harsh realities. That may not be the best way and often you might be surprised by what people and children can rise to if given the opportunity. Adults as well.

Do not be afraid of crises. They will happen, mark my words.

See them as an opportunity for personal and emotional growth and development. A rare chance to force you to be better and have a fuller, more enriching life. You CANNOT prepare for them and even if you could do so in a small fashion, when it hits you are thrown into it.

One of the nicest outcomes can be an opportunity for real insight into who you are and what you are doing with your life and relationships. Once the heart is cracked open it can NEVER go back to being in its' shell. What a blessing… love is possible at last!!!

"When I hear somebody sigh, 'Life is hard,' I am always tempted to ask, "Compared to what?" - Sydney J. Harris

Children Of Famous People... What Happens

"The 'good' child may be frightened, and insecure, wanting only to please his parents by submitting to their will, while the 'bad' child may have a will of his own and genuine interests but ones which do not please the parents." - Erich Fromm

There you have it in a nutshell.

We have children for a variety of reasons, not least of which is to make us proud and live a life we approve of. We live and teach our values, most dictated by the culture we live in.

When a child is born into a 'famous' family it is what he learns from day one. The parent may be consumed by their fame and success but the child knows only that the parent is good or not so good for them. Now positive fame brings with it many rewards; wealth, power, position in society and a variety of people that are usually of the same ilk. Family becomes something different for these children.

To try to equal the parent becomes a Herculean task. Being proud and using the fame for one's advantage becomes easy. If we look at what has happened to many children of such parents, we can see a number of them falling by the wayside and never reaching their full potential or just giving up. Let's see some of the examples in living color.

Antony and Cleopatra married in 36 B.C.

She had three children; ten-year-old twins Alexander and Cleopatra, and four-year-old Ptolemy. She also had a seventeen-year-old son from Julius Caesar. He had five children from three other wives. Their children were considered illegitimate in Roman law, as he was married and did not divorce until four years later.

Octavian, who ruled Rome after Antony, had the seventeen-year-old killed. Antony's ex-wife raised the three remaining children of theirs. The record shows that the daughter, Cleopatra, married a prince who became king of Nubia. There is no mention of the other children's fates. One of Antony's daughters with his ex-wife was the grandmother of Nero.

Benjamin Franklin

William was his son and illegitimate, with no record of who his mother was. Franklin and his common law wife, Deborah, raised him. She was already married to a man that had left her. They had two children; a son who died at age four and a daughter, Sarah. William was his father's favorite, and went all over the world with him. As an adult, he too fathered an illegitimate son. He later married a daughter of a wealthy Barbados sugar planter in 1762, and this did not make his father happy.

He was appointed royal governor of New Jersey. Later he and his father did not speak as they differed on political opinions. Franklin disinherited him. William was later imprisoned.

After nine years when he was out of prison, he wrote his father and they corresponded and briefly saw one another. William remarried after his wife's death and his son, Temple, became a lawyer and fathered an illegitimate daughter. William like his father disinherited his son.

Albert Einstein

He had two sons from his first marriage to Mileva. She left him in 1914 and took the sons to Switzerland. He said the bad marriage made him work hard on his theories.

His elder son, Hans Albert, talked about his father as being loving and involved when he was a child. He too became a scientist but never competed with his father who he felt gave up on him. They came to America in the 1930's.

The younger son, Eduard, was four when his parents separated and nine when they divorced. He was a pianist and studied medicine. He lived in Zurich and his father lived in Berlin and saw him rarely. In his teens, he sent admiring letters to his father but then they turned angry and bitter. He was diagnosed as schizophrenic and nothing helped. He never saw his father again after 1933. His mother cared for him until her death. He died in 1965; at age fifty-five, in an institution. Einstein had remarried in America.

Sigmund Freud

He had six children and the youngest was Anna.

She was the most devoted to him and cared for him for the sixteen years he suffered with cancer of the jaw, which was extremely painful.

Interestingly he sent his sons to a family doctor to learn the facts of life.

One son became an architect, another a lawyer, but it was Anna who followed in her father's footsteps and became a child analyst. Against criticism, her father analyzed her and she learned all her techniques from him.

He died when she was forty-four and she became famous for her work on emotional development of children, and she was the leading child psychoanalyst.

Lucian Freud, a grandson, was a famous painter, and great granddaughter Emma, was the host of a hit British talk show called "Pillow Talk" which she did wearing pajamas in bed!

Gypsy Rose Lee

As a stripper, her son, Erik, had an unusual childhood, touring and seeing her perform.

She had divorced her second husband when she was pregnant. She told Erik that was his father.

She then married a third time and he took that man's name.

It wasn't until he was seventeen in 1961 that he learned who his real father was.

His mother stopped stripping at age forty-two in 1957 and she divorced again.

A psychiatrist told him the man he was told was his father refused to pay him, and Erik confronted his mother. She told him that he must never contact his father, and it was Otto Preminger. She choose him to be the father, but did not want him involved after that.

When Erik was twenty-two, and Preminger, sixty, he learned that his son was told the truth and he contacted him. They then worked together but Gypsy made them keep the secret from the world. When Gypsy died of lung cancer in 1970 Preminger publicly announced that he was adopting his son who was then twenty-six.

So, fame has its rewards and its downfalls, just like the rest of the world, only fame brings it to the world's attention.

"The finest inheritance you can give to a child is to allow it to make its own way, completely on its own feet." - Isadora Duncan

Do We All Hate Copycats?

"We forfeit three-fourths of ourselves in order to be like other people." - Arthur Schopenhauer

That old mantra that imitation is the sincerest form of flattery may work for some people but I know a whole slew of others who really hate being copied.

Now copying can take place in many forms and arenas.

As children we look to parents, and then as teens, to peers for acceptance and fitting in. As adults it gets more complicated.

It can be as simple as following the advice and experience of a mentor exactly, or as insidious as plagiarism calling a work your own. There have been numerous examples throughout history dealing with creative works of art, literature, journalism, and so on where the true artist was 'taken over' by a forfeiter. Often the real cannot be deciphered from the fake or copied piece. An expert would be required to determine the authenticity, and even then there have been mistakes made and heavy prices financially and emotionally exacted.

Now the other copying that takes place is on a one to one basis. Here the person emulates the style of manner, speech, dress, or taste of someone else and adopts it to suit themselves.

If you are a male and a business associate imitates your practice or way of doing business, you may be in for competition. The new kid on the block may even go you one better standing on the shoulders of what he learned from you. That can be a hard pill to swallow.

If you are a female that can happen too but more often than not females emulate one another in manner, fashion, or style.

What is especially funny to see is when someone copies your hair style, for example, and they look awful. If they dress like you but do not have your figure that too can be amusing to observe. If they copy your manner, it may or may not suit them. If you are competitive, which we all are in some form or another, it can be really annoying and friendships have gone awry as a result.

If you are an innovator and have worked really hard to be the individual that you are, and someone comes along and usurps it, it can make you furious. If you are secure and know you will always be the best at what you are, then it is not such a difficult task, emotionally.

If you are in fact an innovator you will probably always be one step ahead of the pack and you can keep that in mind. There will never be another you; not in totality!

Something most of us never knew is that Shakespeare probably read Ovid's 'Pyramus and Thisbe', which was written somewhere in his lifetime of 43 B.C. to 17 A.D.

It is the story of two young people who lived in Babylon as neighbors. Their families were hostile to one another but the two fell in love as teenagers.

There was a crack between their houses through which they communicated when they were unable to see one another. They had a meeting place and it was at night under a mulberry tree filled with white fruit that was outside the city gates. It was near a stream by a cemetery.

One night Thisbe, hidden behind a veil, waited for Pyramus to come. All of a sudden a lioness fresh from a kill with bloody paws appeared to drink from the stream. Thisbe was frightened and ran into a nearby cave dropping her veil.

The lioness got caught in it and ripped it to shreds.

Pyramus arrived at the meeting place and found the bloody ripped veil. Unable to find Thisbe and overcome by sorrow he plunged the sword into his chest, spraying blood over the white fruit on the tree, turning it purple.

Thisbe having recovered from her fright, went back to the meeting place and discovered Pyramus.

Unable to control her agony she took his sword and killed herself.

Her dying words to the gods were that they be buried together in a single tomb and that the tree should always bear fruit of a mournful color; purple. To this day the ripe mulberry fruit has a dark purple color to commemorate their unrequited love. Sweet, no?

Sound familiar?

When was the last time you read Shakespeare's Romeo and Juliet? He wrote it probably between 1591 and 1595.

Does it make it any less wonderful as a story? I think not.

So there's a case of a copycat that worked in its' time and place.

New ideas are old ideas that are improved upon. Original is not often from scratch.

We can learn from those who do things well, or have figured out ways to make us look, feel, or behave better. Nothing wrong with that.

A little competition along the way keeps the juices flowing and lets us know we matter to others, and they are observing us. We too need to follow the examples we admire and want to emulate.

In the end we are all just who we are with, hopefully, improvements as we move along.

"Don't waste your time thinking about who you ought to be; just be content with who you're becoming." – Anonymous

Do Jackasses Know They Are Jackasses

"IF FIFTY MILLION PEOPLE SAY a foolish thing, it is still a foolish thing." - Anatole France

The world is full of them; they are everywhere. The problem is to first of all, recognize them for what they truly are and then to give them no credence.

What is so interesting is that they often come off initially as non-jackasses and it may take time to discover the true person.

Jackasses come in all sizes and backgrounds. They can be educated, have money, and in fact be entertaining at first.

So, how do we determine they are the real thing… a jackass?

One of the most important criteria is what are their true values. In this country, we have slews of them because we worship money. The people who care most about dollars are usually big jackasses trying to impress you with what they have or can buy. It can be subtle or downright obscene.

Listen to what they talk about, and most of it is about money or who they know with money, or where they have been or are going, and how they travel.

Observe the obnoxious jewelry some of these women wear. And remember jackasses have their equal in the partners they choose.

Others are impressed with themselves and their education or what they have accomplished and they make sure you know it.

In my own world, I know a short not attractive man who has a PhD and makes sure EVERYONE calls him 'doctor.' How ridiculous. Out of hundreds that I know with a multitude of degrees he alone does this.

Pompous people are always jackasses. They need 'whatever' to make them feel important and want you to be impressed. What a joke.

Real people who are truly accomplished or creative, the height of it all, never push your nose in it. Most of the time they show interest in you, not in flaunting themselves. Most of the time you are surprised to learn about them and what they have done. Low key is the expression.

Real people are confident, caring, curious, and insightful. It was Plato who said, 'The unexamined life is not worth living.' How many jackasses look at themselves and really see who they are and how they relate to the world?

Often it is true that what we hate in others is what we don't like in ourselves. Hard to believe that but facts are facts.

There are SO, SO many people out there who are the 'walking dead' who just go through the motions of living. How many do you know who are full of joy, and connection? I have been around a while and both personally and professionally as a counselor, I have seen few. Pity.

Do jackasses know they are jackasses? Maybe. My hunch is that even if they realized it or had it put to them in some form, they would find some way of excusing it, ignoring it, or just not dealing with it.

If they are 'caught' early enough and mature and become worldly, then just maybe they can be saved and grow beyond it.

The need to be one is very strong and comes from insecurity that may go way back. It is a poor substitute for being a fulfilled person, who is comfortable in this world with all kinds of people. It is not easy. Some jackasses hide behind humor, sarcasm, or being argumentative; just to show they matter.

Some are 'charitable' and like to give money to causes, but always with their names in big letters. This is not too bad, as others do benefit from their largess. It is always better to have someone else tooting your horn. Jackasses need the spotlight on them and are usually very narcissistic.

Now don't get me wrong, we all want to be accepted and appreciated and thought well of; it's how you do it and in what realm.

The people that are not jackasses are easily recognizable just like the jackasses are immediately perceived. Sometimes however, they can fool you for a while. That is when it is dangerous to be involved. You can be surprised, disappointed, and even hurt. Most of the time they don't have to lie, the truth is right there in front of you. Anyone who is full of themselves is probably someone to watch out for.

People who are fulfilled and content with who they are have nothing to prove or shove in your face.

It is extremely important not to let the jackasses of this world get to you, even if they are in positions of power. They can do damage. Just because their egos are puny doesn't mean they can make you less than you are. Let it be their problem and see it for that. You want your life to have a happy ending and be meaningful.

Jackie Onassis said it well, "Complete use of one's faculties along the lines leading to excellence in a life affording them scope. We can't all reach it but we can try to reach it to some degree."

Emotional Cripples Are Vultures

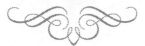

"Those who are unhappy have no need for anything in this world but people capable of giving them attention." - Simone Weil

This is all about those people who have grown up and remain children, or are so needy that they might as well be infants.

It all has to do with what they did not receive emotionally as children. My refrain is always, (God if you believe in one), help those who do not have a loving mother.' They are doomed from day one. Now, many do surmount that sorry beginning, or make up for it later, but that is a huge mountain to climb.

If your basic need for love and acceptance has not occurred in childhood, it becomes a lifelong search. Now there is no constant in all of this and there are always periods of conflict and feelings of rejection but they are usually surpassed by enough good feelings over the course of childhood and young adulthood. When this does not occur, the individual becomes an emotional cripple.

What does this mean and look like, you ask?

Let me elucidate.

These are the selfish, narcissistic people, male or female, that need the world to notice and cater to them. They are a drain to be with. Whatever is given, it is never enough and the hole inside is never filled. They are full of hurt feelings and they accuse you of not understanding, being 'mean' or just not caring enough. It is a continuous problem.

They miss a 'mommy,' or 'daddy.' Not just any parent, but a nurturing one.

They are on edge and waiting to be hurt. What is said is misinterpreted or misconstrued. Often they are just plain stupid or illogical.

Many of these 'uncooked' underdeveloped people are quite charming, often bright, funny, or sociable when first encountered. Their problem is deceiving. They can often be accomplished.

It is not uncommon for people in the helping professions to hook up with them. On some level, helpers are always ready to 'help' and be sympathetic. Nurturers fall into the trap easily.

Once there, the enabler or 'strong' more mature one may not realize their mistake for a while.

Sometimes they continue and are satisfied to feel important and controlling for a lifetime. Some continue to be the 'teacher.'

Others may grow up or have needs of their own and see that the partner cannot offer anything in a grown up responsible way for them. Respect is lost. Often the business of daily life, having children, money issues, social life, or other factors hide or mask the real cancer in the relationship.

As people age, illness, or crisis occur, the stronger partner has to exert more effort emotionally. That may or may not be possible. It can cause huge resentment or overload at times. If the weak one becomes incapacitated, that puts an added burden into the mix.

The 'crippled' one will take and take and take, like infants who will take whatever is offered. There is no limit or end. They cannot help it.

They will suck out the very life force at times. They are the vultures without a dead carcass.

The other danger here is that children see and emotionally copy what they grow up with. Of course, their own personality and life experience can often assist in remedying their own futures.

While the 'crippled' are pathetic and often sad humans, they do not do this to be mean. They are trapped and cannot change usually. The emptiness is too vast and has existed for too long to change. What is interesting is the numbers of so-called 'successful' people who lead those lives of 'quiet desperation.' Search though they may, they can change partners any number of times but they will always find themselves wanting, as their needs have not changed.

Some of these people put on a big façade and try to come across as strong in control people while the child inside is crying.

The weak one usually cannot change and certainly, after a certain age it is virtually impossible. Promises don't make it happen.

What are the choices? There is always choice.

Some seek professional help, which may or may not give more than insight, with the feelings lingering. Some try to make up for it with other activities or finding love substitutes, which can be like the finger in the dyke and suffice. Others find that a crisis jolts and causes a major change.

The partners also have choices. Take it for what it is. Enjoy the role of mommy or daddy. Find pleasure elsewhere, or move on. While the water found its' level in the beginning the tide may rise for one and not the other.

The worst solution is to finally recognize the true situation, resent it more and more, and do nothing about it. That is a death knell emotionally for the strong or whole one in the partnership. But the meshing that is insidious will not vanish and at some point will exact a high price with two people unfulfilled. Prometheus had his liver eaten over and over again by a vulture as he lay on a rock. I would suggest if you are in a relationship that is emotionally crippled, YOU are the one that needs to get loose and get away from the vulture!!

“It's never too late to have a happy childhood.” - Wayne Dyer

Family and Holi... Daze

"They will forget what you said They will forget what you did, but they will never forget the way you made them feel." - Attributed to Maya Angelou

So now we've all just been through Thanksgiving and a bunch of other holidays are on the horizon. Much of the time will be spent with family. Great?

Well, maybe… or maybe not.

The stories of stress and unhappiness that occurs at this time of year are abundant. Reason; there is usually a problem between or among family members, and even though we choose to be together old relationships rear ugly heads and more often than not, there are unresolved issues or uneasy feelings that are aroused.

If you are the one doing the dinner or whatever there is certainly pressure to have the place looking good and the meal yummy, but if you are the 'attendee' you are concerned with how you will get along with everyone and especially how you will deal with areas that are not so amiable.

We can never escape our past. Whatever went on there remains with us in our emotional reactions. True we can learn to handle them constructively and as we mature, if we do, we don't have to get overwhelmed or give in to bad reactions BUT don't kid yourself, feelings will arise as though you are still six or sixteen.

If the people who made you feel badly years before are there and they have not changed, mainly parents or siblings, mark my words, you will want to say, or do something, like run away and never come back!

What Friedrich Nietzsche wrote, "Family love is messy, clinging, and of an annoying and repetitive pattern, like bad wallpaper." He knew that it is certainly true in real life.

Of course the parents have reactions too as George Burns said, "Happiness is having a large, loving, caring, close-knit family in another city."

No one has a perfect childhood and there are no perfect parents. Each generation follows different experts and bemoans the former generations, 'mistakes'. We are all victims of our parents when we are children and the patterns that are established are there forever.

Here my experience gives me a bias that I believe holds true. It is primarily the mother who makes for a loving, and binding family.

Anyway, here we are, gathered for that holiday meal.

The bickering or downright unhappy parents, the meddling grandparents, the siblings who we are still angry with, or competitive with, and any ancillary aunts, uncles, cousins or friends, are all there in your face.

My solution is to have a BIG glass of wine, force yourself to remember something positive they did, and have others around to deflect the intensity of a one on one, and then tell them how happy you are in your own life.

Now if none of that works tell them you are going to a restaurant next year!

From the parents' point of view, it is usually that they are not feeling appreciated enough, for whatever.

From the adult child's point of view, they are in another world and don't care a hoot about their parents' opinions. If they still do maybe they haven't really grown up enough and still have to 'please' the parent. I haven't touched on in-laws here as I have another blog all about that relationship; so read it...

The two sides should just know they are both RIGHT!

Siblings can be more difficult because you are all in the same time period and can only deal with the here and now and remembering the pains of the past. It is only when each of you is comfortable in your own skin and with your own values and life that you can be strong enough to fight off any lingering bad spots.

It was a favorite of mine, Colette, who said, "A happy childhood is poor preparation for human contacts."

Just look at it as a graduate education and SMILE. The people who are NOT happy hate to see YOU happy and smiling!

Happy holidays and remember, "Always be nice to your children, because they are the ones who will choose your nursing home." - Phyllis Diller

You really don't want to be alone, without family, at holiday time… or do you?

Gee URU... Forget Guru

THERE ARE ALWAYS POINTS IN life when we want someone to help us, think for us, decide for us or figure life out. Some help or advice here and there can help but in the end it's up to YOU!

Albert Einstein said, "We can't solve problems by using the same kind of thinking we used when we created them."

A Chinese proverb says, "If you are planning for a year grows rice. If you are planning for twenty years grow trees. If you are planning for centuries grow men."

Robert Frost wrote, "In three words I can sum up everything I've learned about life: It goes on."

Few people raise children to be truly comfortable with themselves and all others in this world.

With our values of independence and materialism we get caught and often feel unworthy or unhappy, and unfulfilled.

Recently Joe Cilio, a 2010 graduate of Haverford College gave this year's commencement address there and he spoke about being nice to others and why that is necessary for happiness. When he raised the question about why you should try to love when the world is full of horrible things he answered it by saying, "Because you have to. Living a sensual, open life full of kindness and love feels good." Yes, it does, but how to get there?

No one can do it for you and it never comes quickly or without pain along the way.

To want instant gratification doesn't do it. None of us is perfect or so special that connection with others is not a possible goal. That's all we've got in the end. That is the be all and end all of what this life is about. True, you need a certain amount of resources to be comfortable, or more to live without fear of the car breaking down or the children needing braces on their teeth, or to live a very gracious life as some people desire, but it is always ONLY the human connection that brings a happy heart.

There was a recent poll that found that people who liked their work didn't care that they didn't earn a six figure salary. They were happy with their jobs and life apart from work.

Do we teach that to children? I don't think so.

Gurus are there to assist when there is a problem or guide you toward a goal of contentment. It is different for each of us.

When I see people for counseling I can help them showing how they got to be the way they are, look at their value system, and explore the choices involved and what each one offers. The real hard part, they have to do; live it! If it's not working the way you want, you can do something about changing it. No, not fast and not easily, but doable.

Sometimes a crisis will force people to change, and sometimes insight and really looking and working on an issue will do it. We continue to learn all the time and while there are some people who are sixteen for life most of us do grow emotionally. A partner whom we love and who loves us, can lead us to heights we never imagined on our own. But only if we are brave enough to risk our true selves. That is why marrying young is not a good idea. We're not finished developing yet, and as we change what we want and need will change.

How often are we lost in someone or even look deeply into another's eyes for any period of time? An exercise I used to do with couples was to have them stare into each other's eyes for a full two minutes without speaking a word. You would be amazed how hard that is for most people. We are busy people, chasing all sorts of things; money, education, leisure time, sports, and so on, and that means the real "I" doesn't get the attention it needs. A guru can't do that for you.

So, sorry, but YOU are your own best guru.

Get A Grip Or Add an 'E'

"THE ONE WHO COMPLAINS THE loudest is generally he who contributes the least." - A.G. Sertillanges

That's right, if you have issues yourself, you like to complain and then getting a grip turns into having a gripe!

Look at the world and what goes on, then break it out into your own little universe and see what gets to you.

Today it's easy to be mad at everything. No one seems to do anything right. No one cares. Just when you think you have a situation solved, guess what; it's not.

I was recently in a bank when an elderly man came in with a list of the things he needed taken care of. He kept explaining, and the teller, a young attractive woman, kept nodding and listening. As his exasperation wore on, I thought he was going to have a heart attack trying to get through to her. He was almost jumping up and down having apoplexy; she then calmly turned to him and said, "Have a nice day." Nothing was done!

It's everywhere.

The film, 'Wild Tales' is terrific. It is six vignettes about general everyday life situations that get out of hand when they are not handled well. The emotions take over and all hell breaks loose.

We experience these affronts all the time and there is no one to talk to or help with changing the 'systems.' Frustrating doesn't even come close. The time, energy, and emotional wear and tear shows in all of our society. We can gripe and that can become a way of life. That can then spill over into all of our life and often does.

Just look at the murders every single day that take place when guns are available and become the way to solve problems or grievances. What ever happened to arguments and fistfights?

Some of it is cultural.

If you look at India, they seem to have people who have a different attitude about life and its' areas of concern.

Africa also has a different mentality when it comes to resolving group or individual differences.

Sometimes just surviving takes up all the time and energy.

The English 'grin and bear it.'

Muslims pray. Catholics have confession, and many just suffer in silence.

We Americans are spoiled and want 'instant' solutions.

Well, a lot of life doesn't respond to 'instant' solutions.

Psychiatry has taught us we need to be happy. All the time? At what cost? As it affects others?

So, take a look at your gripes. What are they about?

Are they worth talking about? Worth fighting over? Worth being angry and missing any moments of love?

What do you use to get a grip?

Stepping back and assessing the situation? Taking responsibility for your part? Alcohol? Drugs?

Sports or exercise? Activity you enjoy? Friends and talking? Just knowing that this too will pass and life will go on often works.

It probably won't be on the eleven o'clock news!

Naturally, my concern is when it interferes with what's truly important in this life; you got it… passion with love.

So many couples get caught up in petty gripes that they cannot get a grip on themselves and they let good times dissolve into toxic patterns. This can all be stopped if recognized early and worked on. It is just bad behavior!

As a counselor I hold individuals responsible for their lot in life when they can have control and don't use it to their and the relationship's benefit. That's just stupid and self-defeating in the long run.

We are our own worst enemies. Do not gripe too often, and especially about the same things over and over. Give it up and get that grip!

"The one serious conviction that a man should have is that nothing is to be taken too seriously." - Samuel Butler

Holidays and Family Can Be...

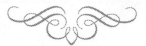

"LIFE APPEARS TO ME TOO short to be spent in nursing animosity, or registering wrongs." - Charlotte Bronte, 'Jane Eyre'

Fill in the blank.

Holidays usually bring a variety of family members together. What happens and how they behave is what this is about.

In order to understand the interactions, we have to first look at the history of the people involved.

Grandparents may represent the origin of the family's value system. Of course, they are from an earlier generation but they may indeed have set the stage for all that follows.

If they are respected and have lived well and wisely, they are looked to and appreciated.

Then there are the parents. They may be stepparents but all that really counts is the way they relate and feel and display their feelings to one another. They will tell you by their behavior what the next generation's marriages will be like. emotionally. Watch with care how they interact. Are they affectionate, playful, sexual, kind, or all the opposite.

The house into which you were born has a flavor, if you will, and you carry that forever. What you do about it is later up to you.

Then there are the siblings. They remember in their being, how they felt about one another as children and that message is engraved. Often you will see them revert emotionally to those childhood patterns. Some parents don't know how to make loving siblings. The biggest element here is whether they have emotionally separated from the parents. If not, they are children forever. It is usually during the teen years that it should occur but it may be later. It can be mild or fierce but it HAS to happen. We all want parental approval but in order to be an individual or grown up, you have to forgo a lot of it at some point.

Listen to the conversations and what is said. Is the talk superficial, shallow, or just intellectual? Is emotion involved? Do you talk about what really matters in your life?

Few of us have learned how to be truly comfortable and secure in our skins. Few are emotionally free and can abandon themselves in the moment, and few are mainly mature, SO what do we get?

We get people who are trying to impress one another, doing one-upmanship, arguing about big or nonsensical things, or not engaging at all in a real sense. There are subtle mannerisms as well, that take the form of sarcasm or joking. Hear what is said and watch the body movements. Who looks into whose eyes, who is uncomfortable and who is really empathetic and caring?

Water always finds its' level, and people are only comfortable with people like themselves. For some you might as well be speaking a foreign language; they just don't get it. Others never want to hear anyone but themselves. Others sit in judgment as a defense from looking at themselves.

Then again, you may not miss what you don't know.

It takes wide-open eyes, and minds, to connect, be interested in another, and share what matters to you.

Watching TV, texting, and talking on cell phones has not helped people, let alone family members to connect on emotional levels.

Being able to be comfortable in this world, with all sorts of people, and many who are vastly different from you, and your background, is a real achievement. You are no longer a narrow, limited person when you master that. Just watch the people who always have fun and people enjoying themselves with that person.

We are all victims of our parents as children; their values, ideas, behaviors, and relationships. The issue is to LOOK at your life and find out what makes you joyful and then work on getting it. It is hard and scary work and can take a long time. Some, maybe most, never complete the task. We have no school to go to and doing it alone is rare. And yes, you cannot and should not love everyone!!! Being whole in this sense is a process and never ends.

If you read the great philosophers and writers and truly fully developed accomplished people's lives, you will see it... always. They may have problems and yes, difficult relationships along the way, but they basically 'get it.'

Old scars can remain but there is salve to help heal them. Covering them with bandages does not cure; it merely hides. The wound will always be reopened.

To learn to love and enjoy another person, family or not, is the goal I would wish for, for all of us!!

"We must develop and maintain the capacity to forgive. He who is devoid of the power to forgive is devoid of the power to love. There is some good in the worst of us and some evil in the best of us." - Martin Luther King Jr.

It's Called Work for A Reason

"YOU ARE YOUR WORK. DON'T trade the stuff of your life, for nothing more than dollars. That's a ROTTEN BARGAIN." - Rita Mae Brown

There are troubling signs today in the world of work. Yes, women are better educated and many people are in colleges, but what happens in that real world of work?

It seems in former years there were clear ideas of how to improve upon your parents' lives, find useful employment and a feeling of pride and loyalty where you worked and with what you did. Not so today. How come?

In examining the situation, I have talked and read a great deal and explored the questions with a variety of age groups and backgrounds.

Let's start with the older group. Our America likes and reveres youth so the employee with age and experience is seen as out of touch and not able to keep abreast of all the new technology. That may in fact be true to a degree. With new workers searching for jobs, they can be found easily and bought at a cheaper rate. They can also be part time so that employers do not have to pay additional benefits.

What goes out the door is replaced with a neophyte. They may be creative and fabulous over time but not necessarily. And the older loyal one may indeed be burned out and disgruntled. Okay, so the company moves on. The old relationships, both good and bad, as in any similar situation are broken.

There may be secrets that also leave with the ex-employee.

Now the new one may have some experience from elsewhere or they may be a fresh face. Fine. Lesson one; learn the ropes. Learn the job and the people involved. Learn how to maneuver and get approval. This is not an overnight task or an easy one psychologically. Many of today's young people have never really had to work, and do not like work!

They are used to being catered to, think they are god's gift, and should be head of the company soon, and so on. There is no feeling of doing something good, important, creative, or interesting for a whole bunch of these newly minted employees. And work at the bottom is boring a lot of the time.

Now there are still the old standbys: doctor, lawyer, no Indian Chief, but you get the idea.

We do not do a good job letting young people find what they are really good at, how to get to a variety of work situations that they might enjoy or develop from, and we still make the almighty dollar the big goal. Nothing wrong with earning money and equal money for all who do the same job BUT is that the case? Not really, in many companies the scales are not equal. Many women have to work, and many men feel they could not support a family with what they earn. Starting a new venture is a BIG problem today.

Why not vocational schools with real trades that you could be proud of delivering and what about apprenticeships? Heaven knows this world needs SO much for improvement; both technical and human.

We all know the really smart kids and we know that they will always find a way, maybe with ups and downs and that's fine too. Do we prepare them for any of that? Where are the risk takers? Who helps with any of this?

I think the people who eventually find something they truly enjoy feel they should pay for the pleasure and use of time that work offers. They are the fortunate ones.

No, every day cannot be fulfilling, but even rotten times and mistakes offer challenges and learning that can expand horizons.

We have so many older people with experience that could help move our country forward that are going to fallow. That to me is a pity.

When you think about the America that was and where we are now it is sad. We became fat, dumb, and superficially happy. Where are the leaders? Who is doing anything?

There are small projects that are trying and good, but we need more and work is work and we need to teach about that world.

The other side is the social aspect. Work offers meeting and talking to others. Making friends, or even having romances. All bonuses.

Great article in the New York Times Magazine, May 4, 2014 by Ryan Pfluger, "The Tale of Two Schools." It had students from an expensive private school meet with a student from a poor school in South Bronx. They compared their experiences, lives, and goals. Fascinating, but no surprises. America needs all the talent it can muster and our current system is just not measuring up. We HAVE to CHANGE it!!!

"The world is full of willing people, some willing to work, the rest willing to let them." - Robert Frost

The In-Law is Never Like Your Own

FREQUENTLY IN MY COUNSELING PRACTICE, I would hear the comment that the in-law parent loved the child their offspring married, "Like my own." Rarely but sometimes I even heard it from the in-law child.

In some cases, there is indeed deep caring and respect between in-laws. More often than not, the opposite is true and in many cases real dislike and combat occurs. The whole issue boils down to whom does the child really love best, care about, or is afraid of more... the spouse or the parent?

It is especially precarious in a new marriage, a marriage of young people, and when the adult child ain't an adult! This process of separating from the parent should normally take place during adolescence but sometimes it never happens. The child remains too attached to the parent. We all seek parental approval in some form for all of our lives but the too close relationship between adult child and parent makes connection to a spouse difficult.

It is really a problem if there is only one parent, if that parent lives through the child, tries to remain young through the child, or if the parent has a need to control. This can be seen in many forms. Control can be accomplished through causing guilt feelings, withholding affection, approval, or with money. It is all insidious. If they have brought the child up well they can trust their child's judgment, if not, they can't parent for life.

When a parent has been a good and mature parent, they have a rewarding emotional life of their own apart from their children. They don't need the child as a substitute partner.

Sometimes if there are real mental or health problems they become the "legitimate" excuse to hold on too tightly.

In most instances, the in-law becomes the "bad" one. Parents will usually find a way to excuse, love, and forgive their own child, but not the in-law. The really tricky part is for the child to fight off the parent and meld with their partner. Not easy. This can be made even more difficult if the marriage partner fans the flames and is not feeling close to the spouse because of all the in-law turmoil. It has always been fascinating to me to see the repeated pattern, more often than not, between mothers and sons. That old Oedipal story.

So what to do?

It is good to be able to talk and get out genuine feelings and set expectations. No one works by radar. If they want to see you on Sundays for dinner, negotiate it. My advice was to tell the wife that she needed to remember that her husband goes to bed and has sex with her, not his mother. The wife can learn that as a couple they can stand on their own and make their life together and that his mother made him for her to love.

If the parent is wise, and grey hair doesn't make one wise, she will realize that an ongoing relationship, and a good one, with her son has to be through her daughter-in-law. True the in-laws do not share a common history and may in fact be of different backgrounds, but the new history can be very special... and just see what grandchildren can do!!

It's All the Rage

"One privilege of being associated with people whom a person loves is that of being angry with them." - Arthur Jersild

What gets you angry? Furious? Ready to kill?

What do you do about it?

As the quote says, if you can't get really angry at someone you certainly can't love them.

The opposite of love is indeed indifference.

Now there are usually different things that get guys upset as to what gets females upset.

With males, it is usually feeling unappreciated and jealousy believing their female is involved with another man. There have been many murders over just that.

With females, it can also be feeling unappreciated and then there are a myriad of other nuances that create anger. Their list is longer and there may be more unreasonable items included in that list. Call me biased or sexist, I don't care. I've been at this a long, long time.

I would teach females to really appreciate males and their contribution sexually. The penis is the BEST body part ever invented! And if he is turned on by you… appreciate his response. True it can be a ready reaction to many females but when it is with you, make it special and include the loving part.

With females, they need to hear the words that they are desirable and loved. Whatever gets in the way of that causes hurt, resentment, and anger or fury.

The pay back and reactions can go from minor to cursing, saying awful things, shutting him out in every way, and boiling inside to Mt. Vesuvius eruption.

With males, there is danger because they are usually bigger and stronger and can hurt or cause physical damage.

Because he is used to the manner in which his mother treated him he will react the same way he did when his mother showed displeasure or anger toward him. If his current partner triggers that old emotion, his response will be what it was growing up…unless he has worked on it. Also, when alcohol or drugs enter the picture there can be out of control reactions.

There is a wonderful comedian, Bobby Collins, who does a routine about what we say on the outside as compared to what we might be thinking on the inside.

But, in real life it isn't funny. Anger is part of life and how we deal with it shows our maturity, control, or helplessness.

If the same things keep on happening you need to take a look at the root and maybe, just maybe, try to change it.

Many emotional repressions lead to physical responses and dangerous outcomes.

When they say you can die from a broken heart, it is literally true. If anger eats you up inside; it does.

Having worked in a hospital for years I could almost pinpoint the illness and its' onset based on what was happening in a person's life. Spooky!

The people who walk around with resentment and anger inside and repress it over years get sick in one form or another. It HAS to come out somewhere.

When couples report little dissension or adolescents don't get out their anger no one can move on or connect in better ways.

Anger is a natural response as none of us can have all our needs met emotionally all the time. There are times when each of us needs extra coddling or understanding. Being thoughtful, apologizing, trying to do better, or being just plain considerate as we are to others, will do it.

It takes two to be angry. It can't happen alone. There has to be response; even if it is silence. Ignoring it or debunking it will be more infuriating as that means there is no credence or justification for a reaction.

Being loved will get you through it. Loving your partner, child, or friend, will get you through it.

The best outcome is to talk the issue through when the heat is off. Looking at the issues and honestly sharing the reactions is a learning experience and is necessary for intimacy and growth together. The concepts will be seen for what they are.

So, go on, get angry… it proves you love!!

"Never forget what a man says to you when he is angry." - Henry Ward Beecher

Rah Rah College

"WHAT IS LEARNED IN HIGH school, or for that matter anywhere at all, depends far less on what is taught than on what one actually experiences in the place." - Edgar Z. Friedenberg

Have you been around, or are you a kid applying to college these days? If you are you know what a horrible, stressful period this is.

If you are applying to one of the prestigious schools, like the Ivy League, it can be positively awful!

Every trick in the book is tried from coaching, getting professional help in writing an essay, to finding wealthy donors to the school, and various people to write letters of recommendation. It is a consuming take over your life horror show.

You and your family have been preparing for this since you were born. The plan had always been for you to get into the 'right' school.

After the agony of the SAT's and other preliminaries, the wait is on.

You and your friends are in the big competition. Who will 'win?'

What is the prize?

Today with everyone wanting to go to college and the costs escalating out of sight; is it worth it?

Many are asking that very question.

Why not vocational schools? Why not apprenticeship programs? Why not trial and error in life's experience?

Well, there are several answers.

School should be a place where you expand all of you. Who you are, what you may want to do with your life, how to earn a living, and how to pursue your passion.

It is also a testing ground for your acceptance, sexuality and decision making. It is a socialization process.

We are not 'educated' about what really matters in life beyond the basic tools.

Schools can be for dummies who can memorize facts and regurgitate them well.

It can be a place for conformity.

It can be… misery.

What if we taught students how to experiment, not to the point of hurting themselves, but to try new and different things?

What if we taught them about relationships that may or may not include sex?

What if we taught them that people who are 'different' from themselves have much to offer?

What if we allowed them to be really 'different?'

Can you imagine the freedom to be creative that would foster?

Yes, we are a competitive nation. Yes, being smart and proving it are important.

BUT, what if you are not one of those who wants or can go to college, let alone a 'good' one?

Some of our most productive and 'successful' people have never gone to or finished college.

I am not advocating that as a goal for all but just maybe we should look at the issue more broadly.

A liberal arts background certainly expands your horizons and makes you a multi- dimensional person, opening your eyes to new ideas.

The socialization is invaluable as you mix with a wide variety of people. The contacts for the rest of your life perhaps are invaluable. You are in a certain milieu.

Now without college maybe there is a world for you that takes you to other places. Life experience.

Maybe only those really smart ones who will go on with additional education for specific tasks should be in college?

Many of the campuses today are riddled with drugs, especially with the rich kids. Many are full of drunken parties. Many are full of rampant sexual activity. Maybe that's all good learning experience and learning how to behave once on your own. Maybe not.

All in all, it is the whole of life to be curious and want to explore the world and continue to develop oneself. That's the real education. Maybe we should have mini schools along the way at various life milestones and changes? Maybe that's the best that 'education' can offer.

Look at where real change for the better has come from throughout history. Much of it… not from college people.

I do not dispute research, especially scientific research, and what it has done to advance our world, but that is a small group of very well educated people. Rah, rah, for them!

So, do not make yourself crazy over that acceptance phone call… look at the broad picture and contribute what you have to offer in the best way possible. Then you and the world will be better!

"The object of education is to prepare the young to educate themselves throughout their lives." - Robert Maynard Hutchins

Self Help for Pessimists

"Death the last sleep? No, it is the final wakening." - Sir Walter Scott

Why write such a gloomy topic on Christmas Eve? Because that's when a great many people are sad and unhappy, especially when others around them are joyous, making it even more unbearable.

If the truth be known other than children who still find delight in 'things' many people are just not happy.

Sometimes it's the remembrance of former pleasanter times that compounds it too.

Not all of us have it right or even stop to take a step outside of ourselves and examine our own lives, so we go about our daily motions and think all is fine. Maybe it is, BUT then again if we really looked, maybe it's not.

Have you ever seen a mouse in a tank with a snake? You would never forget it. It knows what's coming and it sits and rubs its paws together until it is eaten. That's what life is like. We all know what's coming and some of us choose to find transitory happiness and make the best of it. That of course includes finding real love. Then the world is Technicolor.

You may know the work of the philosopher, Schopenhauer, and if not, here it is.

Basically to make life bearable you should lower your expectations. Problem is we have fairy tales and Hollywood making that difficult.

He says we are in a world always on the brink of destruction. Our wills are continually demanding things that the world cannot satisfy. Even when we briefly satisfy our desires they are short lived and we become bored.

If you look at all the famous people who have committed suicide you will get his point…let alone the ones not famous...

He was right saying wealth won't do it, and there is no such thing as altruism, as we are all selfish and want to satisfy our own needs.

Back to Schopenhauer, his ideas about getting through this life include:

Live in the present, making it as painless as possible

Make good use of the only thing we can control, our own minds

Set limits on anger, wealth and power

Accept misfortune and only dwell on it if we are responsible for it

Seek out solitude

Keep busy

Now you have the ideas and the TOOLS.

He interestingly, lived alone twenty-seven years except for a series of poodles!

We like dogs or pets because we can project any of our thoughts or feelings on them and they love us unconditionally. How nice. Try that with anyone else….

So, ho, ho, ho and merry whatever.

With a new year on the way there is much to think about and while some of us make resolutions others of us will try to find solutions. There is much work to be done both within ourselves and the world around us.

The time was never better to begin. It all has to do with both mind and feelings and the feelings will always win out, both on a personal and grand scale.

"Feelings are not supposed to be logical. Dangerous is the man who has rationalized his emotions." - David Borenstein

The following is a short list of some people you might recognize that decided to end it all, on their own:

Salvador Allende

Mark Antony

Diane Arbus

Capucine

Cleopatra

Kurt Cobain

George Eastman

Vincent van Gogh

Ernest Hemingway

Adolph Hitler

Richard Jeni

Alexander McQueen

Freddie Prince

Mark Rothko

George Sanders

Virginia Woolf

Sometimes we are kinder to animals than to ourselves when 'it's time.

Sibling Rivalry... It Never Ends

"GOD GAVE YOU CHILDREN so death won't come as a disappointment." So said Joan Rivers, and many of us would agree. One of the most difficult aspects of being a parent is living with sibling rivalry. This begins as soon as the second child appears. It automatically usurps the center of attention from the first-born. No matter what it cannot be avoided. It depends on how it is handled by the parents that determines the degree and outcome over time.

If the child is the sex the parent preferred the attitude will be different than if it is not.

If the child looks like the parent or someone they like it will affect the relationship. If the child has a personality that the parent responds to in a favorable way, that will play a part.

Siblings always eye one another and measure themselves against one another in a variety of ways. How they look, their accomplishments, and above all the stage is set by how they feel accepted and loved or favored by the parents. Many dynamics can be played out here. If the marriage is a solid one, the parents will behave as a unit. If not, one may favor or play a child against one another. Often a child will be favored or not favored at different points in their growing up.

My own personal favorite was taking a long car trip with my two daughters who are about three years apart and hearing commotion in the back seat with one screaming, "She's looking out my window!" There is just no dealing with that. When each child at some point says, you are nicer to her or him then you know you are doing a good job.

As small children, there is stuff like what each child has as gifts for example that set them off. The values that the parents live by are ingrained into their children at young ages, so if a father thinks being a good athlete is a high priority and one child excels in this fashion the other child will naturally resent the brother or sister and try to gain the father's attention and affirmation in other ways, sometimes with little or no success. This of course, affects the sense of self-worth.

Many clients I have worked with favor one child over another as one will live up to the parents' dreams.

One of the most difficult things is for a parent to love and truly accept a child who is different from them in looks, values or accomplishments. Sad examples exist where parents have actually emotionally removed themselves from the lives of their children. This often happens when they do not approve of the choice of a mate their child has made. So when children do not feel they are accepted for who they are and a sibling is accepted and in a different position, they act out.

The two or more children can take sides for or against a parent, or against one another.

There are any number of examples of siblings who revert to childlike patterns no matter what their ages when in a family setting or around parents. Think of all those holiday dinners and the tension or out and out verbal subtle and not so subtle messages. The real feelings are always there.

When adulthood occurs it is the wise ones that put aside childish slights or hurts and feel confident in who and what they are that makes the playing field equal. The siblings accept their own and their siblings' differences.

The oldest will always have privileges and different responsibilities, and then if they succeed it will go on to the next and so on. If the first one messes up the hopes of the parent may be transferred to the next or another sibling. The baby will always be the baby and these children may never really grow up.

Nora Ephron said the successful parent is one who raises a child who can pay for its' own psychoanalysis. I think it is a parents' job to make each child feel good about themselves and although a bit of sibling rivalry can be healthy and push people on too much of it can erode a family's true happiness, and that is the fault of the parents from long ago.

Spoiled Rotten! As Adults

MANY OF TODAY'S YOUNG PEOPLE have been given much by parents... because they had it to give. There is nothing wrong with wanting your children to have a better life than you had. This is true not just with material things but in the way of praise and giving children the message that they are great in any number of ways.

The kid who comes home from kindergarten and presents his parents with some picture that is scribbled is oh'd and ah'ed over as if he is a junior Picasso! The child who has a beautiful face is looked upon as a movie star and the bright child gets to believe he is Einstein. Now don't get me wrong, letting a child know they are special and loved is a good message, even if it is exaggerated.

The ego is built upon these messages and the child learns early on he or she is loved and appreciated and may indeed have talent or brains. All that should be encouraged. If the child is given many material things which parents do to show their wealth, have others see what they can afford, or to make up for being absent or not there for other things the child needs, in time, for example, they learn that is what matters in that family. Nannies don't deliver the same messages and certainly not in the same way. Sometimes grandparents can contribute to all of this as well.

So what does the child learn from this? They learn they are God's gift to the world and that they matter, and more importantly, they learn what values the family holds and lives by.

I once had a friend, one of the world's wealthiest men, tell me he was not leaving a huge fortune to his children as, "It makes them lazy house dogs!" Bill Gates and others in that league have said or delivered the same message. It takes away initiative and the child has no drive to develop on his own and become his own success.

At any rate what happens when these children become adults? Well, in fact the world usually teaches what the parent can't. It can be a big shock to discover you are not the center of the universe and there are indeed others who are richer, smarter, or prettier.

What to do then? The smart ones adjust and work on their own growth and the ones not so smart become angry, frustrated and can give up. Material things will never bring true contentment, just a bigger house to be miserable in. It is sad that many Americans have money as their prime goal in life.

Sometimes spoiled adults seek a partner that will continue the childhood message and they will be takers, not givers. Look at all the young narcissists we have now. It is beyond selfish and self-centered. They believe the world owes them, they hate authority, and they are demanding, not gracious people.

Then as parents... Often they vie for the attention with a child and resent the child as a result or they repeat the pattern and grow another generation of narcissists! The opposite is the case when children do not get the attention they need and they search and try to grasp it from others, all of their lives. BUT the lacks from parents usually leave a hole that is never fulfilled.

So what to do?

Give praise and things and at the same time teach appreciation and compassion. Show children those that do not have. It will go a long way to make a completed, contented individual and a better world.

The Business of Women

"Women are at last becoming persons first and wives second, and that is as it should be." - May Sarton

As you look around today you are aware of the different role of women, especially here in the U.S.

They are educated and they work, and they run households, and rear children! No easy task all of this.

Whatever you think, women are different from men in many ways; and especially in their brains. They are better able to do multiple tasking than men are. They are definitely more empathetic and better collaborators than men.

So the question becomes why are they so few in number with power, or powerful positions?

Even when they have top positions in the work world, they are paid less than men are.

This is a long-standing situation and although addressed it has not significantly changed… yet.

My own theory is that real women have a nurturing nature and their drive is to be loved, mainly by a man, and to have and rear children.

When you find a woman who is not driven in that fashion she usually has a lot of testosterone and is not what I would call feminine. Being female is multi-faceted and the world of work has now rooted out the women who can do it all, so to speak.

There is a new horizon in the work world and companies like Business Talent Group are making the adjustment so that women can use their talents and education and still be really feminine.

They have top-level people doing projects and not having to go to a place for many hours a day or week. It is a great concept. Talent at your own pace when you want to use it.

And by the way, this new format also serves men well.

Women who like men can use their femininity and still be totally competent when working. They do not have to compete in the same old ways.

This allows them to be spiritual if you will, and connect with the people and things they love without being worn out and driven.

This also allows them to have the time and energy to 'let go' which in turn allows for full sexual delight!

Much of life is boring and we have few 'special' moments.

Work definitely compounds that process. This is probably truer for women than men. The title, 'mother' is one of the most demanding and emotional connections for the majority of women.

If work impedes that, it is a tug of war.

Some women give up one or the other in order to be 'successful' today. Men do not have that choice. They are out there making babies, and slaying the dragons… and they like it!

For a woman to be out there in the same way diminishes her in her female role, I believe.

Once children are on their own, and once she is supported emotionally to do 'her thing' the job can take on new significance, and be more manageable.

The main issue to keep in mind is that while women can try to be 'Superwoman,' something will have to give.

Even with the best help or nanny, the role of 'mother' will take precedence or feelings of guilt when it is not foremost.

The woman in business of any sort has a tough road. She is torn in several directions. Even with a partner who 'helps' and is understanding she carries a huge burden.

Working part- time or taking time off does not usually help her career.

Big money however still takes a great deal of time and effort; a project here and there will not put her on the top rung. She will still be competing with men, and not just for compensation.

A new system may be the answer to a new beginning in how we all view and use 'work.'

When we look at the 'millennials' and their desire to work for themselves, and needing praise, it is not such a bad future. While most has been written about the males here, the females are part of the over-all picture.

Our world needs talented, committed people of both sexes to solve what is going on everywhere. If we cut off a large segment, namely women, we do all of us a disservice.

Women need to be women… and they need to use their abilities to their utmost without sacrificing one for the other.

"Once made equal to man-, woman becomes his superior." – Socrates

Get Certified

"MAN USES HIS INTELLIGENCE LESS in the care of his own species than he does in his care of anything else he owns or governs." - Abraham Meyerson

We live in a world where we must be 'licensed' for any number of things; driving a car, being in any kind of a profession, yet for the most important aspects of life we are left to our own devices.

We do not have to do ANYTHING to be a full person, a partner or parent. Why not?

My guess is that in a 'democracy' you have the rare privilege to screw up your entire life and affect others in a perverse or bad way!

Could this be changed? I believe it could certainly be made better.

If I ruled the world people would have to learn about themselves. They would examine their backgrounds. They would look at their needs, and they would see who they really are. It would be a goal to be comfortable with oneself.

Without that there is NO way anyone can find happiness and learn to love; which should be the ultimate human goal.

The steps to being a 'person' would be followed by being a partner.

How to share hearts is not taught anywhere and the examples most people have in growing up are usually falling short of real love and intimacy.

So, what happens? They repeat the narrow lives they have learned at home. Pity!

Yes, we know things that can help make you a better partner.

I would certify people as lovers. Yes, I would. Those that learn would have a certification and seek partners who are also 'certified.' Why not?

And the biggest task of all; that of preparing the next generation would also not be left to chance.

What is entailed in being a parent would be learned from what to expect at different ages from a child to what emotional needs ought to be met. Imagine a world in which children had 'certified' parents who knew what the heck they were doing!

Yes, there would always be some 'baggage' but it would still be better than what goes on today.

Now who would do all this teaching and what do they know?

We have all sorts of 'experts' out there and they can differ in ideology but there are some basics that are available and have been tested over time.

On this 'journey of learning,' I would include not only being self-aware, but social awareness, what really goes on in relationships, how to deal with hurt, and anger, and decision making.

The practical aspects of life such as responsibilities, managing money, and sharing duties can also be taught.

I have a friend who had a very important position and told me he didn't know anything about money management until as an adult he really got messed up. That's one way to learn but not what I am suggesting here.

On this 'menu for life' the business of sex would also be taught in a real way so that people would know what to do for themselves and their partners to achieve the highest level of satisfaction.

Now those that want to stay uninformed need not apply. Not everyone wants insight or a genuine look at their relationships. They are content to be 'dumb.' That's fine with me... stay and live out a limited life.

We are not all the same and we all don't want the same thing out of life; too bad for many.

BUT, for those that get 'certified' they have a license that is more important than any other. And they will be appreciated like any connoisseur or qualified person in any other field; only this will be the highest degree ever offered.

Boards of 'experts' could put together the syllabus and it would be reviewed and updated frequently and those that are qualified would report their success in life. Others would then want to follow the example.

Maybe universities could be involved or public education. Anywhere where learning is valued.

Wouldn't it be great to carry around a card that says you passed the test and are looking for a partner with the same skills?

Think about it…what do you wish you had learned about all of this and how would your life be different today?

I bet you have things that you could list!!

"The happiness which is lacking makes one think even the happiness one has unbearable." - Joseph Roux

The Middle Muddle

"THE FIRST HALF OF OUR life is ruined by our parents and the second half by our children." – Clarence Darrow

Rather negative and depressing… right?

Blaming others for our life situation is an easy out. The really difficult part is taking responsibility for the life you lead. That takes courage! It also takes a willingness to look at, think about and examine yourself from time to time. Sometimes unhappiness or a crisis forces that. Other times you may have to just take a step back and ponder.

The middle years are an especially tough period. That is when you usually have teen or young adult children and aging parents.

The pulls go in both directions and, heaven forbid, maybe at the same time they are both wanting parts of you or stressing you.

The emerging adult may be emotionally separating and putting you through the wringer. At the same time parents are aging and not what they used to be.

With the child you want to still have some influence and control. With the parent you have to battle their wish for continued independence when it may not be possible as in the former fashion.

Either way you have an emotional battle on your hands.

With the child you are still the parent. With the parent you are still a remnant of the child.

The old hurts, and anger even, does not disappear.

You have to be careful not to want and act out 'revenge.'

What you can do and not do needs to be accessed. What you can live with needs to be addressed.

Then in the mix is your life with or without a partner.

The pressures of any of this will take a toll. Your partner may be helpful or in many instances also putting demands on you.

You are in a full-fledged war battling on all sides.
Taking care of you is not easy during this period.

Who do you turn to for sustenance? What brings you relief or pleasure? You really need to take time to work that part out for your own wellbeing.

I had one client who finally said it was her mother or her, after she took her elderly mother in to live with her. She came to realize it was not doing either one of them any good. Once the difficult decision was made to place her mother in a care facility they were both better off.

I have had other parents who put guilt on their young adult children for their own unhappiness, or even, bad health problems. Not fair! They are trying to grow up and be independent and test the waters. They can make bad decisions and learn from them. They need to experiment in their world which is different from yours. You need to allow it.

The thing that gets you through it all is, you guessed it… love!

When there is a foundation of caring and loving that is what will rise to the occasion.

The love for a child from day one will be remembered and appreciated. Just being there is good enough during much of this period. While it is true the times are trying and the harder you hold on the harder you make it for the child to grow into an adult; they have to be strong to tough it through.

You have to watch much that you may dislike or even hate, to allow the growth to take place. And true some do fall and never get up, but the majority work it out and become their own person. In the end you will respect their accomplishment.

Now with the aging parent it is painful to see once successful, vibrant, in control people, fail.

They will hold on with their bare knuckles and even fight you for their independence and right to rule you. That is a really painful battle. When money is involved and they control the purse strings it can be absolutely awful. I have worked with families where there were fortunes and even then there were issues and battles that were truly unnecessary. It can be a horrible ending to what should have been a contented life's end. People can be extremely foolish with silly ideas and values.

What really matters in this life? In the end we all know what we face. How do we want to do it?

For my money it should be with kindness and loving gestures… always!!

The thing to remember is that you will not remain in the middle for life. Life moves on and you will too...then you will be on that other end!! Watch out because you know who will then be in the middle!!!

"Even the happiest child has moments when he wishes his parents were dead." - Allan Fromme

Money... Matters

"If you make money your god, it will plague you like the devil." - Henry Fielding

While money is important for this life it has many ramifications; especially here in America.

The first question is how the money was obtained.

If it is inherited wealth that may set the stage for a life of expected privilege and never having to 'prove' oneself. A life of idleness and indulgence may not offer fulfillment in the end. Ambition may go.

True, the fine points of living may be taken for granted and the attitude of never having to worry about money will be ingrained. That part makes life easier to be sure and only having grown up that way will instill that manner within you.

For those that have worked for their money they learn the value of a dollar and then it becomes a question about what they do with it. What people do with their money tells a lot about them. Money is a way of showing what really matters to you.

For some, they become the 'takers' and withhold their money.

Others become 'givers' and are that way in all aspects of their lives.

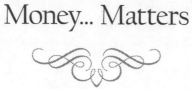

Some are free in some areas and withholding in others. You can see it.

What is extremely interesting is the people who have to flaunt it and try to prove their worth and impress others as opposed to those who have nothing to prove.

For many, after acquiring whatever their goal is they continue the 'chess' game to enjoy the accumulation and show they are 'winners.'

Everyone gets to decide how they wish to live and then go after that lifestyle.

Some are happy with McDonald's and others have to have the French Laundry regularly. We all get to decide. Some never experience the full gamut of what is available and that may be the limitation they settle for all their lives.

It is only through experiencing a full range of choices that we know what's out there. Some are not curious and others really do not care.

They did a study, (naturally), about money and happiness. It showed that after a reasonable amount of income and living comfortably there was no difference in those people as opposed to those with millions of dollars.

Dealing with your money and protecting it is a full time job and takes knowledge and like everything else, experience.

Being able to stand on your own two feet feels good. Women have learned that.

Money doesn't care who has it. Look around! Class and taste do not come automatically with dollars.

It certainly is important for comfort, gracious living, health, and things like educating children to give them a good start in life. Nothing wrong with any of that.

Then see how happy, and for how long, buying things, or going places keeps anyone content.

We have made money so important here that people will do almost anything to obtain it; legally or otherwise. Watch the news!!

Many people do not enjoy what they do to earn it.

It would be good to have that passion; loving what you do and many of this generation are looking at just that. Good!

When there is passion, whether about how you spend your life making money, or in relation to someone you truly love then and ONLY then will you have a fulfilled happy life!!!

"Money is human happiness in the abstract: he, then, who is no longer capable of enjoying human happiness in the concrete devotes himself utterly to money." - Arthur Schopenhauer

Am I Normal

"Life is pleasant. Death is peaceful. It's the transition that's troublesome." - Isaac Asimov

Have you ever asked yourself this question? Most people have at some point in their lives. That's normal.

There are definitions of psychiatric disorders listed in the Diagnostic and Statistical Manual for Mental Disorders commonly called the DSM. It is updated periodically to add or subtract a listing. They too have difficulty in some of these decisions!

It is perhaps easy for anyone to know when someone is really 'crazy.' We are not talking about those people here.

What we are talking about is everyone who is human who gets into tough spots and has bad times and can't get it 'together.'

Now who among us doesn't have their 'down' times? Who doesn't go 'haywire' from time to time? Who doesn't want to kill someone or themselves every so often? Answer; everybody!

So what is normal?

One category that the DSM uses is a definition of a 'borderline personality.'

These people it says suffer from:

Problems with regulating emotions and thoughts

Impulsive and reckless behavior

Unstable relationships with other people

These people it says have high rates of co-occurring disorders such as depression, anxiety, substance abuse, eating disorders, and suicidal or completed suicides. Almost two percent of American adults are thought to have this problem every year. Two percent, my foot!! We all have some of these issues any given time….

What does that say about our culture? What do we learn and what do we live? What are the values that we hold dear?

All of this can get confusing. That is probably why most people go through the motions of living and never look at their lives, to evaluate it from an emotional perspective. The 'okay' life is what many lead. The boring, hum drum existence suffices for the majority, perhaps.

My own rule of thumb is that if your life is not fulfilling, and by that I mean, in your heart, and it doesn't get better over time, you need to do something about it.

Now psychiatry can help in its' many forms from a good friend who accepts you totally to a doctor who can prescribe medication. There is help out there.

Yes, it is not easy to unburden yourself, and there are not a lot of people you can trust with your 'raw' self, but if you dare, you can get relief. You will feel better. Only you can know how your heart feels.

The outside world really doesn't give a damn. It will not be on the eleven o'clock news.

People who are fun may be a little 'crazy' at times but that's fine. They are not boring.... they are the unique, interesting people we all like to be around.

The people who have opened their minds and hearts are readily noticeable. They draw others to them and they are happy and joyful.

When you see the malcontents, what I call 'pickle pusses' you recognize them right away. They are like dead carp. No personality. Always finding a problem, critiquing others, rather than looking at themselves, or just downright unhappy, or miserable. The 'walking dead' are in this group. They have given up and think they have settled for what everyone else has and they lead peaceful dull existences. Yes, they are 'normal' but at what cost? They have dearly paid a high price.

This life is meant to be grabbed with both hands and jumped into with both feet. Splash in the mud, be spontaneous from time to time. Let it all hang out. Share your 'self', mind, AND body, with just one other that you love and you will be loved in return.

Water always finds its' level. Emotionally if you can love you will find another who can love. If not, you will lead a VERY normal and EMPTY life!!

So, yes, be a bit 'crazy' at times. When in love one is always 'crazy' and that's a good thing. Do not fear it.

However, if you are unhappy and things are not going the way that makes you feel good most of the time, and the same problems keep reoccurring; talk it out. I promise you will be on the right road. You will not be weak then, you will be stronger in the end.

"When we long for life without difficulties, remind us that oaks grow strong in contrary winds and diamonds are made under pressure." - Peter Marshall

And Baby Makes... Trouble

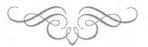

People always think of babies as those cute little things that we play with and bring along for the oohs and ahhs of the family and friends and strangers. Well, I'm here to tell you it ain't all like that.

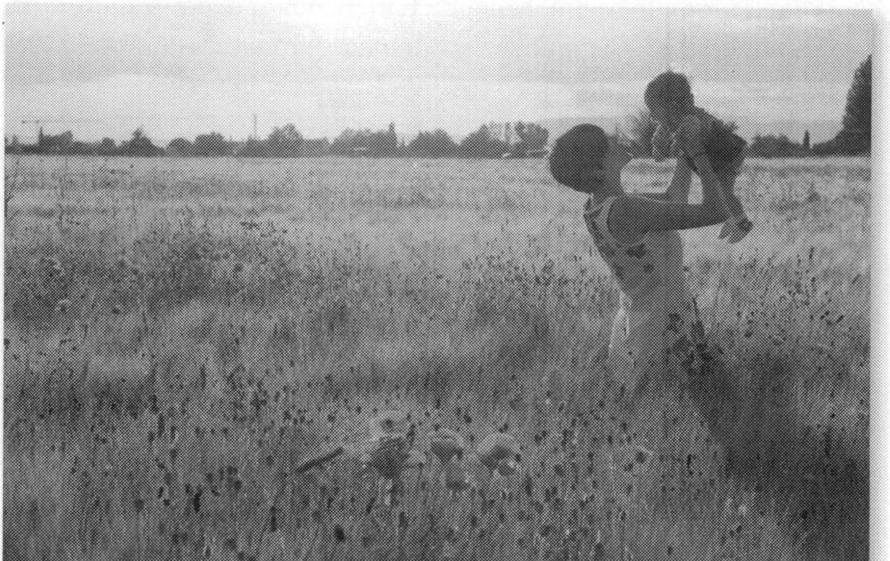

Again we get no preparation for what being a parent is really all about.

There are many reasons for having children and rarely is it to raise a responsible next generation. Ask people why they had children, and you will be surprised at the answers.

When my friends tell me they had a child or grandchild I respond with, "Great, someone else to worry about and spend money on!"

Now I'm not a cynic; just a realist.

One day early in my counseling career, an elderly woman came in to talk about her adult son, about forty years old, whom she worried about caring for himself when she died.

I asked to see him and he came in and slouched in the chair across from me. He did odd jobs to make money and I began questioning him.

I said maybe he should have a real job.

He responded," And what then?"

I said he'd have money on a regular basis.

He said, "And what then?"

I said he could have his own place to live apart from his mother.

He said," And what then?"

I answered that he'd have funds to buy things he liked and needed.

He again said," And what then?"

I went on telling him he could do whatever he wanted.

"And what then?" came back.

Finally, I asked about what he really enjoyed.

He said he liked to go fishing a lot.

I then said he could do that if he had a job.

With that he sat straight up and looked me in the eye and said," Lady, I do that now all the time!"

I was left with wondering who had it right, me or him. I was getting up early in the morning leaving my young children to go to school and work and here was this guy doing what he liked. It was a lesson for me.

Worrying about children no matter their age never stops. From the minute they arrive until your death they can be a source of great pleasure to be sure, but a worry a good part of the time.

Plus, a lot of them are quite frankly a pain in the ass.

They are ALWAYS unappreciative on some level. That's the nature of the relationship. They learn to expect as coming to them, whatever the parents provide. They cannot be saying "Thank you" all the time, or even a little unless they are taught.

We all want them to have better than we but that's not always the best for their lives.

Teaching about standing on their own two feet, being responsible, compassionate and making this world better might be in order.

But you know, as a general rule, we don't think in those terms here in the United States.

Children are the victims of their parents and once they are past five or six the dye has been cast, and while not impossible it makes change difficult. Of course the generations cause change and that can be for good or not so good. And then there are influences like the peer group during adolescence, but the core usually is set and gone back to in the end.

We need a school for life as it truly is, and we need to look at our goals along the way.

Dream on if you think a baby makes life wonderful. It changes everything, and especially the relationship between two people.

So, be prepared, and then decide to have a baby, after you have taken care of a friends' newborn for a full week at least. Your family and friends will welcome the offer!

Perfect Doesn't Exist

"Have no fear of perfection- you'll never reach it." - Salvador Dali

For those of you who drive yourselves to distraction you need to hear this.

Searching for 'perfection' can be beneficial in some ways but it can be quite harmful in other ways.

Looking for the perfect dress, the perfect home, the perfect job, the perfect mate; all nice ideas but totally frustrating in the end.

Some areas can be felt as perfection at the moment or even for a while but your idea of perfect is only that; your idea.

It can be very satisfying but realistically someone else or a lot of someone else's may disagree. You have to stand your ground when it comes to this.

There are some forms of perfection to be sure. Mostly they exist in nature. Look at a gorgeous sunset, a rainbow, a beautiful tree, a landscape, flowers, and so on. They are perfect in form and beauty.

And yes, we can find that dress that looks wonderful and we view as 'perfect' at any given time.

We can find the home that we feel is 'perfect' for our wants and needs at a certain point in time. And we can work on ourselves to an ideal that we believe to make us 'perfect' or close to it.

Read or ask any creative person if they ever believe their painting, written work, or music is perfection and most will answer, 'No." Achieving that final point is almost always viewed with hesitation, believing 'it' could be better.

Now it is good that here in America we have high standards in all areas of living and achievement and that's fine; except when it isn't. It isn't if you are not capable to reach that end or if you do not judge yourself accurately or if you make yourself 'crazy' over it. It is also not okay if your aggressiveness to get 'there' hurts others, or makes you so competitive that you lose sight of what really matters in life. The balance of being 'perfect' in some areas may inhibit you from blossoming as a full human being capable of loving and being loved.

That brings me to the idea of the perfect mate.

Is there such a thing?

Indeed, there is; for a time.

No one is 'perfect' forever. And that's a good thing or else we would all just stagnate and not grow ourselves or grow in tandem with a partner. So, perfection, is temporary. Get it? Learn it. Accept it. Deal with it and do not get caught up in the end goal or you will lose the fun in the middle!

Perfection is like much that is wondrous in life. it is captured in short moments or spurts.

Think of the best meal you have ever had. Think of the prettiest thing you have seen. Think of the nicest time you shared with someone you love. Think of your most ethereal moments.

What's New About Sex

"HISTORY REPEATS ITSELF. THAT'S ONE of the things wrong with history" - Clarence Darrow

When we look at what is happening today with sexuality we are often amused, shocked, or mystified.

There is no reason to be as it has always been so. The differences today exist in the ways in which the information is transmitted.

The media, the films, and the internet have all contributed to a wide distribution of visual and written material on the subject. That does not mean however that any behavior is new or that any attitudes are vastly different from time immemorial.

People have not changed and our needs and desires have not changed. We are still the 'animal' that we have always been!

While it is certainly true, that science has offered us a great deal and put a spotlight, literally, on the acts involving sexuality itself, the interactions are the same. Some problems can be solved dealing with every aspect of sexuality and its' outcomes, (pregnancy, diseases, and so on), the real intimacy and interaction between two, (or more), people has not ever changed.

Take a walk down memory lane… history.

Read and look at the pictures in the Kama Sutra from ancient India. Read their love poems.

Eastern philosophy combined sex and spirituality in a way that doesn't exist today. The skilled lover was the one that made sex more enjoyable. It's always the more you know the better!

The practice of 'tantra' was taught where the male does not ejaculate and therefore prolongs the pleasure for himself and his partner. Try that today!!

Three thousand years ago in Egypt the Turin papyrus was written. It showed sexual positions. Sort of an early, 'Playboy' magazine. Hathar was the female goddess of spiritual love.

The Greeks and Romans were lustful.

Over two thousand years ago, the first brothel was in Pompeii.

There were sex slaves and public baths.

Prostitution was readily available. The poor had dark and dirty curbside activity, while the wealthy had 'call girls.' Most were slaves. Prices depended on desirability. Nothing new here!

In 40 A.D. Caligula taxed prostitution. Now there's an idea for government today!!

The noblemen rarely slept with their wives and had private clubs and 'swinger' parties. Often there were slaves in the home that were used sexually.

Sometimes, the 'respectable' wives had lovers, as sex with husbands was rare, but they were often punished if found out. Again, what's new? Well, in many cultures, that has changed… for the good!

There was graffiti, pornography and many brothels, actually forty-one in Rome alone with a six-thousand population!

The brothels, interestingly enough, were owned by the noblemen and were motivated by greed with a policy of cash only!!

Talk about history repeating itself…

Today, while being bombarded with sexuality in all its' forms, we are still shy, hung up, not informed and sexual neophytes. That has to do with attitudes.

We fear what others will think, we receive little or poor information, we are not free with ourselves, and so we have issues. The other side is too free with our bodies and not 'there' in our minds or personal development. We do not know how to relate intimately with another.

What is taught? What is the role of religion? What are we afraid of?

All of it leads to being shy, frightened, out of control, or ashamed. That's the pity of it all.

History can teach us a great deal. Who studies that side of history?

When our history is written, what will be the message about our sexual behavior? I think it is a mixed message. It's all out there for the viewing, but what goes on in the bedroom is still very much a sorry state in many cases. What it could take to teach people when they are young would not be difficult and SO enjoyable for the rest of our lives.

My theory would be that no one should leave school, especially college, without the knowledge of how to be and bring your partner to orgasm!!! That would be coupled with communication skills that would lead to deep connection on that level as well.

How about that for a political slogan?? Would you vote for that candidate???

"We Americans are the best informed people on earth as to events of the last twenty-four hours; we are not the best informed as to the events of the last sixty centuries." – Will and Ariel Durant

Too Much Sex... Possibility

"LOVE IS FRIENDSHIP SET ON fire." - French proverb

Today people are hooking up. They are young and having sex a lot. The question is, is that a good idea?

Who's to say?

A recent study showed that college students are not having relationships but they are having a lifestyle of unemotional, unattached sex. Of those that were, interviewed 41 percent felt it was not a good way to behave.

They used words like, "ashamed" and "empty" and for some, "abused." Some 23 percent expressed an ambivalence, and 36 percent said they felt "satisfied."

Most felt they were okay with it as it was a big part of campus life and they wanted to fit in.

Older traditions like getting to know the person, and having long conversations, and dating were not the norm...

Old- fashioned commitment is rare.

There are some long term relationships on campuses and many were formed after a one-time hook up or serial hook ups. Most students reported they would have preferred to have sex after at least one date.

Many students interviewed said they wished they could have old-fashioned dates!

It is hard to find a student who will say they don't want to have sex before getting to know someone and they are not comfortable or confident enough to say they are holding out for something more.

Now where does all this lead?

In talking to a number of male and female college students I was told the girls that have easy sex do get a reputation, like the good old days. The boys get a free pass. Too bad, for both sexes.

For me I believe they will pay a heavy price at the end.

Call me whatever, BUT without romance, longing, and the flirtation and so on it is just a slam, bam, thank you ma'am and while both males and females can get a physical release that won't be enough later on.

Where will they learn romance? Where will the discovery of one another come from, and when?

It's like anything else in this life… too much becomes gorging and not pleasurable.

Think of it like having a yen for chocolate. When you think about it, wait for it, and then have one piece you can savor it. If you have a desire for chocolate and I give you a hundred pieces do you really enjoy it? Do you want to keep repeating that experience? Well, I think sex can be viewed in the same way.

Longing and appreciation make the act better; believe me.

Now sex coupled with love is really something to sing about.

Listen to songs and read poetry, and great love stories. Most are not about jumping into bed immediately or using your body as a commodity.

The body is attached to a mind and the mind has a heart to deal with and those FEELINGS are what we are about.

There is a place for lust and it can be built upon, and we do need to feel desired and appreciated. It's all about how you feel about yourself and how that other person makes you feel important to them. If it's just for the use of your body, (for males, and females too), you will NEVER be fulfilled.

In relationships it's up and down, and communicating, and expectations, and letting the other one really know you.

Being comfortable is important... Then the body responds with joy.

If it's just sex, and you take it for what it is, I think it will be harder later on to truly have deep, loving relationships.

Sexual attraction starts it all, but as a young person, the hormones speak and there may not even be much of an attraction, especially for males.

When the pain outweighs the pleasure it is time to move on and being honest about how you feel is necessary.

Being sexually desirable is a good thing but how you use it is what counts!!

You do not learn about love by hopping in and out of bed. It is a slow process… good sex, and love, is not about hopping. That's just too fast!

"I'm old-fashioned and a square. I believe people should not engage in sex too early. They will never forget that first sexual experience and it would be a pity to just throw it away. So what's the rush? Hug and kiss and neck and pet, and don't rush into a sexual encounter." - Dr. Ruth Westheimer

Who Are The Real Perverts?

"The nature of men and women - their essential nature - is so vile and despicable that if you were to portray a person as he really is no one would believe you." - W. Somerset Maugham

As promised, my report on the second part of the film: "Nymphomaniac."

Even as a relationship therapist and sex educator for decades, I felt you needed a strong stomach to view this film. It's not just that it is graphic, but the aspects shown are probably getting us all ready for the film, "Fifty Shades of Grey" that will be coming out.

It is full of nudity; male and female, and full of what we think of as perversion.

It has both Uma Thurman and Christian Slater in each of the films which is interesting in and of itself.

There are scenes of married sex, the birth of a child, sadomasochistic sex, a pair of black men with HUGE erections, homosexuality, betrayal, lost love, and more. Ready to run to see it yet???

So, indeed, she is a nymphomaniac who tries therapy to break her addiction and runs out claiming that will not work and that it is in fact, a fraud and hypocritical. She calls it all as she sees it and is brutally honest about what society teaches.

In each of the two films she describes her life to an older man who takes her in and befriends her.

In contemplating it all I was surprised at some of my reactions.

When they showed the many scenes of her being whipped on the bottom by a young man for his sexual desires I was reminded of the very wealthy and powerful Alfred Bloomingdale. Yes, that one with his name on those stores!

It was well known that he paid two prostitutes regularly to be nude so that he could beat their rears with a belt. This went on for years, and his mistress of thirteen years reported it in her biography! His wife Betsy was the doyenne of New York society!! Did anybody call him a pervert? He, who founded Diners Club and was one of Reagan's key fund raisers and friend.

Then there is Jean Paul Getty, who was absolutely horrible to his five wives and four children, neglecting them all. He was even miserable to the many women in short lived relationships with him.

Did anyone call him a pervert? To the contrary; he was sought after by the rich and powerful, and the cultured. Does money do it? Is it that they were men?

What of all the 'parasites' that are married and offer little to their spouses? They have the name and share the riches but so many never enjoyed or shared a decent sex life, if at all, with those hard working guys. They are more perverted than our heroine who at least was honest and authentic, and gave of herself to pleasure both him and her.

True, there are perverts; pedophiles who act out their needs on children, and the rapists who take out their aggression by force. Indeed, there are perverts BUT let us be clear; they are not the willing pairs that can actually enjoy doing what society calls 'perverse.'

In fact, some of what our heroine does can excite and put fire into a sexual relationship.

Now, what is missing, is that elusive element called love. This is serious and what allows any sexual behavior to be ok. When in love NOTHING is perverse, if the two parties want to engage in it!

I have counselled people who look so ordinary and often, meek, who have done things in and out of bed that you can only imagine. The bed is the secret place where the real you is bared; literally and figuratively. As a therapist people feel safe to tell me their secrets, but how many people discuss that area of their lives with anyone, let alone a partner? How do you know what he or she really enjoys and might like? How much experimentation really goes on? How close can two people become when they share pillow talk and ACTION?

Let us be clear; sex is the most powerful drive on earth and the most fulfilling only when coupled with feelings of true love.

This film shows that in the end when her feelings of closeness and caring are betrayed she takes revenge. It is a strong message and one that captures it all in a crude, brutal portrayal, but it says what is important and her being a nymphomaniac is only a means to the end. It was her drive that she couldn't control.

We all want and do, 'pay back' the people who hurt us emotionally. It can take many forms and she found one. I won't spoil it if you are going to see the film!

"True love is like ghosts, which everybody talks about and few have seen." - Francois de la Rochefoucauld

When No Means... Maybe

"We are never so defenseless against suffering as when we love, never so forlornly unhappy as when we have lost our love- object or its love." - Sigmund Freud

We all know that to love and be loved is the 'It' of life, but to first find it and then to maintain it is never an easy task.

The finding it is now in a whole new sphere; the internet, cougar night in Silicon Valley and new sexual interest drugs for women. Whole new world… some good, some not so good.

Many people are experiencing the joylessness of sex as a result of the instant hopping into bed. When sex and you become a commodity the lure, the romance, the delight disappears.

Looking just at sex on TV shows, the manner in which we are engaging with one another in this arena is without emotion. Sex has been relegated to a transactional, utilitarian obsession. Anything goes, and it is there in living color for all to observe. Michael Douglas saying his throat cancer was a result of cunnilingus was another example of what would never have been disclosed just a short time ago.

Sexual voyeurism is rampant in many forms. In some cases, it may enhance the viewer's desire or give them a new idea… that's not bad;

but when it desensitizes the act and there is no feeling of intimacy and caring and longing it falls short and gives a poor message.

Sex today makes me nostalgic for sex just yesterday. It should include longing and fun. Does it for you?

Today instead of looking for Mr. Right, many are settling for Mr. Right Now!

Where does this lead?

Are you saying yes instead of saying no? Does he hear, "No," or does he hear "Maybe?"

Now sex is vital in my book, and yes, sometimes it can be just sex for sex, or without much caring over time, BUT when does that line get crossed and you are no longer able to get to "Yes" with real intimacy? It seems many have lost the art of communication. The iPhone and texting are not the same!

The other area where this gets played out is when two people disagree or have a heated argument and then it becomes who 'makes up?'

Most of us get bent out of shape when our emotional needs are not met. What gets you hurt?

Figure it out. It will help. We all have Achilles' heels.

When that awful feeling bubbles up recognize it. Then deal with it.

Teach your partner what they have to do or say to get you back on track. When we say "No," we are often looking to play cat and mouse and have our partner come to us with a hug, a flower, a poem or whatever to make it right again. Partners should hear," Maybe" in their heads when they hear that "No." It is often a call to be shown how much we are truly loved. Love is being close 'in spite of' not 'because of.' And yes saying "I'm sorry," is important. Then talking after a while maybe with a glass of wine!

Women want to be wooed and men just want to be accepted without harassment.

So, in both realms, sex, and disagreement, "No" is not the final answer, unless you really want it to be.

Living with ups and downs, hateful feelings, and loving feelings are all part of the package. Being grown up also means living with ambiguity. If the negative outweighs the positive that's a horse of another color, and may be a sign of something more sinister.

We have no guarantees in this life and real love is one of the few oases we have for fabulous feelings, and sex is the physical wonderful expression of it. Use it wisely and be sure what you mean when you say, "No" and maybe just have it as a come closer message, that he has to 'fight' for.

"In lovers' quarrels, the party that loves most is always most willing to acknowledge the greater fault." - Sir Walter Scott

When Sex Isn't Fun

CAN YOU IMAGINE WHAT BARBARA Hutton's seventh husband said on his wedding night?

My hunch is it was, "I know what I'm supposed to do. The question is, how to make it interesting!"

That's right, sex should be at the least, interesting.

Is it?

For many people it is boring, boring, boring. That is the reason so many people look for new partners. Then there is that initial conquest and excitement.

Sex should be fun and satisfying for the partners involved. In truth if you are not involved sex looks ridiculously silly. The movements and sounds...

Once you share your body in that intimate way and hopefully with that miracle of love included it is a glorious experience to be repeated, dreamed about and cherished!

What gets in the way of that? Lots of things.

A bad day at the office, anger at a friend, children fussing, money problems, a house that needs work, and most of all not feeling loving toward your lover.

It is necessary to put everything out of your mind to have great sex. Now that doesn't mean some males, especially, need it for physical release and anyone will do, but for the most part I am referring to an intimate caring relationship that has sex as a cornerstone.

Knowledge about sexuality is SO important.

Sometimes sex isn't fun because of medical or aging problems. Men can have 'premature' ejaculation. I think that is ridiculous. There is no such thing; it's just fast sexual release. To be simultaneous with a female takes time and maybe the 'squeeze' technique where the head of the penis is held to slow it down, helps that.

Maybe as aging sets in he can only have an ejaculation with masturbation. Sometimes he can climax without ejaculating. If 'it' won't go 'up' or stay 'up' you need tender care and talking to see what feels good.

For women they can have vaginismus, or painful spasms of the vagina. They can also have vaginitis, inflammation of the vagina. None of this makes a female want to have sex. She can also, especially with aging, be 'dry' vaginally. All that makes her not want to be close.

There are many lubricants in drug stores to help with this.

Many females report having more intense orgasms as a result of using a vibrator.

When I was a young marriage counselor we had a psychiatrist come to the agency once a month to review and give insight into a case study. One day it was my couple he addressed and asked about Freud's, 'penis envy.' He wanted to know had I ever thought of that.

My response which left him silent was, "Worship, maybe; envy, never!"

That working penis is a truly miraculous body part!!

Females can only work from the inside which is why the male thrusting is totally male. Some females, even with all the equality, or lack of it, are not male! They should never be. Gender is destiny in most cases; transsexuals notwithstanding. Being male or female is wonderful in its' own right. Enjoy the differences.

No matter the age the fun of sex can be there. The cable TV series, "Grace and Frankie" is a good example. The heart will guide you and the body is in tandem. Being desired is the stuff of life. Being relevant makes you youthful and alive. Being in love and enjoying sex means you are doing what is best in this life!!

In relationships there is always compromise, wrath at times, trust or lack of it at times, disappointment and a lot of ambiguity. Living with all of that is what makes us human and offers us experience leading to a level of maturity. And no one is mature all the time, nor should they be. Playfulness and being 'goofy' is part of the package too. Just being; and being free, is the goal. It will get played out on many levels not the least of which is in the bedroom... or kitchen... or beach... or...

So, if sex isn't joyful and fun take a look at why. It can and indeed, should be!!!

"Sex may be a hallowing and renewing experience, but more often it will be distracting, coercive, playful, frivolous, discouraging, dutiful, and even boring." - Leslie H. Farber

Young Sex Can Never Be Safe

"THE YOUNG ALWAYS HAVE THE same problem - how to rebel and conform at the same time. They have solved this by defying their parents and copying one another." - Quentin Crisp

Once the decision has been made to lose your virginity, male or female, a whole new world opens up… literally and figuratively!

The U.S. government stopped funding for abstinence sex education programs in 2010. That was a message. The message is, there is little research that shows that kids will not have sex and that the real issues are birth control and things like the number of partners involved and so on.

It is a fact that today over half of the babies born here are to single women, under thirty, living with a man. That's another message!

My concerns are more about relationships and learning about having great sex. Does everything have to be immediate? Have kids lowered expectations in relationships? Has sensation replaced emotion?

Forget drugs… the brain when one is in love makes dopamine! That makes us feel fabulous. We are built to love.

Now where does sex come into all of this? Everywhere.

But first, we have to look at what the two people involved say, feel, and do to one another.

You cannot underestimate the importance of having a solid connection emotionally.

How you meet, get to know one another, take time to look at what you want from a relationship and get through the difficulties of any relationship, will all be factors that will come and go as you enter into the realm of sex.

The beginning is always fresh and new and a learning process. No one starts out being a perfect partner or sex partner. There is a LOT to learn and only time, experimentation, communication, and practice will get you there. Love is the biggest risk anyone ever takes. Putting sex into the mix can make it wonderful and exciting or it can cloud over other issues that will be really important later on.

We all want to feel special and desired. We all want to feel complete with a lover. We all want to feel secure. None of this is automatic and for all time. It is especially true for young people having sex.

So, when I say young sex is never 'safe' I am not talking about birth control. I am talking about putting your heart in a 'safe' place... someone else's hands!

What do you talk about to initiate the sex act? Who does what to whom? Does it feel right? Does it feel good? How do you feel the next day?

Males respond in their way and that is readily seen and felt. Females are responding internally and they need sweet words and time to relax and really enjoy their sexuality. It takes learning. Learning about your body and your partner's. What feels good and where are the places on the body to touch, lick, or kiss.

It takes a long time to know how to 'abandon' oneself to love and lovemaking. Males need to learn that what they say is as important as what they do. The sex act for young men is over quickly.

Females need to learn that a man giving her his ejaculation is his way of saying he really wants to be with her.

Men like pornography, and women like romance novels!

Pleasure is good for you… and good sex is VERY pleasurable. Just touching and being naked is a testament to what being fully human is about.

Young people should do what feels right to them. The relationship needs to develop and sex needs to be talked about as well as practiced. How else can you learn?

There is NOTHING that is WRONG if two people want to do it and like it!!!

There is no part of the body that is not explorable with the hands, mouth, tongue, or anything else that feels good. Do not tell your parents I said this!!!

At any rate, use your mind, heart, and body well so that the rest of your life and relationships will benefit from the experiences you have in the beginning. Like everything else in this life, the more you know the better. Connoisseurs are not born they are cultivated!!

"The last step in parental love involves the release of the beloved; the willing cutting of the cord that would otherwise keep the child in a state of emotional dependence." - Lewis Mumford

Listen Up Guys

"THE HUMAN RACE HAS BEEN set up. Someone, somewhere, is playing a practical joke on us. Apparently, women need to feel loved to have sex. Men need to have sex to feel loved. How do we ever get started?" - Billy Connolly

It was Freud who pondered the question, 'What do women want?' He never answered it. I however, after over thirty years as a relationship therapist will attempt to assist you guys with some of my insights.

First of all, consider why I start this with a quote about sex. It's because without that there is no real relationship of intimacy between a man and woman. And there are all kinds of sex; from the perfunctory to the total fabulous loss of self, sex. You need to know things about women. No one teaches you what really matters in this area and what really makes for a good life.

Women can do great damage to you if you do not understand some things. They can be irrational, emotional over anything at any time, they can be demanding, and they can be controlling. Watch out for all the signs and then if love is there; learn how to handle these aspects. Let's see if we can figure some of it out.

Whenever a female is not getting what she wants from you, she will act out or become silent. If she withholds sex she is not a REAL woman, and knows nothing about love.

Now what does she want from you? It's not the little things that you argue over, or the details about whatever… it is ALWAYS that she does not feel loved the way she wants to be. A real woman only wants to inspire love. Now how is that defined?

It can vary but the studies show that WORDS are your most powerful aphrodisiac.

Now if your deeds do not work together with what you profess there is a problem.

We all USE one another for our purposes, but when in intense love that USE is taken over by wanting to please the partner primarily. It just happens. When you are there you will know it.

No matter how upset, how angry over whatever, how hurt… the magnetic force to be close will get you over it. The 'glue' of sex will conquer all. It will.

So now you need to learn, and better to learn early, how to have great sex. Again, no school for this ultimate of life's joys.

Masters and Johnson did research that showed that there was absolutely no difference between a vaginal or clitoral orgasm. You of course, need to know where the clitoris is. Do you? Well, it's that small raised part of the vaginal opening down from the naval. Massage it the way she likes, softly, or vigorously. Ask her. Ok, now get started. It takes a woman longer than a man to get 'there.' Average time about fifteen minutes. It can seem an eternity I know, but it's worth it.

Women can achieve multiple orgasms, and need no time in between. Women know penis size means nothing when it comes to 'doing' it. The pleasure from orgasm cannot be measured and need not be discussed after the fact. By the way, it is fabulous for your brain and health. Nice fringe benefit!

Women who are comfortable with their bodies, and confident in themselves who enjoy their sexuality are the best partners. You guys know them and will want to be totally 'into' them!

A real woman does not demand declarations of love, or expect you to read her mind. She wants you to listen, has a life apart from you, is interesting and relates openly to you, and talks about her feelings.

One of the area's most men are not aware of is the fact that women like variety. The early relationship had it. Otherwise it is dull and boring and just a habit for release. Both partners should be free and open to experiment and have fun with one another. Sex actually, if you are not involved, is kind of funny.

Over time you will develop a 'style' in bed. Alter it from time to time. Surprises are not bad.

In a recent U.S. survey, they found that 14 percent of men were not satisfied with their sex lives and only 16 percent were very satisfied. You can bring that statistic up!!!

In that same survey eight out of ten men preferred performing cunnilingus to having oral sex. There's a surprise for you!

Sixty-five percent used lubricants and forty-two percent used vibrators. Won't go into the other stuff that can go on in bed. When two people want to do it; NOTHING is off limits!!!

If you want a crystal ball look at your mother and then look at hers. See any similarities? Like them? Like their marital relationships? Beware, you are about to repeat emotional history, like it or not. It takes a heap of insight, work, and bravery to change it. Yes, times and attitudes, and things change but the human beings we are have not evolved terribly much… for good or bad.

So, listen up you guys… learn and enjoy, and make her orgasmic. Do not be a selfish lover. It will all pay off, trust me.

"No woman ever falls in love with a man unless she has a better opinion of him than he deserves." - Ed Howe

Keeping 'IT' Alive

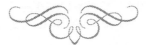

"If you want to read about love and marriage you've got to buy two separate books." – Alan King

"The secret of a happy marriage remains a secret." - Henny Youngman

"I know nothing about sex because I was always married." - Zsa Zsa Gabor

Yeh, yeh, yeh… ain't love grand?

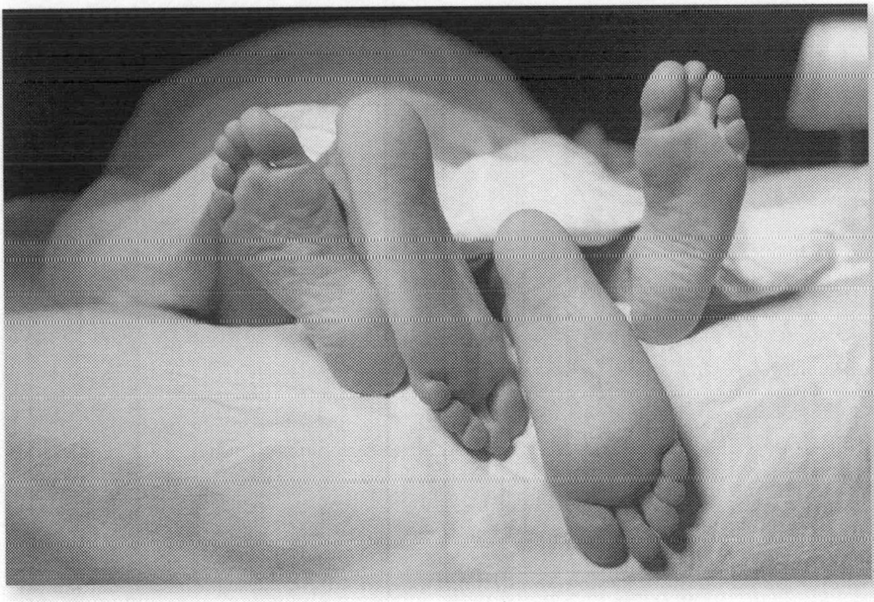

The lusty days of early love and marriage to the one you adore will wax and wane. There is no getting around it.

When someone is available, and you see them in all their glory night and day feelings change and can erode. Most often this occurs after about five or so years. That is when we become vulnerable to an outside influence and may become attracted to others. Of course if you are not really emotionally close you can just be going about your business and not even be aware of the changes.

Now the people who really love and who can still get excited and get it on together know how to deal with this problem. They are the relationships that are 'juicy' for years.

They talk about it, make sure the secretary is old and ugly, plan fun projects together and keep themselves marketable. They do not walk around the house in ratty nightgowns and they always smell good. They complement one another and are as nice to each other as they are to friends.

By the way, research shows that women are more attracted to pleasant smells than men so they should not be the only ones wearing perfume!

It is easy to slip into complacency and have a perfunctory sex life. It is difficult to keep improving oneself and like Scheherazade keep him interested.

Men for the most part are turned on by sight…looking at the body parts they like. It is not difficult for them. Women on the other hand need to hear sweet nothings and feel they are loved. Men who learn how to love also like to know they are appreciated.

The biggest help is letting your partner know and SEE that they turn you on and that helps them.

Humor helps as well as a playful attitude.

Now specifically what can you do?

Well, you can be interesting, fun, and do things to share with one another.

You can take courses, be involved in activities and talk about new and exciting ideas.

You can plan events, be with people you enjoy and entertain, get a pet, travel, buy sex 'toys', watch sex films, read books about new ways to 'perform', and buy a new house.

If none of this works maybe you need a new partner!

If you are bored, you may be boring!

Try cute ways to let your beloved know you still love them. Notes in pockets or on pillows, a fun gift in the cereal box, write "I love you" on the mirror in lipstick, pin a place to meet on their underwear, or send flowers…guys like that too.

Food can be great, cooking a favorite meal together, licking stuff off one another….

Bubble baths with music and candles work too.

Music and dancing….

Wine or champagne makes the world prettier and inhibitions loosen.

Read poetry or write a poem.

As long as you are good in bed "It" stays alive. After that, you have a really good friend!!!

"When love comes to an end, weaklings cry, efficient ones instantly find another love, and the wise already have one in reserve." - Oscar Wilde

Mistresses... Then and Now

"A MAN LOVES HIS SWEETHEART the most; his wife the best, but his mother the longest." - Irish Proverb

There are any number of theories about mistresses and we will explore some of them here.

The saying goes that a mistress is to enjoy, a concubine to serve, and a wife to bear legitimate children. In all of it, the woman's feelings are somewhat irrelevant. There is also no alternative word for a man in this situation.

It seems women are 'split' and never really equal to a man. Men, it is said, fear women and see them as dangerous to their power and control.

A lover is usually seen as illicit.

What is also usually true is that a woman is testing her seductive powers while a man cannot be wrested from his old way of life.

Now none of this is always the case and throughout history, there have been any number of examples of all of this. Most of the time it holds true that one woman cannot be all things, and marriage and passion do not seem to go together even after a short period of time. It takes thought and work to keep a relationship vital over time. Usually the woman does the better part of keeping the fire going, if she is smart and knows how.

It is that old saying, 'A cook in the kitchen, a lady in the living room, and a whore in bed.'

Having a mistress or a male lover always indicates something missing emotionally, and sexually, between the partners.

Helen Fisher examined 853 cultures and found only about 16 percent monogamous.

Historically there have been many mistresses who changed history.

Diane de Poitiers born in 1499 married at fifteen to a man forty years older. He introduced her into the French court where she became a teacher to Henri II. Diane became a widow while Henri married Catherine de' Medici and was unhappy.

Diane and her young lover, Henri, had a passionate affair and she advised him on many official matters. She was a real early cougar!

After Henri's death from a jousting accident in 1559, Catherine confiscated the chateau he had given Diane and banished her to the countryside where she died still beautiful at age 66.

Barbara Palmer was beautiful and ambitious, and became King Charles II of England's most infamous mistress. She met him after she married at age nineteen.

She and Charles had seven children together, five of whom he acknowledged, and her husband accepted the situation.

Charles married in 1662 but the love affair continued. She amassed a small fortune and had other paramours including an ancestor of Winston Churchill. Charles finally let go of her in 1674 and she died at age 68 in 1709. One of her descendants was Diana, Princess of Wales!!

Madame de Pompadour met the recently widowed king, Louis XV, at a masked ball. He quickly moved her into an apartment with a secret stairway at Versailles. She became a patron of the arts and literature.

After five years she was no longer Louis' lover but he was loyal to her until she died at age 46, of pulmonary failure.

The list goes on and on.

Today there are any number of mistresses, and we only hear of the ones who are involved with famous men.

Think of the recent situations in our own history. There's Bill Clinton, who made over a hundred million as well as, Mark Sanford, John Edwards, Eliot Spitzer, and so on. There are those French who seem to accept such situations with different attitudes than we Americans.

At any rate, this is a human condition, which shows no sign of changing.

The analysis of it all boils down to the theory that it is usually a woman who has a poor relationship with her father, and is jealous of her mother and wants to outdo her and find ways to gain her father's caring. If she does not please her father, his conditional love can be uncertain and could disappear.

The reasons for these relationships include career women who do not have time for marriage, someone who works for a lover, a one-man call girl, and a masochistic one where the woman wants marriage but chooses a man where that does not appear likely.

When two people are married to others and become involved romantically, that seems to work better and longer.

There you have it… mistresses.

The counter part is the woman taking on a man as a lover and we will deal with that another time. Maybe he becomes the 'mister guy!'

"No matter how happily a woman may be married, it always pleases her to discover that there is a nice man who wishes she were not." - H.L. Mencken

Male Cougars Turned Female

Excerpts from Benjamin Franklin's "Reasons to Marry an Older Woman"

1. Because they have more knowledge of the world, and their minds are better stored with observations; their conversation is more improving, and more lastingly agreeable.

2. Because when women cease to be handsome, they study to be good.

3. Because there is no hazard of children, which irregularly produced may be attended with much inconvenience.

4. Because through more experience they are more prudent and discreet in conducting an intrigue to prevent suspicion.

5. Because in every animal that walks upright, the deficiency of the fluids that fill the muscles appears first in the highest part. The face grows lank and wrinkled; then the neck; then the breast and arms; the lower parts continuing to the last as plump as ever; so that covering all above with a basket, and regarding only what is below the girdle, it is impossible of two women to know an old one from a young one. And as in the dark all cats are grey, the pleasure of corporal enjoyment with an old woman is at least equal and frequently superior; every knack being by practice capable of improvement.

6. Because the sin is less. The debauching of a virgin may be her ruin, and make her life unhappy.
7. Because the compunction is less. The having made a young girl miserable may give you frequent bitter reflections; none of which can attend making an old woman happy.

8th and lastly, they are so grateful!!!

"Advice to a Young Man" June 1745

So do you agree with all of this?

When women age it is now not uncommon to look well, thanks to plastic surgery. They are not irrelevant and go on with their lives and are not boring or "retired" as many older men. Many today are not "parasites" doing little while their men work and produce a lifestyle they enjoy.

Many older women have finally learned how to enjoy their sexuality and they are freer than they were when young. They have also learned how to abandon themselves. Many are then able to teach their partners what to do for mutual pleasure. Finally; fun!!

To know that a man gives his "all" when he has an orgasm with you is a great step forward and older women can learn that.

While men have chosen younger females as sex partners for years for any number of reasons; women are now doing the same thing.

A marriage or relationship is never in jeopardy from the outside, it can only be lacking or erode from the inside. So when you think about all the scandals, remember the "other" party was only there and didn't have to do a thing to attract and have a relationship begin. Where it goes is another story.

John Edwards and Rielle Hunter are only a recent example but he handled it foolishly. Love and sexual need make people, even the smartest, do crazy things.

If a woman is involved with a younger man she does run a big risk as she will age differently and probably more unattractively than the man. That makes him go looking for a younger woman. So be advised you lady cougars…you can have fun, maybe even find love, but it may be temporary. Younger men may be using you just as so many younger women used older men for a variety of purposes.

Like I always say, "Some people should come with warning labels!"

Male Sexuality from an Expert's Experience

THEY SAY THE WAY TO a man's heart is through his stomach. I however believe there's a different route. The following is my interview with Dr. Julian Slowinski Psy. D, who has been dealing with male sexuality since the 1960's.

L.H. How did you become an expert in this area?

J.S. In the 1960's I was a teacher at a Catholic Prep school and I read a book about a psychiatrist, Dr. Harold Lief who was introducing sex education in medical schools, and thought it would be a good idea for my curriculum in religion and biology.

Later in the 70's I met and ultimately worked with Dr. Lief at the University of Pennsylvania after training and a Psy.D in clinical psychology, specializing in impotence and sex therapy.

Since the 80's I have been in private practice specializing in sex therapy and couples' therapy.

In 1999 my book, "The Sexual Male Problems and Solutions" was published.

L.H. What specific problems do you treat?

J.S. Both males and females, who are coping with desire, arousal, and orgasm, with males mostly problems with erection, or ejaculation. With women problems with vaginal pain disorders is a big issue. I also deal with gender issues and transgendered people.

L.H. Is there much work from a psychological point of view?

J.S. Yes. Anxiety short circuits sexual functioning, and of course relationship issues are a big component. Feelings of shame, guilt, or trauma, can also be huge factors.

I make sure my patients are cleared medically so that we know that is not the problem.

L.H. What actually works for some of the sexual problems you treat?

J.S. Well, Viagra and those drugs can be very helpful for a number of men, injections into the penis directly of hormones can help some, testosterone in shots or gel form for desire, is useful in many cases, and things like the vacuum pump can be used. The penile implant is also a possibility. Medicare may even pay for some of these remedies! But the combination of drug therapy coupled with counseling works best, I believe.

L.H. Besides a twenty-year-old blond what can help men as they age to still enjoy a sex life?

J.S. All of the above.

L.H. Is it ever boring to hear the same complaints over and over?

J.S. Not really, each case is different. Each couple is different and I see them alone and together as the situation warrants.

L.H. Do you see the issues as different categories?

J.S. Yes. There can be sex problems like," What is normal?" There can be sexual difficulties especially disagreements with the partner, and there can be sexual dysfunction; the plumbing not working.

L.H. What are your views about marriage and fidelity these days?

J.S. I believe there is more stress from our American culture on people these days, and that affects relationships and sexuality.

There is availability and people are more exposed to one another and that can get in the way of many relationships.

Young people engage in sex of a variety of sorts, but intimacy is a problem. There is a lot of pressure on young girls to have sex, oral sex in particular, these days.

L.H. What would you like people to learn about their sexuality?

J.S. Good sex is what you and your partner feel good about…not what the "experts" think.

The World Health Organization has a definition I like. "Sexual health is freedom from fear, shame, guilt, and false beliefs."

And I believe that sexual health is part of a loving, respectful adult relationship. It's part of living life with vitality and joy.

L.H. Thank you so much, and amen or ah men!!

Orgasm And Feminism

"ONCE MADE EQUAL TO MAN, woman becomes his superior." - Socrates

So what's the deal with feminism? What does it mean and how is it translated into action between the sexes?

I have lived long enough to see a huge transition in the ways in which women and men relate to one another.

This thing called feminism is the basic reason, and a lot of it has to do with wonderful advances in the field of human sexuality, such as birth control.

As a result, women are no longer victims of their role as mothers, unless they choose to be.

With the advent of furthering their education they also have moved into different realms.

People like Gloria Steinem wrote about the issues and others followed. Attitudes changed and so did behavior.

Now, I for one, believe in women using all their talents and becoming accomplished in whatever field they choose, but I also believe there are basic differences that need to be both acknowledged and given in to, so to speak.

Some changes are wonderful. It used to be the rare woman who went to college, let alone graduate school. It used to be the rare woman who was respected in her field. It used to be the rare woman who was sexually free and enjoyed that aspect of her life. Fortunately, much of this has changed. BUT, and it's a BIG but, there have been some changes that I think have diminished the true nature of most women; to be sensuous and desirable to men.

I have watched aggressive women act in ways that I think take away from their ability to be what I call, feminine. You know it when you see it or feel it.

True, not all women want marriage or to be mothers. That's fine. Today we have options like never before. Good ones too.

Really equal in education or profession and equal reimbursement should be the standard.

Equal in expectation in bed… that's a key to what being feminist is about, or should be.

Recently I had a great conversation with a young woman going on twenty.

She has a boyfriend for over two years. They enjoy a sexual relationship.

When we talked, as I always do, about the intimacy, she said she was a feminist and he learned to please her as well as himself!

I was curious about how that happened. Not the usual behavior of young men, even today.

She answered quite simply," I taught him!" What an education! This guy is set for life!! And how smart of her to go after what is so important for women.

Now there are women who act more like what we traditionally think of as men as opposed to being 'full' women. Many of them seek power in areas such as business or politics. The qualities needed for success here are different from what we think of as truly female.

You can look at some of them. Many are not very attractive, but some of that is changing too… slowly.

The story of one woman is relevant here and not well known. It is the history of Hatshepsut the most powerful woman Pharaoh in Egypt. She ruled for twenty-two years and did wonderful things for the country.

She was born in 1508 B.C. and died in 1458 B.C. She married her step-brother who was a child, which was common then. Her father had no son so when he died she was twelve and became Queen. Her husband was sickly and he also died after ruling for fifteen years.

She had a daughter, and no son. The closest male heir was a nephew who was also still a child. She became regent and was the real ruler. After a few years she crowned herself Pharaoh. She was not yet thirty. The nephew was too young to object.

Interestingly she had an adviser who was believed to also be her lover. Good!

She had many buildings and statues built as a way to assert her authority and she dressed as a male along with a fake beard!

Her death was attributed to bone cancer from creams she used for a skin condition.

The nephew became Pharaoh, had many of her self-statues destroyed and became a good leader in his own right.

Look around at today's 'leading' women.

Today female politicians can wear dresses OR pants suits!!

"I don't mind living in a man's world as long as I can be a woman in it." - Marilyn Monroe

OMG I'm Gay - OMG I'm Transgendered

WHILE THIS IS STILL AN issue for many in America, I believe it should go away as a problem.

Because we have a Puritanical background and so many Americans are religious, it becomes an issue. It makes life for good people sad and difficult unnecessarily. What I want to say at the outset here is that no one asks to be different from the compact majority. It makes life hard, especially for children. But, more importantly, these things cannot be changed. It is the rare person who is truly gay or transgendered that can change. No matter what method is tried; talk therapy, aversion therapy, hormone or other injections, none of it works in the end. You are programmed with whatever is in you to be what you believe you are; gay or transgendered.

The two are different in that one does not require surgery to have the body match the brain. No one really knows the cause.

Being gay means you can pass as a male or female and no one is the wiser unless the individual goes to some length to stand out for whatever reason. To finally, usually after years, accept the fact that you are gay means wrestling with being different and then, whom to trust enough to tell. Sometimes they tell no one for years. In some places, we have all heard how they are taunted and even killed because of other people's ignorance or irrational fear.

Families likewise have terrible times dealing with the fact. While the individual may think something is wrong with them, the family may believe their child is gay and may try to ignore it or wish it away. If they come to terms with it, they may believe they have done something wrong or carried a gene that caused the "condition."

It is not easy on either side, and one of the things we try to do if we have the opportunity to counsel families is to have them attempt to accept and appreciate each other's point of view and feelings. You don't have to like what you can understand and be compassionate about!

Many gay couples have been together in loving relationships for years but the image, especially for men, is that they are promiscuous. This is not always the case and people need to look at each situation before jumping to conclusions. Females seem to stay in a committed relationship for longer periods than men usually.

Having children together, no matter how they are obtained can also be a problem and the child may bear the brunt of prejudice. The parents have to be strong and help the child combat whatever is thrust at them. Not ever easy.

The best advice is to find people who are tolerant and supportive and stick with them. Others may be helped to be educated, but if not, move on. What is amazing is the fact it is usually religious people, who preach love and respect that cause most of the anguish!

All of this is true for the transgendered person as well, but with a vengeance! How strong this group must be to go through what they must in order to live fully. Having worked for years with this population I can only tell you what respect I have for what they are made to bear.

At the end they have the additional problem of finding a way to pay for costly surgery to make them whole. It is a terrible problem that can go on for years. Most are persistent as they cannot live any other way. Again, the telling and the family connections require a raft of concerns and emotional upheaval. Many families just cannot accept their child ever again and that is tragic indeed. The person isn't changing, only the shell.

Here again society does not understand it is not about sex. It is about who they are as people.

Most of the males to females find the one stage operation bearable and they go on with their lives. Often they are without men, but occasionally live as lesbians, which the outside world has a really hard time understanding.

They need breasts and often have facial plastic surgery, all costly. They spend time learning female movements and have to adjust their voices.

The female to male group has more and costlier surgery and often does not have a penis constructed. They more often than not usually find female companions. Interesting. Many thoughts about why this may be the case.

They need mastectomies and hysterectomies and can often end up balding.

The penis in the male to female group is not "cut off." It is a different use of the skin that is inverted to make a vagina. It works and looks fine. They can be orgasmic as the nerve endings and prostate are left in, and "massaged" during intercourse. They take hormones for life.

The female to male group has to have several operations and the construction of a penis can be done in several fashions from using the clitoris, to making a penis from skin, and even installing a penile implant for erection. Ejaculation is not possible but a form of orgasm is. They too receive hormones for life. Neither group is able to bear children.

So the message is fuck it! Be what you are and get strong enough emotionally to deal with friends, family and the world.

Perversion... True or False

"WE ARE SLAVES OF SEXUAL desire and can only achieve fleeting satisfaction. Suffering is the essence of life and we inhabit the worst of all possible worlds and death is the only cure for the sickness of being alive." - Schopenhauer

The definition of perversion states that any sexual activity that is regarded as abnormal is perverse.

Sex is the defining act of connection between people. How it is manifested and under what circumstances varies greatly.

For the majority of people, it is a rather straight, (no pun intended), forward act with a short variety list. However, for others it can take forms that are unique, alien, and in some cases downright disgusting for many.

In life there is an endless range of possibilities given our body parts and imaginations.

There is nothing under the sun that has not been done! You name it... any item, any orifice, and anything animate or inanimate has been tried in a sexual fashion.

Just watch a current TV show about sexual occurrences that sends people to a hospital ER.

In your wildest dreams you cannot imagine what some people have done to achieve sexual pleasure or new ideas. It is truly amazing.

We all like variation and especially in the area of our sexuality. It can become boring and with people with limited knowledge, experience, imagination, or daring that is usually the case after a bit of time.

When sex is consensual there is nothing verboten. NOTHING!!

Sex is a hidden subject for many and talking about it is not the norm, not even with a professional counselor. I have heard of all sorts of situations and whenever the behavior is not the 'norm' there is hesitation and embarrassment surrounding it.

It is the ultimate test of who you are and how you feel about yourself and most importantly, your capacity for love.

Good sex makes you feel 'alive.'

It is pleasurable and you want to repeat it again and again.

So people do so many 'weird' things to achieve that feeling. It reminds me of all those young people who cut themselves just to feel `something.' How tragic.

To feel this way, we go to any extreme and any length to get that total 'letting go.'

Nothing else comes close.

The reason throughout history, and any variety of culture and religion have had `rules' is because the drive is the most powerful on earth, and some groups want to have control. When you read about the numbers of people watching what is deemed 'pornography' and what has gone on behind closed doors we are aware of the hold sex has on us.... if we allow the feelings.

Some are taught to repress the feelings to their own detriment and lack of joy. Others are schooled to believe that certain forms are `dirty' or 'bad.'

Yes, people have had sex with animals, they have tried bondage, they have come close to strangulation, and anything and everything has been inserted into any orifice. All in the pursuit of sexual excitement and gratification.

Read the biography of Salvador Dali if you want to see most of what I am talking about. It is amazing! He is only one of those we know about who was famous and creative in more ways than art forms!

Being orgasmic is one of life's great gifts.... but it doesn't happen automatically. We need to learn how to please ourselves as well as a partner. Who teaches that course?

The wide sphere of sexual practices is a fascinating study, from the Kama Sutra, to Murat.

Sade and on and on.

What is also fascinating is how the experience coupled with the memory lasts and lasts.

While the act itself is not of long duration its after affects are.

While it is a silly looking activity unless you are involved it is divine.

Once you have known full abandonment with someone you love who loves you, you will have experienced heaven on this earth. That is why people do ANYTHING to have that feeling.

There are seven deadly sins; lust, gluttony, greed, sloth, wrath, envy, and pride.

We may all have some of these at some time in some measure, and that's okay.

It's only when it is out of hand or hurts another that we should be concerned.

For my money the real perversion in this life is not sexual; it is what we do as people on this earth, to one another.

There have been wars someplace on the planet for almost 97 percent of the time we have existed!! That's perverse!!!

So, the sex part is not an issue in and of itself. Do what pleases you and your partner and you don't have to tell anybody!

"Everything in the world is about sex, except for sex. Sex is about power." - Oscar Wilde

The Nitty Gritty of Sex

"EVERYTHING IS ABOUT SEX." - Benjamin Spock M.D.

Now this is a true statement and anyone who knows anything and anything about history knows this is so.

Go back to Athens 411 B.C. and Aristophanes' play Lysistrata about the women refusing to have sex with their partners in order to stop war! Good idea for today?

Some very brief highlights in our American history include the problem with VD during the First World War.

The next World War saw sex with Europeans and a change in our U.S. practices. Women went out to work and met other men.

Kinsey studied it through questionnaires. Birth control freed females. AIDS caused difficulties, and Viagra now helps problems. Next comes virtual sex and robots.

HOWEVER, there is still the real nitty gritty of two people sharing that most pleasurable of experiences once they know how. That's the part that Masters and Johnson examined. They, by the way, were thought to never be in intense love. They divorced after twenty years and he married for the third time at age seventy-nine to his true love from his youth. It's a great story.

Now the how to…

First of all, there should be feelings, hopefully loving ones that the two people share. That includes not having other things on your mind and setting the mood and being able to 'let go.'

All the problem areas will be discussed in a later blog with suggestions about overcoming them to reach your full sexual potential.

The start of lovemaking should include a quiet comfortable place with nice smells and soft or dark light. You need time.

Caressing, hugging, touching, kissing are all good here. It leads to arousal and desire for sexual connection.

Males get there fast and visually respond to a female's naked body. Females respond to sweet loving words.

The next step is touching anywhere that feels pleasant. It can be with fingers, hands, mouth, feathers, ice, whipped cream… you name it.

The idea is to talk and say what feels good to one another. It also offers variety.

Once aroused a male can reach orgasm quickly with vaginal penetration or oral closeness. She can kiss, lick, or suck any or all of his organs; penis, scrotum or any other part of his body that he enjoys. Whether you swallow the ejaculation or not is a personal matter. Have tissue nearby if you need it. Cigarettes and alcohol make the fluid bitter. Red meat, spinach and foods high in iron make sharper flavors.

Some alcohol like a glass or so of wine helps relax people and lowers inhibitions.

The mouth is cleaner than the genitals but Herpes, for example, can be transmitted through oral sex. Most people do not choose anal sex.

Many men report liking her finger in his anus as it massages his prostate and feels good. There are any number of creams and gels to make this even better. Look at the KY section in any drug store.

To slow him down there is the 'squeeze' technique. When he is close to orgasm, the female can squeeze the area near the glans end of the penis for a few seconds and not stimulate him for several seconds after.

The female needs at least fifteen minutes of clitoral stimulation to get to orgasm. This can be with the penis, the fingers, tongue, or vibrator. Actually, it has been shown that a vibrator offers the strongest orgasm. He can participate with her in any form. Brookstone has a section of what they call 'massagers' that are used as vibrators and drug stores sell them along with sex shops. The chargeable ones that are quiet are best. There are creams to enhance clitoral response that can be put on before sex. They too are in drug stores in the KY section.

That business about vaginal versus clitoral orgasm seems to be unreal, and women can be multi- orgasmic with one contraction after another. They also usually release a clear warm liquid at the point of orgasm. The 'G' spot at the end of the clitoris is said to help this. Of course you may need a GPS to find that 'G' spot, but no matter.

After orgasm and don't worry about that simultaneous stuff too much; it can just happen with time, there should be cuddling, kissing softly and tender words. That makes it all just wonderful and memorable until the sought after next time.

So, there you have it… a start to supreme happiness and contentment. Practice!!

There is a really good book by a friend and colleague, Chris Fariello PhD, "The Lovers' Guide." Nothing is left out of this illustrated encyclopedia.

"Lord give me chastity---but not yet." - Saint Augustine (354-430)!!!

Affairs Are For Caterers

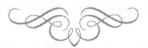

"A LOVER, WHO HAS CONFIDENCE in his mistress feels no displeasure if she absents herself, is occupied at a distance from him; sure that she is his, he prefers to possess a free being than to own a thing. For a woman, on the contrary, the absence of her lover is always torture; away from him she is dispossessed… even when seated at her reading or writing… he is abandoning her, betraying her."

This quote from the longtime lover of Jean-Paul Sartre, Simone de Beauvoir rings true for many who are in the situation of mistress or men having an affair. It does not hold true when the individuals are secure in themselves and what they offer their partner, for the most part.

However, there are times when an affair can turn sour and often there is real hurt or even murder, but for the most part, there is just some discomfort and real pain.

The problem is the 'lover' is never the primary person when there is a wife or husband. Comparisons are there and time and opportunity are difficult to come by. There is often guilt as well.

Maybe we all expect too much from this business called love.

A real intimacy involves sharing oneself honestly and being loyal to a partner. If it is an in- depth affair over years that part of a relationship will be split and the intense part may well be with the lovers.

Great lovers in history have not had an easy time of it.

Rudolph Valentino had two divorces and a poor sex life and died at age thirty-one.

Casanova wrote his biography listing having had relationships, of one sort or another, with over a hundred and thirty women!

Lovers come in all stripes and colors. All ages.

If the twosome is under eighty, there may be a good chance of them ending up married. Some over eighties have done it too! Leaving a family is not the norm for most men in affairs. Women do it more easily.

Men fear being dominated, (like with mother), and loss of control. Women fear loss of love and abandonment. Father's love is conditional.

So, what goes on in these relationships?

What should a woman, in particular, know before getting involved, if she can think before acting.

She should know how they will get their messages to one another. How much time will they spend together? What is he willing to do for her? What does he want, (besides sex), from her?

The problem usually is; she is catering to him, while he is catering to a wife whether he likes her or not. Therein lies a big problem.

The mistress becomes resentful and feels used. This can be talked about and they can work it out but it needs addressing.

He too, may feel a lack of attention from her and resent her life with another man.

An affair can be wonderful and fill in what is missing at home. It indeed can keep a relationship going at home in a better form than it would be without the affair. Certainly, being in love and loving makes us happier and content.

Everyone wants that special kind of love and while an affair is not riddled with all the mundane business of life it can be fulfilling and not just for sex!

Even the clergy understand this.

A man comes to a priest for absolution for adultery. Another priest asks, "Did he tell you her name?" The priest says, "No." The second priest asks, "Was it Mrs. McCabe?" He answers, "No." Asked then, "Was it Mrs. Riley?" "No." "Did he get absolution?" "No, but I got some good leads!"

Ha Ha…

Some famous affairs have gone on for decades. Sometimes the spouses are told or know, but often it is a secret. No one wants to be hurtful usually.

You see males have built in advertising to light up anytime. Females can only do promotional work behind the scenes. They both work their side of the coin and it never dies when people are sensual. To act on it depends on the individual situation. Today affairs are commonplace. It's what we do about them that matters. Being alive includes being turned on and turning another on to you!!

"Sometimes our light goes out but is blown into flames by another human being. Each of us owes deepest thanks to those who have rekindled this light." - Albert Schweitzer

Can You Have Too Much Passion

"Love is passion, obsession, someone you can't live without. If you don't start with that, what are you going to end up with? Fall head over heels. I say find someone you can love like crazy and who'll love you the same way back. And how do you find him? Forget your head and listen to your heart." - William Parrish

No matter when it comes you will know it. Now some people never give over to it totally but here we are talking about those who have.

The studies show that when madly in love the brain releases dopamine and that is the feeling that some drugs provide, hence the reason for taking them. Even seeing a picture of the beloved can cause people to feel less pain, as an example. Pretty heady stuff this love business.

It has been said we are an animal built to love. So, the question is can there be too much passion? Well, yes and no.

If it overpowers so that you cannot get on with work or life it will interfere but if it's compartmentalized it is perfect and wonderful... until of course it isn't then you want to die!

Some have said to stay in love never marry, but that is not always true. There are some, albeit not the majority, where being together twenty-four seven can be full of passion. You have to know how to do it!

If life takes over in the world of mundane and perfunctory, forget it. When it goes, it's gone. Trying to get it back won't really work most of the time. What some called 'love' in the beginning wasn't what we're talking about either, especially in first or young marriages.

If it all becomes banal it doesn't have the 'juice' in it. Then you will see substitutes for it… in work, a cause, eating, shopping… you name it. Poor substitutes to be sure. It's sort of like those poor children who cut themselves just to FEEL something. Tragic.

Lots of people 'settle' for comfort but not comfort and joy… (for this season).

You never want to be so mature that you can't feel passion. Sex and love have to just be downright silly at times. Actually if you came from Mars and watched people engaged in sex you would think it was really ridiculous!

Passion is worth whatever sacrifices have to be made in its' behalf. Anyone who's been there knows it and once experienced you can never go back to the 'living dead.'

Relationships end from the inside out never from the outside. You can do anything with anybody but if it's genuine with your loved one no one can come in between. No one can offer what the two of you deliver to each other… therefore no threat.

"I was nauseous and tingly all over. I was either in love or I had smallpox." - Woody Allen

Right… that's it.

I wish I could help people before they married when they're dating as an audition for marriage to look at it all and connect with the feelings. Difficult and I've been at this over thirty years, counseling, teaching and lecturing. We don't do prevention in America; we only throw money at crises.

It is changing a bit lately. Women are different and their relationships are not the same as before. They know about being orgasmic, and they are not dependent 'parasites" on their men. It has meant a difference in the attitudes of men, some I don't prefer. We are not equal in our feelings and in what we contribute to a relationship.

"For women the best aphrodisiacs are words. The G-spot is in the ears. He who looks for it below there is wasting his time." - Isabel Allende

Learning how to abandon oneself and to be totally uninhibited is not easy. Like good cooking, it takes information, time and practice.

A college freshman recently told me she went to a 'sex toy' party at her school. My reaction was bravo! That will be the best education and one that she will use for the rest of her life!

Passion may need rose colored glasses but they make us all look prettier, so put them on and enjoy!!

From Mother To Dominatrix

"MOST MARRIED COUPLES CONDUCT THEMSELVES as if each party were afraid that the other one could see that it was the weaker." - Alfred Adler

Laugh if you will, but the leap is a short one from mother to dominatrix and many, many men are in that position.

Mothers dominate their households and especially the children, for the most part. Young boys learn early on that they need to please their mothers. If not they can be deprived of her love, affection, praise and even hurt. It is a pain young boys seek to avoid... at any price.

Sometimes there are domineering fathers but they are often punishing in a different way and it is not the emotional pulling away, that the mother does.

So, young men learn right away that they have to please women. They have to first of all choose another woman, from their mothers, and that also does not often sit well with mama. They have also learned, by rote, day in and day out, what a woman is and they will duplicate the example they have emotionally lived with; mother. Even if the partner seems totally different, and of course offers a sexual attraction, at least in the beginning, trust me, they almost universally marry mother in the end, especially in first marriages. The emotional pattern will rear its' head soon enough.

That is why the old saying of look at how he feels and treats his mother is true; next, it will be you!

So, here he is, in a relationship, and in the beginning it looks and feels okay. Give it a bit of time, often sooner rather than later, the bloom is off the rose.

The business of having and caring for children, making a living, daily life, all change the original duo. Now comes the hard part.

He does not want to suffer her displeasure so he does her bidding.

She wants things done her way, when she wants it done, and gets her message across in her fashion.

It can be a look, a guilt trip, a request that may be a demand, or an outright fight. She has the big bargaining chip; sex and affection. If she withholds either, she too suffers but she may in fact not care. He cares and needs it.

Either way it is not usually, "I would really like and appreciate it if you would..." Or" thank you for..."

He can jump to her tune, play the game or be passively aggressive and sabotage the wish. Maybe he takes it out on others, kicks the cat, hits balls in sports, avoids her, gets sick, or drinks. Whatever way, he will seek comfort in some form, or in another's arms or bed. The early patterns, once established, are never easily broken, if at all.

How many men have you seen going through the motions of life and without what I call, "juice?" Hen-pecked doesn't even come close. They are a sorry lot and they are everywhere.

They can be captains of industry, rulers of the world, but with the spouse, they become spineless, even if they hate her!

Now true, some men are tyrants, but they are a different breed; but also fighting off mother, in another form.

The ones who 'get it' are the rare breed who have looked at it all and especially themselves, and have a mature willing partner to work on it together. Talk and more talk does the trick.

Being good bed partners helps tremendously and will cover a lot of hurts and pillow talk is great about feelings that really matter. Otherwise, lots of luck!!

Who is in control, who makes the major decisions, and who is willing to be vulnerable are all part of this important issue.

Mothers take notice… free your sons to be loving men!

"It is very difficult for the average person to realize that friction with his spouse is based not so much upon minor contemporary provocations as upon the earlier frustrations and resentments of his childhood." - Dr. Karl Menninger

Girls Who Just Wanna Have Sex

"A long life deprives man of his optimism. Better to die in all the happy period of unilllusioned youth, to go out in a blaze of light, than to have your body worn out and old and your illusions shattered." - Ernest Hemmingway

This was written the year he committed suicide. Thirty-five years earlier he wrote, "How swell life gets after the hell is over."

I know a lot of people who are over fifty, let' say, who do not and have not had sex in a long, long time. Most of these women probably never really fully enjoyed it. Now they make do and are "happy" with what they have; a husband or man in their lives, a nice home, children and enough resources to enjoy their lives of hairdressers, and restaurants and whatever else they fill their time with. The men probably make do too, or find other women on the side.

Not so for this generation…

Recently I had a long talk with a young college girl about what goes on with her peers. I had asked her to critique the "Sex for Dummies" book by Dr. Ruth Westheimer

She said she knew most of what was in the book and thought it was for an older group as the gender attitudes have changed.

When I asked," How so" she said that girls were much more aggressive today and many had attitudes like the guys and sex was just for sex whenever they wanted it! There are aggressive older women also but that's another story. Finding older men on-line is a whole new area today as well.

No surprise to me but how did that change the capacity for real relationships and what about intimacy and longing and romance?

She wasn't sure, and yes the girls who have sex like guys do, did get a 'reputation', mainly among the other girls, she thought.

Well, one girl doesn't have all the answers, so I looked at what girlfriends and boyfriends search for on Google.

No surprise there either, for me.

The girls want to know; why doesn't he call me, then, why doesn't he like me, and thirdly, why doesn't he ask me out?

After that they want to then know how to get him to propose, how to have him spend more time, or how to get him to love them again.

The boys ask;

How can I get my girlfriend to give me head, sleep with me, followed by wanting her to lose weight!

See the difference?

Following these responses, the girls wanted their boyfriends to trust them again, be more romantic, stop smoking, be more affectionate, last longer in bed, stop drinking, or how to break up.

The guys followed up with;

How to get her to trust them again, love them again, shave, break up, forgive them, kiss them, and lastly to love them.

Fascinating, and the genders are still doing the same old stuff. Girls want commitment and guys want sex.

So, now with the females so liberated and 'equal' to the males, where does that leave us?

I'm not sure.

Women today are independent, educated, and earn money. They're strong and tough and run homes. work, and manage children. If all they need a man for is sex, and prefer that to a vibrator, how do males feel about that? Used? Not important? It can't be positive in my thinking. It's the reverse of what we have always had.

Sometimes sex just for sex could work, but for women I still think they want more. We'll soon find out as this generation grows into adulthood. Stay tuned!

"There is only misfortune in not being loved; there is misery in not loving." - Albert Camus

Give Yourself Permission

"So, too, our whole life is an attempt to discover when our spontaneity is whimsical, sentimental irresponsibility and when it is a valid expression of our deepest desires and values." - Helen Merrell Lynd

We live according to rules. They are set by our culture, our background, and those around us.

The people who don't give a damn are usually the very rich or the very poor. They have nothing to lose. They can write their own ticket, so to speak.

It is those in the middle that conform and want to do the 'right' thing and save face.

Most people have areas of self-doubt or things they do not like about themselves and issues about how they 'measure up' against others.

It takes a lot of life to accept who you are, and be comfortable in the world.

Now it is true we all need to obey the law, usually do not want to harm others, and want to be viewed in a positive light. By conforming, we live out our lives. We follow the rules and lead constrained lives for the most part. Pleasing others is taught at young ages.

What I am hoping is that we can learn to be spontaneous, joyful, and sharing people.

When alcohol or drugs enter into the picture many open up and 'let it go' in a variety of ways. That may be fine but we can live full, connected, expressive lives with that in moderation, as well.

When you see how someone behaves, we immediately know how they were raised and what they are like. Their 'instincts' or immediate responses are there.

One of the difficult things today is that people have learned how to satisfy themselves but have not learned that pure happiness comes from being close to someone else in a truly deep emotional fashion.

To share yourself openly, and totally, is indeed frightening and many go through life without doing it.

The question is always; 'If I allow my partner to see or learn this or that about me will they still care for me, respect me, and love me?'

There are no angels walking the earth. We are all but specs of flawed material, here for a whisper of time... SO…

Try it a bit at a time. It doesn't have to be all at once and it doesn't have to be so guarded that the real you is protected. You will learn that as you unpeel, like an onion, the other person will feel they too can let out their secret selves.

It is when this has occurred in a consistent manner that you will 'trust'; it will feel safe and you can then feel totally accepted, and loved.

Then spontaneity can occur, and how good that feels.

To just 'be' and say what you feel and think in the moment and act freely is what it's about.

Yes, you can be foolish at times, and yes, you can be goofy, and yes, a lot of it doesn't make sense, but so what?

In the end you are authentic and more importantly, accepted!

Then and only then is life beautiful and FREE!!

We are not all creative in the utmost sense but we are all unique in special ways. Finding that and sharing it is joyous. When that happens, the world is a rainbow and everyone sees it and benefits from what you dispense. You are not unhappy, spreading misery and boredom. You are not living a mundane existence. You have gone beyond that.

You can dream and really have fun… every minute… almost.

Life will hand out it's sorrows and crap will happen, make no mistake. Life's duties will need attention, make no mistake about that either. Conflict is inevitable. HOWEVER, the joyful part will get you through and allow you to really share it all with another.

If you have tried and perhaps been disappointed, or 'burned' by the person you thought was 'it', it will take time and experience to risk it again. But do it!

This is a once around game… no second lives to try again… it's now or never!

Being responsible and stable is important but starving real love with passion, will never satisfy. Without it, you have NOTHING!!

Nothing that matters. To love is the height of this life… go after it.

Do not lead a puny scared life; sing and dance, hug and kiss, make fabulous love, and, let the 'magic' in!!!

"To be free is to have achieved your life." - Tennessee Williams

Hooray For Pornography

"SEX WITHOUT LOVE IS AS hollow and ridiculous as love without sex." - Hunter S. Thompson

That's right… no sex… no love. When you are in love you want to make love… a lot!!

The movie, "Nymphomaniac," produced in Denmark is what anyone would call graphic and pornographic. It is FULL of raw sex. A young girl has sex anytime with anyone in every conceivable fashion, except for homosexuality.

She is not terribly attractive, and has a thin body, much like a young boy's.

Her partners are young, old, fat, thin, attractive and homely. In other words, there is no discrimination in her choices for her behavior.

Her closest emotional attachment is to her father and her mother is described as, "cold." No surprises here.

The film has artistic pieces relating to nature, the animal kingdom, and music.

What is missing is her development and growth.

Now, I am no prude when it comes to viewing graphic sexual activity in film, the concentration of it, makes it almost ho-hum.

My feelings and, in my therapeutic practice, have always been that there are things to be learned from pornography. It is not just stimulating for men either. As it is the essence of the life force the word itself should not have a negative connotation. It can be educational, uninhibited and fun. That's right, fun!

There is no foreplay, intimacy, or see-saw in any relationship in this film and that is the problem, as I see it.

Men like confident, and curious women. Women like the same in men. A lover can show he will be a good lover just by the way he dances and moves his body. She too. Eating with gusto and a variety of foods also gives a peek into sensuality.

Sitting by the phone waiting for his call, getting ready to see her, and doing considerate things make it special.

The rule of thumb is if you know how to love you will be found, and then sex forces the relationship to grow or become stale.

There is no shame or guilt in good sex coupled with love. By accepting one another with all the 'faults' you become enmeshed. That means you do not want to be without that person.

Now we could go through a whole list of the sex lives of people you would know but that is for another blog. There are many surprises there.

Those people who do not enjoy their sexuality are to be pitied.

Loveless is lifeless and as stated earlier, love without sex ain't love!! Not the kind that matters in this sense.

Sex is not a theme park with counting numbers. It is part and parcel of the life force and those that can't abide it, or refuse it, or deny it in any shape or form from birth to death do themselves a great disservice, and will never have truly lived.

The beginning is indeed when the baby feels comfort and pleasure by being touched and held. That naturally develops into other forms as the child grows. The adult then is prepared for real closeness in its' many forms.

Yes, it is true, many people do not learn about their bodies or a partner's and never learn about pleasure, so they naturally do not want to engage in sex. And true there are poor substitutes, but once you really 'get it' literally and figuratively, you will NEVER want to be without it. That is true until your dying day. Thank goodness!!!

The end of this particular film shows the female lead saying after a steamy sexual encounter where she is orgasmic, (she always is)," I felt nothing."

That's it; you can feel nothing without closeness, and intimacy, and that all translates into LOVE.

Stay tuned because there is a part two to this film and I will be happy to report on that when it comes out.

There is a place for sex just for sex, but in a lifetime, it will never be enough.

"Sex alleviates tension. Love causes it." - Woody Allen

Hooked Up Or Fucked Up

"IN SCHOOL, YOU'RE TAUGHT THE lesson and then you're given the test. In life, you're given a test that teaches you a lesson." - Tom Bodett

There was just an article in the Sunday New York Times about sex on campus and girls who 'hook up.'

That's the term for having sex just for sex; without emotional involvement. That can be okay for some or for a while but what is the outcome over time?

I don't think we know, but we have a damn good hunch.

Love includes the brain, the heart, and the body. The most powerful sex organ is the brain.

It triggers whom we are attracted to, and what our thoughts are, and become, about that person.

Many long-term relationships begin with a physical attraction that evolves into mutual appreciation, but some can also go the other way. Whatever; the feelings get into it.

Because of the changing role of women, the goal for a college education is no longer getting the Mrs. Degree, but working hard toward a future career. As a result, many young women are opting to use their sex drive to have sex and use a guy's body to get it!

Many reported needing to be drunk or close to it in order to perform. Great!

By senior year a study found that 4 in 10 students are still virgins or have had intercourse with one person. The study is at Online College Social Life Survey. Nearly 3 in 10 said they never had a hookup in college. However, 20 percent of women and a quarter of men said they had hooked up with 10 or more people. Great!

They found that many of the females engaged in oral sex and the males did not care to pleasure them. They also found that wealthier girls engaged in hookups more than their poorer counterparts did.

Many felt 'raped' afterwards when the alcohol wore off, and many had 'reputations' with both men and women as a result.

Many of those that engaged in hook up activity felt their lives were and would be too busy for a while for a relationship and they wanted to see if someone 'better' came along and they wanted to end up married to someone that was finished growing up. Not bad reasons.

My theory is that finding the person that you can really love is a more important goal than anything else, and difficult to find at any age.

A recent book, 'The End of Men' by Hanna Rosin argues that the hook up strategy is for ambitious young women to have an enjoyable sex life while pursuing their academic and professional goals. Great!

Many of the women said the warnings not to get emotionally involved came not from the feminist culture but from their own parents. Great!

Some of the women said they never wanted marriage. Great!

Let me tell you; guys still control the scene, and most of this hook up stuff goes on at fraternity parties.

Using sex for whatever purpose needs to be understood and at college ages that's not so easy.

Nationally women outnumber men in college enrollment by 4 to 3 and outperform them in graduation rates and advanced degrees. Men, in the minority, hold the power in the sexual arena and they prefer casual sex to long term situations. No news there.

So, what about longing, waiting and agonizing over his calling, that sweet kiss, the heart throbs, and all that goes into ROMANCE?

If you look at sex on TV, you can see the fun and playfulness is missing. Pity. It ain't sexy!

A movie, "The Look of Love" stars Steve Coogan. When asked about playing the role of the British soft-porn baron, Paul Raymond, he said he realized it was possible to see too many naked women. True, believe it or not. Direct quote, "By the end of shooting, I just wanted to go for a hike in the hills, alone."

Ladies, invest in a vibrator. You don't have any emotional attachment there and it works!!!

"The belief that youth is the happiest time of life is founded on a fallacy. The happiest person is the person who thinks the most interesting thoughts, and we grow happier as we grow older." - William Lyon Phelps

How Do You Make a Man or Woman

"I think it can be stated without denial that no man ever saw a man that he would be willing to marry if he were a woman." - George Gibbs

As a therapist, for over thirty years with a sub- specialty dealing with transgendered people I am pleased that Bruce (Caitlyn) Jenner has brought the issue to the forefront.

When I began working with this population there was little knowledge or acceptance by the general public. Today there is at least some understanding of the dilemma this group faces.

When I first went on TV talk shows with my clients and their families, they were treated with ridicule and derision. Today that has lessened somewhat.

My book, 'Transsexuals—Life From Both Sides' has personal stories from my male and female clients as well as family members. It also includes pictures of finished surgery for both males and females.

Most transgendered people know something is wrong from early childhood. Many struggle with what that 'something' is for years. They try all sorts of possibilities and try to 'fit in.'

They suffer, often alone, and in silence. They can be bullied, ridiculed, and many seek relief through a variety of means including suicide. It is an extremely emotionally painful existence.

It is only when they discover what the real problem is and that maybe they can confide in someone that relief begins.

The steps to correct the gender are easier for a male that wishes to be a female than for the female who believes herself to be a male.

There are standards that surgeons will follow before doing the final step; surgical correction.

Transgendered people take hormones for life. These grow breasts for the new women and soften their facial features; It takes one operation to cut through the penis and scrotum to invert the skin to create a vagina. The prostate is preserved so that during intercourse there can be sensation similar to orgasm. I co-authored a research paper on that topic. They can never become pregnant.

For the new man the hormones create facial and body hair. They can also become bald.

This group has to undergo mastectomies and hysterectomies. Building a penis can take several operations and inserting a pump for erection to take place can also be included. They can never father a child.

So, after all of this are they happy?

You bet. They have had to see a mental health professional and have two letters from two professionals to approve surgery. They have also had to have lived in the desired role for at least a year.

The really hard part is being accepted in the new role.

Some look better than others. Some relate more easily. Some have support people, and jobs.

For the parents, it is certainly a trying acceptance and often there is guilt about what they did that might have caused this. They did nothing!

It is like homosexuals; you either are or you aren't.

What I have found especially interesting is that every one of my new 'males' has a partner. It is unusual for my new 'females' to find partners. Some are lesbian and while the public has a hard time understanding that, it is not bizarre. Some born females are also lesbian!

I have also had married couples stay together after surgery.

Children can be confused but can come through okay in the end if handled well.

So, we can make a man or woman but what really makes a man or woman?

Is it a penis or vagina? Is it the ability to have children? Is it the way you look, act or think about yourself?

Haven't we all see the stereotypes? The 'real' man and the 'real' woman. How many fall into those categories?

We come in a variety of forms and behaviors.

The oldest person we operated on when I directed a program was 70. She became a matronly woman.

Some of my petite 'new' women looked great and were sexy.

Some of my 'new' men were weight lifters and others were doing what are thought to be traditional female jobs. It's a rainbow!

Now back to Caitlyn.

She looks beautiful. She is older. I'm not sure how much therapy she has had. She has always liked publicity and attention…whether male or now female. My hope is that she will bring about a public awareness that will be understanding and kind. The world today could use all of that no matter the source!!

"Basically, society has to get rid of that myth of the dominant male and the submissive female. When both sexes realize that either one can be on top, we're all going to enjoy our relationships a lot more." - Gloria Steinem

Passion Is Both Hot And Cold

"Love is of all passions the strongest, for it attacks simultaneously the head, the heart, and the senses." - Lao Tzu

Are you a passionate person?

If so, you know longing, despair, and at times wanting to kill yourself!

Now we're not talking here about being passionate about a cause, or a career, or anything other than a lover. This blog is only about this stuff.

My question has always been can just anyone be filled with passion? I am not sure.

In my life and career, I have seen too many what I call, 'dead carps.' They go through life with little in the way of abandonment, pure joy, personality, or loss of control. Whenever you see someone with those traits just imagine them in bed!! Yuk!!

A good clue is watching people dance, or if they eat with gusto. It can be a clue. Just listen to what people talk about. True we all have houses to run, dinners to plan, children to raise, insurance to pay and so on BUT the people who are LIVING just take all of that in stride and it consumes a small part of their world. Yes, if money is a problem that's a different story. You can't be free, creative, and full of love if you have real issues to contend with that drain your capacity for love. However, even with big issues to contend with, a passionate person shares it all and that makes it better.

Now, passion can go both ways… hot and cold.

Listen to all the murders that we hear about. That's passion gone awry.

Let your lover hurt you in any fashion, or feel you are not given what you need emotionally and see how you react.

When you 'risk' it all and unchain your heart and are ready to be totally out of control, and can abandon yourself in another, you will know passion. When you share passion, it is the ultimate joining of heart and body. There can be NO passion without sex. Not just any old sex but SEX with passion, on both sides. The pull to be close is like a magnetic field. The feel of one body against another and touching is the root of it all. And there can be no true love in all its' majesty without sex. Many people cannot 'surrender' therefore they are the living dead all their lives.

Pity.

It is scary as hell and only the brave can succeed. But boy, is it worth it!!!

All the creative people that have ever lived knew it, wrote about it, and composed music for it, and so on. That is what lasts in a culture.

There is the wonderful story about Richard Burton and Elizabeth Taylor, who married and divorced twice. There was much passion in their relationship.

At the end he was marrying someone else and told Elizabeth he would always love her but the passion was so consuming he could no longer handle it. He called her at least three times a week, after he remarried, for the rest of his life, which was not long after that.

A famous P.G. Woodhouse quote says it all.

"His soul, as he walked, was a black turmoil of conflicting emotions. This woman had treated him in a way, which would have made even a man with so low an opinion of the sex as the late Schopenhauer whistle incredulously. But though he scorned and loathed her, he was annoyed to discover that he loved her still. He would have liked to bounce a brick on Prudence Whittaker's head, and yet, at the same time, he would have liked to crush her to him and cover her face with burning kisses. The whole situation was very complex."

"Passion makes the world go round. Love just makes it a safer place." - Ice T

Sex First Talk Later

"We like someone because. We love someone although." - Henri De Montherlant

You may have seen a recent study that stated that talking after sex was perhaps more important to the relationship than the sex act itself!

Well, imagine that.

There's that story about the brothel for women where for one hundred dollars the man will caress you. For two hundred he will kiss and fondle you. AND for three hundred he will listen to you!

So what is this new generation experiencing with jumping into bed, and THEN getting to know the person?

Maybe it works as well as anything in the past. In former generations the females, if they were 'good' girls, were virgins until marriage. Hence many young marriages. What were they saving it for? Did it work out? Was it any better than the relationships that go on today? All good questions.

The issue as I view it is that once sex is in the picture the relationship takes on a new perspective, especially for the female.

Does he love me, will I see him again, am I the only one, and when will he call, are all areas that come into play.

Whatever you think, the guy still has a different role and attitude than the female. Even the most assertive or aggressive female is at his 'mercy', like it or not. She however controls the sexual opportunity unless he uses force. It is a trade-off, of sorts.

Sex is never an emergency but it is a powerful drive, maybe the most powerful.

True some females don't like or want sex but the majority have working hormones, and the guys have a strong drive. If not, something may be wrong.

It could be the lack of intimacy and not feeling loved, cherished, approved, appreciated or maybe a medical problem.

It boils down to whom do you want to be involved with and how to make it happen and stick.

While we usually only deeply love once or probably twice in a lifetime and life is made up of moments of happiness, sex offers a wonderful closeness and joy.

If after meeting someone and having sex with them you discover a whole bunch of stuff that you really don't like, what to do then? Jump into bed over and over again until, maybe Prince Charming arrives?

We do not teach reality over fantasy and if you find you are a matter of convenience, romance will surely be out the window.

Can you be honest and yourself? How do you resolve differences and maybe rejection? Or how do you reject someone? Again, all good questions. They should all be considered BEFORE you get into anything that may involve commitment of any sort.

You know it was Socrates that said, "The un-examined life is not worth living for a human being." How many of us do that? Being young could help if you take a step back and look at what you are doing. It will give you a jump on life.

·Now if drugs, or alcohol are involved that colors the situation.

Where is your will power? What are your values and what is your ultimate goal? Again great questions to ponder.

We all develop patterns of behavior based on many factors; how we feel about ourselves, what we know of the opposite sex, what our parents lived, and so on. If you repeat situations that do not work for you, you definitely need to EXAMINE or get a professional to help you do it.

When you get in bed never forget your parents and his parents are also there with you in a form.

Another important issue to look at is pride and it may be a good thing or a factor that prevents you from moving closer to someone. Control is another piece of this delicate puzzle. Who has it and under what circumstances?

Life will teach you what no one else can. 'Mistakes' can be wonderful for learning.

Loving someone includes sex and the only question is how it fits into your situation.

Great sex does not happen by magic but the magic will be there when the right person is in bed with you.

Males like freedom and females like commitment and when they finally get to the point where each is content it is fabulous!! Nature rules!!!

In breaking his engagement to Agatha von Siebold, Brahms wrote to her: "I could not love thee, dear, so much if I did not love my freedom more."

Selfish Lovers Should Fuck Themselves

"Sexual pleasure, wisely used and not abused, may prove the stimulus and liberator of our finest and most exalted activities." - Havelock Ellis

The opposite of love is selfishness.

When we choose someone to love one of the primary areas to be aware of is how selfish the person is. Now true we are all acting in our own best interest and when giving ourselves intimately, in every respect, we also experience pleasure. The difference is whether or not our beloved's happiness is what is most important, and what you are willing to do to bring it to them. It should be without limit. If there are problems, they should be communicated and worked on because there is NOTHING that love cannot conquer!

When someone is selfish, there are reasons.

They may have been given too much as children, so that they believe they are the center of the universe and everyone is there to cater to their needs. They are not appreciative as it all is just naturally expected. The opposite is also true; they may have never had their emotional needs met so they are empty inside and need to be constantly filled.

You can only give love if you have a full cup yourself.

In order to entrust your heart to another, you have to be able to abandon yourself and reveal who you truly are. In order to feel safe emotionally you have to test and over time believe the partner is capable of caring which he has demonstrated to you on many levels.

A lover in bed that is not concerned about your orgasm is a sure sign they, (usually he), is only interested in what you deliver for him. If selfish in bed, he is probably selfish in other areas as well.

Males are not educated about how to bring a female to that ecstasy because it is an easier and more natural task for him. His orgasm does not require the same process as a female's.

He is usually not taught how to pleasure her body and where or how to touch what areas.

There is an organization that is quite intriguing called, The One Taste Method.

They have groups that meet all over the country and teach what they call the OM, (orgasmic meditation), method.

This is a process where a partner, (male with heterosexuals), learns how to touch the genitals of his female partner for about fifteen minutes, bringing on her orgasmic response. Now that's an education!!

There are other organizations as well.

While the response in sexual activity can occur with or without love, wanting to share more with a partner shows a selfless person.

This is also possible with toys or vibrators if he is not physically capable. It doesn't matter how. We are only talking about actual sex here but there are other touching ways that people can show they love one another if sex is not possible for any reason. There can be no true intimacy without touch and usually really good sex.

Females can learn how to prolong a male's response, and how to keep him excited over years, but he really has to learn how to bring her to her peak sexually.

The old adage that a woman's best sex organ is her ears is also true. She needs to hear how you feel about her. She can see her male's reaction physically. Her genital moisture is also a sign for him.

The other many ways of being loving include all the things you know. Listening, being helpful, flowers and candy, cards and notes, and the small and large material displays of 'I love you.' Any and all of them should be included in a repertoire of revealing your love. When people really love, they cannot do enough for one another. It is the 'doing' that counts, with genuine love and wanting to show feelings.

If you are with a selfish lover, and many women are, you can decide to not care about what he does not do, or you can attempt to teach him, and if all else fails, in the end, you may decide he should just 'go fuck himself!'

The act of physical love means a great deal and both males and females revel in what it brings. Without it why bother at all?

Being attractive, wanted, sexy, and desired is good for you. The orgasmic response makes the brain and body healthy in ways they should be. Why would anyone not want that?

The selfish lover takes but cannot give.

It depends on what you think about yourself, what you will tolerate and be able to live with. There is only so much overlooking, forgiveness, and justifying that you can do. Over time, resentment will rear its' ugly head and then things turn sour, no matter how many orgasms are or are not, involved. If one partner refuses sex, pure anger will occur and can be let out or repressed causing physical harm to the body over time. This is often the reason why the search for another partner happens.

The selfish people usually end up hollow and empty inside and rationalize or philosophize about their lot in life. Because of their limitations, they may live out their entire lives 'making do' or putting the blame anywhere but on themselves.

The thing is that once selfish eyes have been opened, so to speak, and they have experienced sex coupled with love, their 'self' is happier; they can never go back. That would be the epitome of misery. That's a good thing!!

"Love is an attempt at penetrating another being but it can only succeed if the surrender is mutual." - Octavio Paz

Sex Is In the Head

"Knowledge is power" - Sir Francis Bacon

"The big difference between sex for money and sex for free is that sex for money usually costs a lot less."- Brendan Behan

Think about it… everyone is a prostitute… of sorts.

We all have sex for a variety of reasons and good sex includes knowing what and how to do IT. Great sex includes love.

BUT we all do IT for a reason and that reason means we are prostituting ourselves for our particular needs. That's true whether you want to believe it or not.

Look around at the people you know. Really look at their relationships and what they have going for them.

How many are married because they wanted security? How many are together for the children? How many are there for company? How many are there to have… sex? You fill in the blank.

The initial reason may have changed dramatically over the years as the individuals and their life circumstances and their emotional and intellectual development progressed. One person for life is a foolish promise and the premise is ridiculous. You must choose and re-choose the person. It can be quite a challenge.

Now about the sex act itself. What's in your head???

What kind of education did anybody receive about that? How is the trial and error method working?

Where does control, pain as part of it, or other fetishes fit in? There's a lot more to it than body holes and poles!

Yes, it can be simple and the missionary position gets the job done BUT what a difference if the guy really knows how to excite his lady. What about the clitoris and massaging it, and what about slowly caressing her ALL over to bring her to that final release of ecstasy? The smells and the sounds and the discharge of vaginal fluid make him over the top happy. Does she know the Kegel exercises; squeezing the vaginal walls in and then out to make them firm? It helps.

For her part does she know how to use the squeeze technique to slow him down? Holding the shaft of the penis head as he rises and falls. Pressure under the base near the anus gives him pure delight, licking the scrotum… and so on. Who teaches all this and who is free enough to learn and do it?

Not a whole lot of people.

Sex can be embarrassing.

As a therapist and sex educator for over thirty years I have heard it all.

I once had a prostitute come for counseling as she was having a problem with her husband. She had been married about ten years and had the face of a beautiful, fresh farm girl.

She prostituted for money for her husband's drug problem. He knew what she did.

When she talked about the details one curious thing came out. She said that the most money she received regularly was from a well-known older man who only wanted to look at her, touch her while she was clothed and talk. So what's that about?

People are lonely and many feel unappreciated and cannot be themselves and still have a good sex life.

In a working relationship that is ongoing good sex can make up for a lot of crap, and compromising. It is the glue that keeps it going and makes it last.

If you want to be sexy use everything at your disposal, ALL THE TIME!!!

There are creams, bubble baths, candles, dinners, gifts, sweet talk, and lingerie. You think of it and it can be incorporated. Whatever pleases the participants is just fine!! Nobody else matters, or quite frankly gives a damn. Those that talk in moralistic tones are repressed or just plain jealous…. probably with outlets that are ridiculous and very poor substitutes. Even creative or work output doesn't hold a candle to lively, satisfying sex. Sex in the head is never as good as juicy sex with a partner in bed!

So, yes, prostitute yourself and while at it have a good time! The older generation had wives that were parasites on their husbands and this generation shares more equally and uses one another in better fashion. I, however still believe that the human species follows their ancestors with the woman being the nurturer and the man the slayer. Instincts don't get wiped out, and sex with a receiver and a thruster are the roles we still play, as our anatomy dictates!

"I need sex for a clear complexion, but I'd rather do it for love." - Joan Crawford

Sex... For Men... For Women

Men use love to get sex and women use sex to get love!

This is very true statement and the differences are probably in the biology of the two sexes. From the childhood, the hormones begin their work and by adolescence, they are rampant especially in young men. The saying, that woman need a reason to have sex while men just need a place is probably true for a majority of people.

Women as they mature can have an equally strong drive, but it is behind the scenes as men's response is right out there. While we have little in the way of really great sex education most of it is trial and error. To learn about sex and love we see parents and most of what we see is not ideal. There may be some type of education in school or from peers but no one deals with the individual and their needs, questions and basic information.

Only in recent human history have women been seen as sexual and with birth control, they have let out their impulses. The need for a relationship and being loved is much more apparent in women as opposed to men. This is probably in the history of the species. Men need to propagate and women need the protection and support of a man. Today some of that has changed, as women are educated, work and support themselves.

Years ago, there were good girls and bad girls. The good girls went to heaven and the bad girls went everywhere! What has happened today is that there is often no wait for sex, no longing and the mere act.

Men are not instructed how to pleasure a woman and women are not knowledgeable about how to achieve sexual fulfillment or orgasm. How sad because a total sexual response is wondrous. It feels fabulous and connects two people like nothing else. It can make up for many other aspects in a relationship that are not what you might think. It is the glue. There is no great love without great sex and vice versa. Good sex is like good cooking… it takes information, experimentation and a freedom to experiment.

Communicating one's likes and needs is a way to achieve results. Being shy, body conscious, insecure, feeling vulnerable, taken advantage of, and not cherished; make sex a problem for women. They want to be adorned. If they feel used, they become angry or guilty. Not feeling admired or virile affects men and their sexuality.

If not satisfied, kings, presidents, and top men in all fields look around and do risky things. Many factors enter into the whole sexual area and few people are able to abandon themselves and truly connect with a partner. How sad!

What is your sex life like? People will tell you anything, but that. Americans have a tough time with it as we are a religious country and most people feel very self-conscious and insecure when truly naked.

Sexy Sensuous...What's the Difference?

"In my sex fantasy, nobody ever loves me for my mind." - Nora Ephron

Many men subscribe to both National Geographic and Playboy, both of which show places they'll never get to visit!

So being sexy or sensuous what is the difference?

In my experience, it is two very different aspects of a woman's personality and capability.

Looking around you see many women of all ages, some very pretty, dressing provocatively with tight, short or low cut clothes. They wear a lot of make-up and move in seductive fashion when men are around. Many have had plastic surgery on their breasts, bodies, or faces. All of this they believe makes them, "sexy."

While they may appeal to some males and be sending out their blatant message of, "I want sex," they may be sacrificing the real thing and may just not know how to get it...love.

It is important to look good and feel comfortable in your body and nothing wrong in trying to enhance what you have, but not to the exclusion of what really makes a man want a woman.

In Philadelphia the Barnes Foundation just moved to center city and in that collection there is a painting titled, "Woman With White Stockings" by Gustave Courbet. It is one of the most, if not the most, sensuous painting in the world. She is lying on her back, in grass, with a leg raised while she puts on a stocking. It is revealing, yes, but it conveys a message of femininity rarely seen on canvas. Go and view it!

Being sensuous may or may not be in the manner in which one appears... It is in the very essence of being a female and having that message conveyed.

How?

Well, it can be in a variety of forms. The subtle way one shows the body but leaves a bit to the imagination. The voice, the intellect, the charm, the lingerie. There is an old saying, "If love is blind how come so much money is spent on lingerie?"

Because it all spells female.

The sensuous woman knows she is all woman and craves men, or a man, and she lets him be all man. She has often been short changed by feminists who made her want to be like men. Can't happen. Not with a real woman! She doesn't want that. Equal rights and pay, yes, but defer to letting a man be what he is in her company. The sexes are different and have always been so.

That will never change!!

A man is a woman's whole life while she is usually only a part of his. Just see who's the one waiting for the phone to ring. When in love it becomes, there are things I can live with, but I cannot live without YOU!

Now to the nitty-gritty, when it comes to actual sex, which is the end game. A book, "Sex Made Easy," by Debby Herbenick of the Kinsey Institute explains every aspect of the sexual act and what to do with certain issues. It is excellent.

One of her first areas deals with knowing and liking your body and understanding how it functions when it comes to sex. This is for men and women.

Here in America we still do not teach people how to be sexually fulfilled and how to truly enjoy this part of life. It is the driving force and still we know and teach so little about it. How many people are comfortable with their and their partner's bodies? How many are able to abandon themselves sexually or even have fun with it?

When girls are given the images of models and skinny actresses as their role models it leads to misplaced values.

When you see unattractive people really in love and wonder why, you need to know about being sensual.

A *joie de vivre*, ready smile, listening ear, entertaining, and interesting dialogue will hold a man's interest a lot longer than a boob job!

Sexy At Sixty... and...

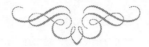

"Man reaches the highest point of lovableness at 12 to 17 – to get it back, in a second flowering, at the age of 70 to 90." - Isak Dinesen

"An archaeologist is the best husband a woman can have; the older she gets, the more interested he is in her." - Agatha Christie

True.

Sex never disappears and the desire is strong in the lucky ones as they age.

What is especially great is that older people bring a lifetime of experience with them and they can share all that they have learned and lived with one another.

Now it may happen to people who are already married and then they have to decide whether they want to act on their feelings. The relationship may be with or without sex. It will have all the usual trappings of, will he call? Who says, I love you, first. The first argument and so on. All part of ANY relationship, until it stabilizes.

While aging affects people differently and health issues can enter into the equation, the drive to be together will overcome all obstacles.

For men they will probably have difficulty having or maintaining an erection. This can be dealt with. There is Viagra and other medications to assist. There are air pumps and penis rings to inflate the penis and hold an erection. There are vibrators that help. Penile implants are also available with surgery. And of course a man does not need a full erection in order to reach orgasm. The best part is that he takes longer for it all to occur and that helps the female as she is always slower. Oral or manual sexual activity is another form of pleasure. Just being naked and touched or, massaged, or bathed is also fun!

At any rate, sex at any age brings closeness and a way of showing affection, caring and love.

For women many have never been 'free' and able to abandon themselves but with age they may be able to take that 'last' chance. Dryness in the vaginal area can often be a problem but there are creams and lubricants for that. Vibrators can enhance and help orgasmic response. Being touched, fondled, kissed, and hugged are all available at any age!

It's always spooky to think of older people with wrinkles, sagging bodies, and whatever else age brings that's not pretty, having a sexual liaison or life, BUT it does and SHOULD happen. Why? Because it is the life force and makes you feel great! Plastic surgery is common these days for both men and women to look good.

The old story that she looked fifty but undressed every older woman shows her age may not be so true these days.

We are fitter.

Being desired at any point in life makes you think differently about yourself. You dress differently, buy new underwear and look younger. No doubt about it… sex matters.

Humor is a factor that is certainly a part of this activity. When you imagine parents, or god forbid, grandparents doing 'it' you could die but guess what… you are lucky if they do. It may bode well for your future.

Now of course probably the majority of people, especially older women, do not engage in this activity. My hunch is they probably only did it begrudgingly earlier in their lives. That's because older women were raised to know little about it all and that generation did not feel comfortable about much of it. Sad.

Today some enlightened older people are getting new messages and want in on it. They also realize it is the last of life and they may want to experience what they have always heard about. Brave ones will jump in.

What is so nice is that with age people can really let loose and try all sorts of stuff, in and out of bed.

As a therapist you cannot believe what I hear. Nothing shocks me at this point but I bet you would never imagine what goes on behind closed doors.

No fear of pregnancy, no fear of children bothering, no worries about money, no fear of neighbors and what they think, no fears of not being accepted for just being you. Little fear of you or him finding someone else to move on to. How wonderful!

There is a quiet dignity about the human struggle that mature people have. Life has taught them what they needed to know to survive and find whatever joy they can have as life winds down. There is a freedom in that.

If they have lived well there is comfort in having raised children that can care for themselves and their children and there is pleasure in whatever has been accomplished.

If they have regrets they can be shared with someone who will understand. The pain that life brings can be talked about and the acts of caring are appreciated in ways that never could have been shared earlier in life.

History cannot be repeated and the new history may be short but it is very sweet. My thoughts are that this may indeed be the best that life has to offer!!!

Go for it!!!

"Cherish youth, but trust old age." - Pueblo proverb

Training to be a Casanova

"I HAVE LOVED WOMEN TO a frenzy." - Casanova.

There it is, from the man himself.

Casanova was born in Venice and lived from 1725 to 1798.

His early life included being abandoned by his mother who was an actress, and being sent to live with a grandmother until at an early age he was sent to become a priest! He was thrown out after a short period when found having sexual relations with another boy.

He worked as a magician, spy, and translator. In 1755 he was accused of witchcraft and escaped a prison sentence by fleeing to Paris.

His life included being a prolific lover and seducer of women.

When he wrote his twelve volume biography he listed 132 women he had made love to!

Now that is not the longest list in history but he is the one most quoted as a 'lover' in the 'biblical' sense.

What is even more important is the fact that he liked variety, always had a mutual break-up, and remained friends with the women after the love affairs.

He never married but did have children.

He liked women and he enjoyed talking with them, and never wanted to hurt them.

Without women he became melancholy.

Many of his loves were well known and he kept their names secret.

At sixty-five he was worn out and then wrote his books.

What do we learn from this?

First of all, men learn to like or not like women from their earliest experiences… you guessed it, from their mothers.

If they had sisters that can also give perspective on their relations with the female sex.

Men who truly like women can learn to love them.

How to be a lover is not taught in any school.

It's a matter of, like all things, knowledge.

How you view yourself, your body, and being interested in women will all come through.

Do you talk to her? What about? Can you compliment her about what you appreciate and like about her?

Are you genuinely interested in her life and what she talks about? All part of the beginning.

Seduction and combining body parts comes as the next step. What do you know about her body? What do you like about it? What turns you on? What turns her on?

These can be talked about. They should be. There are all sorts of enhancers out there today too.

Every guy has had a time or times when 'It' doesn't work.

So what?

It's okay. A female should NEVER make that an issue. Work around it.

There are pills, creams, vibrators and many devices to aid in the process.

Learning about how to be orgasmic, and bringing a partner to orgasm should be taught before anyone can graduate, certainly from college!

Learning about body parts is a discovery that pays off.

Some of this comes more naturally to some. Others have to really study and learn; like anything elsewhere, competence is the goal.

The problem is we are shy, scared, embarrassed, guilty or whatever when it comes to sex.

It is the most intimate of sharing, although many today just have sex; not intimacy. That's fine for some but once you know the difference you won't want to live without it. That means connection, not just with body parts, but with heart and mind.

When was the last time you had sex? With whom? What were your feelings for that person?

What did you talk about?

Have you had disagreements? How were they resolved?

What do you really like about that person? Have you told them? Have you shown them?

Casanova was real; he loved in his fashion. Probably short term for the most part, however there was one long term relationship that carried him into his older age. That one had a different quality to it.

You can be any kind of lover you choose… short term, just sex, or involved totally. When it is real and truly fused love and passion you will know it. It is not easy to find or accomplish, I grant you, BUT worth every heartache engendered! And trust me there is always heartache along the way of real love. That's sort of how you know it's love; you care. You can be hurt, and you still want that person, body and soul!

"Man survives earthquakes, epidemics, the horrors of disease and all the agonies of the soul, but for all time his most tormenting tragedy has been, is, and will be- the tragedy of the bedroom." - Leo Tolstoy

Sexy Presidents

"POLITICIANS LIKE PROSTITUTE, ARE HELD in contempt, but what man does not run to them when he requires their services?" - Brendan Francis

We all know the stories about some contemporary presidents; Lyndon Johnson, John Kennedy, Bill Clinton, and many others before them. They used their sexuality to full advantage; power being an aphrodisiac.

But, I'll bet you don't know about the loves of our George Washington or Thomas Jefferson.

Washington was born in 1732 to a father who had been married and had two sons. His mother was the second wife and they had George and then a sister and three brothers together.

The older half-brothers were his father's favorites.

At age eleven his father died

His mother was not an especially caring mother to him and his education was rudimentary. He disliked his mother and she always wanted money from him even complaining to Congress in later years; lying about what he gave her.

He longed to be in an upper social class.

As a young man he met Sally Fairfax who was a beautiful young woman two years older than he.

She came from a socially prominent, and worldly family.

They fell in love and she educated him about her world.

Although in love her family did not want her to marry George, and so she did not. She subsequently married a wealthy suitor.

She and Washington wrote to one another often.

When Washington met Martha she was a wealthy widow, of one year, with two small children. She had married when she was eighteen and her husband was thirty-eight. They lost two children and he died after they were married for a short time. She was just what he wanted; in a high social position and rich. She was about a year older than he.

They were married about forty years in what is described as a ‘helpful’ marriage but without passion. He was not able to have children.

All of his life he loved and wrote and saw Sally often but it is believed based on the mores of the times that they never consummated the relationship.

When he helped sell her farm after her husband died he kept a small pillow she slept on for all of the rest of his life.

The letters that survive are from him and extremely loving and with a longing for her. Her letters are not found. His last one in 1798 a year before his death is especially moving.

Our other famous beloved president, Thomas Jefferson, also had an intriguing love life.

He was born in 1743 and as you know the author of our Declaration of Independence.

He was tall and handsome.

When he met his wife she was also a widow. She had married at eighteen to a man four years older and he died two years later. She also lost a son who was almost four.

A year later she met Jefferson who was close to six years older than she. She was twenty-three.

They married and truly loved one another. She had many pregnancies and lost five children. Two daughters lived; one to old age.

After about ten years she died and he was thirty-nine. He mourned her terribly and she had told him never to remarry. He became president nineteen years later.

As a result, he had a number of love affairs; many with married women. Maria Conway was a long term love of his. He met her when he was forty-three and she was twenty-seven.

Another big love of his was another married woman; Betsy Walker.

The other love was said to be a slave of his; Sally Hemings. There is much rumor and speculation regarding this affair that went on for years, begun when she was in her teens. It is said she had at least six children with him.

The DNA proves her descendants are from his line but one theory suggests it was his nephews that impregnated her, not Jefferson. Again rumor has it that Jefferson kept her as his mistress for life and the only slaves he freed were her children.

So there you have it. The fathers of our country were red blooded Americans in more ways than one!!

"Tis true I profess myself a Votary to Love." - George Washington

There's No Such Thing as 'Cheating'

"LIFE ISN'T ABOUT WAITING FOR the storm to pass; it's about learning to dance in the rain."- Anonymous

Whenever I hear the word, 'cheating' I cringe. As a marriage and relationship counselor we need to teach people that there is no such thing. Most couples do not even think of such a word, let alone an experience of finding another to fulfill their needs.

Now I am not talking about the people with mental issues that need to keep having new lovers in their lives to make them feel good, and I am not talking about the people who have never been able to maintain a long lasting relationship with depth and feeling and intensity. They are everywhere but that is not who we are dealing with here.

I am talking about the couples who, after a number of years, usually over seven, who need to find a new partner. Many do not consider divorce at first for a number of reasons; children, money, status, shame, fear of being alone, habit, or whatever. So, they fall prey to their emotions and sexual drive.

With women out in the work force it is easier to become entangled these days.

Monogamy is an unnatural state and those couples who have achieved it for many years have figured out the way.

They have grown together and found new and challenging ways to keep love and sex alive and fun.

They can teach us a lot.

However, for the many, and it is many, both men and women, who 'wander' into another's arms or bed, there is another story.

That NEVER happens from the outside, it happens because there is something necessary that is missing on the inside.

Perhaps one or the other is no longer capable or interested in sex. Maybe the relationship was never really intimate. Maybe they had to mature. Some know they can't fill the bill and should know that at some point the partner will, 'wander.' and learn what love is. If the partner is not able to develop and be there emotionally then there is a hunger.

That hunger is always picked up by others who are 'hungry.'

It is a normal feeling and need and when it has to be fulfilled and people are ready to 'risk' it they get together. That like marriage or a long term relationship is also no picnic after the initial high. All love takes knowledge and some doing! Sex will lead the way and good sex, coupled with love, is the height of what life is about for the fortunate ones.

When a partner is insecure, suspicious, too controlling, or being superficially involved, living a shallow life, it is THEIR problem.

On some level they know they are driving the partner to 'wander.'

It is the nature of humans to seek satisfaction emotionally and sexually and that is why many who have given a great deal to a partner and then find a new way to love never feel guilty. They have given enough. There is no short changing here.

Now to tell or not, or to be discovered is another issue.

I am also not addressing the consideration of children here. That will be another blog.

If the relationship continues the outside one has to be clandestine and limited. That is not easy.

If the marriage is to go on after discovery the couple have to reconnect on another level. It is possible and can improve. If the outside love continues in secret it may in fact help the other relationship to be pleasanter and continue as needs are being met elsewhere. Tricky business.

Being desired and feeling that you can love and be loved is indeed a narcotic experience. It also keeps you young and healthy!

A couple of examples are interesting. Hannah Arendt and Martin Heidegger two brilliant creative people had an affair for decades and in the end he has her meet his wife

Ayn Rand had an open marriage and a long lasting involvement with a younger man.

Interesting that creative bright people seem to need this.

There is no shortage of male examples. You can think of them all on your own. Often they are powerful, successful men choosing young, beautiful women whom they believe love them. Perhaps.

The bonobos, small chimpanzees, are the most peaceful, contented creatures on earth. They have sex anytime with anyone!!! Is there a message here?

"If you're already walking on thin ice, you might as well dance." – Proverb

The First Time

The first time for anything is usually both frightening and exciting.

With sex it's definitely both.

What matters are your age, the relationship, and the reason.

Now the age is important because a certain amount of maturation is necessary for both knowledge and where your brain is at when the activity occurs. Too young or too old makes a difference in a lot of what happens.

The relationship is really important because if it is a casual one without much behind it, it will certainly have an effect on the outcome as well as what happens afterwards.

The reason for the encounter is crucial as well. If it is consensual is the primary question. Next comes whether it's for cementing an intimate connection, or to prove something, or to do what everyone else is doing, or to hold on to or try to attract someone to you, will all be factors to explore.

At any rate the first sexual experience is usually fraught with all sorts of horror stories. It can't be good because nobody has experience!! If one has experience they may become the expert… but they may not have what is really needed.

Most couples tell about the awkwardness, the fumbling, and the embarrassment they felt. Most are not happy with showing their naked selves and don't know what to do or say. It is not a warm fuzzy episode in most people's lives.

To be a lover takes time and practice. Read about the great lovers from history and their connections both emotional and physical. There will be a blog later on about this

Problem is when you start out young and end up marrying that person, that initial pattern persists emotionally. Not good for the most part. Better to have some experience and then choose a mate.

What do you need to know after that first encounter?

A lot!

First, you need to know about your own body and what pleasures you.... what and how to touch where. Can't be shy here.

Then you need to be comfortable with the body of the partner. What parts to touch, fondle, lick or suck!!!

Can't be shy here either!!! For girls try practicing oral sex, maybe. Try a banana, a lollipop, and an ice cream cone. Use that mouth and tongue. Guys use your mouth in rare parts of her body and ask what she likes. Guide the hands and talk about it before, during, or after. Most people find that SO difficult. Shame.

A real body works, and toys like vibrators, can augment and enhance the activity.

Variety so that it doesn't get boring can be implemented. An Ice cube over his body, whipped cream on some of her body parts, removable tattoos in strategic places, are but a few examples of creative sex play.

Getting ready is half the fun, and it should be playful and fun. Watch an x rated film, take a bubble bath, kiss and hug all over. Foreplay is also in the brain and what the ears hear, especially for females.

Never, ever, talk disparagingly about a guy's sex organs, or his prowess in bed. He will never forget it and you do yourself an injustice with your sex life in the end.

Females need time, average a half hour, to be orgasmic and guys react quicker so work needs to be done to slow them down. That's not impossible. It's in the brain and thoughts. Practice, practice, practice.

The sum and substance of all of this is to arrive at maturity, (and no one is always mature, or should be, all the time), and include sex as the epitome of a loving relationship shown physically, which feels SO good. The serotonin released makes you want that person and that feeling over and over again. It makes the world prettier and your life happier. Trust me!

The first time is for starters. Learning in this aspect, like anything else, takes time, study, and a willingness to reach a goal. Here it also takes cooperation, and open communication, both verbal and non-verbal which goes on all the time. It should never be for a final goal, such as mutual orgasm, it should be enjoyable all along the way and whatever happens, happens. Being close is the only goal.

Whatever it takes, it's worth it!

The Criteria of Emotional maturity

Having the ability to deal constructively with reality

Having the capacity to adapt to change

Having a relative freedom from symptoms that are produced by tensions and anxieties

Having the capacity to find more satisfaction in giving than in receiving

Having the capacity to relate to other people in a consistent manner with mutual satisfaction and helpfulness

Having the capacity to sublimate, to direct one's instinctive hostile energy into creative and constructive outlets

Having The Capacity To Love - William Menninger

There Is 'Ape' in Rape

"I ONLY MEAN THAT WHEN one thinks coldly I see no reason for attributing to man a significant different in kind from that which belongs to a baboon or a grain of sand." - Oliver Wendell Holmes Jr.

The mere word 'rape' conjures up a shudder, at the least, in most people's minds. And it should!

It is the taking of a female against her wish for sexual purposes. Women can seduce but they cannot rape.

Men rape for a variety of reasons; none justifiable.

While most psychological analyses say it is for control, not sex, I believe it can be for sexual needs as well.

Yes, it is a forcible act which can be done in a variety of forms from mere coercion to physical brute force or with weapons.

It can be performed by a single individual, in small groups, or by armies.

Most analytical people say these men hate women or fear them emotionally.

Some have no means for sexual outlet.

If we look around today, we see young girls wearing next to nothing. When they encourage not just interest but an unwanted sexual encounter many say they 'were asking for it.'

When girls drink or take drugs at a fraternity party, for example, and are not in control of their behavior we read about gang rape.

When armies invade they often rape the conquered women. Lust run amuck!

How about the recent Bill Cosby episodes? Does money, fame and power entitle a man to any sexual partner he wishes? In this case he used drugs to have the women unconscious. Couldn't he get what he wanted otherwise? The new theory is it was a psychological disorder… right!

What about the married men who insist on sex when their partner doesn't want it? That's a form of rape too…even though legal in most places. Many wives see it as a 'duty', and feel they have other benefits as a result. There's tragedy. How many 'fake' orgasms go on in this situation?

Today many think of marriage in its' old form as obsolete.

Today the number of unmarried adults outnumbers those married. One in seven lives alone and mostly in urban areas.

Today there is much choice and also opportunity to meet strangers through the Internet. People want instant gratification.

There are pedophiles who are educated and look like regular people. This is rape at its' basest. To damage a young child is just intolerable.

While the fantasy of being 'taken' and ravaged is fine, the act is not.

Years ago there was a sick joke that ugly girls heard where a rape took place and went there…hoping.

It is true some females who are insecure or not feeling desirable may put up with being 'used' in a sexual manner, when they don't want or enjoy the behavior.

Sometimes it is allowed after a breakup or not wanting to be alone and this is the way to feel wanted again.

There is a place for sex without love and that's fine. Needs are strong and sometimes the urge takes over and males cannot or will not, contain themselves. BUT and it's a big BUT, it is the female who has to screen the men she is with.

This should take place over a bit of time and in places where she is not alone.

Trusting a partner allows for great sex. Sharing emotions and feelings, as well as experiences allows for great sex.

Rape damages both partners in the end, unless the rapist is a sociopath with no conscience.

Getting over such an experience takes time, much empathy, and maybe professional help.

Having a man relieve himself sexually using your body without your participation, is rape!

This life is not a dress rehearsal and whatever it takes for you to go on and be a completed reasonably happy person is always the goal.

While rape can be one of life's horrible experiences; females have creative energy, and it does not have to be a death sentence for you or your love life forever!!

"The ability to make love frivolously is the chief characteristic which distinguishes human beings from beasts." - Heywood Broun

Does Sex Lead to Love

"A WOMAN HAS TO LOVE a bad man once or twice in her life, to be thankful for a good one." - Marjorie Kinnan Rawlings

Interestingly there are many people writing about the demise of courtship, and the ways in which young people meet and connect. The opinions vary as to what it all means in the end and what it may mean for marriage and family later on.

The quick introductions at speed dating places, the dating services on-line, and the whole computer age have definitely changed behavior among today's eligible daters.

The first date is no longer an exploration of who you are, what you do, what you like, and so on.

It's that next step that starts to get the real ball rolling.

That first look and FEELING is what counts.

Now what to do about it is also changing.

Sex, for sex, seems prevalent among a large group of twenty or thirty somethings. Casual, it's called but is it really? For males? For females?

I'm not so sure.

In my experience sharing one's naked body doesn't equal a handshake.

True, women are independent, educated and may indeed have a better job or earn more money than the guy, BUT does that mean he can't bring flowers, pay for a coffee date, or go for a walk? I think he likes doing that after he sees her and thinks he may like her. I also think she likes it, and the attention and caring is appreciated.

So, sue me…. that's what I think!

By all means, have hookups, and go out in groups, and hang out to find someone, BUT, then hone in. Intimacy doesn't just happen. It's a joint event.

AND sex without it is NEVER, NEVER, the same as with it!!!

The real issue is where do young people get their sense of self and their worth, and is it even completed by their twenties? That's the dangerous part, because if not 'gelled' they can do damage to their unformed ego. They can then substitute sex for love or worse, think that's the only way to get or hold a guy. With males they still like the notches on their belts of all their conquests. It is different.

The fear of getting serious can be dispelled by talking and saying that one is not ready for that part of it… hopefully not until almost thirty in my book. Marriage is not the question here.

All of these are' starter' relationships that teach what to look for in the future.

Experience helps.

How you feel about yourself determines how you allow yourself to be treated.

Yes, sex does lead to love, good love in the end.

We are feeling creatures and the heart never lies. We may love the wrong people who are not good for us but that's another story for another time. You cannot fool your heart, no matter how hard you try, BUT you can make it a responsive heart when it's right for you. Sex will definitely lead the way but that's just the start and what you do with it is what counts.

Having fun, showing caring and thoughtfulness will accompany passion and sex in a good and long relationship. Sex overcomes many areas of compromise in a real relationship.

So text away, go on blind on-line dates, do speed dating, and so on and let that be step one. That's 'just the facts, ma'am' as a famous TV detective used to say. Just the facts takes the lid off but it's what's inside that will have you requesting and exploring more as your feelings push you...

It's no longer just the missionary position…it's the whole Kama Sutra today!!!

"Without love, what are we worth?
Eighty-nine cents! Eighty-nine cents worth of chemicals walking around lonely." - Benjamin Franklin

The Morphing Of Sex

"Of all the sexual aberrations, chastity is the strangest."- Anatole France

What makes the world go round? Sex, of course!

Now, as in all other things, sex has changed over the years. You need only to look at the Kinsey report from only sixty years ago to see the differences.

Then, over seventy percent of couples performed only the missionary position… BORING!!

Then merely one third had ever engaged in oral sex.

Partner masturbation and anal sex… forget it.

Female orgasm…don't even think about it.

The frequency… who knows?

Today there is a huge difference in a number of sexual behaviors.

Since the 1960's and birth control there has been a steady increase in female satisfaction. What is especially fun to know is that eighty-five percent of males believe their partners are orgasmic while only sixty-four percent of the females report being orgasmic! Why fake it? Well, they say it makes their male partner feel good. Okay.

Today over ninety percent of men between the ages of twenty-five to twenty-nine report having had oral sex while almost ninety percent of females report having oral sex at least once. Progress?

The frequency of activity is low in the forty age range and is high early in life as well as late in life. Interesting.

All of it changing and for the better. Variety and sex videos and toys are readily available for those free enough to use them. Just thinking about sex gets you ready. The males get excited with erections and the females lubricate and the game is ON!

Alcohol is a social lubricant and can help or hinder. Too much inhibits the male performance and can cloud judgment. Caution is the word here.

When trying to explain to a young person what the sexual release is like it is often compared to a sneeze. The buildup and then the release that feels good. Trust me however, sex and sneezes… no comparison!

As people connect today with the online world there is a danger that intimacy is hard to achieve. One statistic that proves this is that one in twenty-five married men see prostitutes, and almost seventy percent describe their sex lives at home as, 'mechanical.' They have partners that know little about what it takes to keep IT alive.

Good sex and love mean enchantment and complete vulnerability. Who teaches that? This blog!!

Just thinking about, 'letting go' and allowing IT to flow and his or her reactions will help.

The sounds and smells are so special and unique to each couple that they cannot be duplicated.

Our technical culture and mind set do not assist in all of this. Calculation and thinking itself runs counter to being close and having great sex.

That is a problem today. Being poetic, if you will, is not in our nature or culture so easily.

As a result, people look for something more, and they have increased opportunity today to connect with other people. Affairs are commonplace and may, in fact, help keep a dead relationship going…which exists for other reasons…not real love.

So, yes, sexual behaviors, and thinking have changed; mostly for the better.

We know more, we experiment more, and we are freer. Yippee!

The whole area of homosexuality and transgendered love is also in the forefront. Why shouldn't these groups share what heterosexuals have?

The expression of feelings is not new. Love is not new. How it is shown in the realm of sex is new and different. Aberrant behavior has always been there but now we have a media like film showing it in living color to all of us. Hence the new film, "Fifty Shades of Grey." Do we get ideas for our own lives from these things? Probably.

The rule of thumb is if two people agree to ANYTHING it is fine. It is only when someone is exploited that it is a problem or illegal.

The more we know, the more we practice, the better we are at whatever we do. So too with our sexuality. That values and science have helped us move along in this most vital of areas of human existence is indeed a blessing. Just think how long it would have taken for desire to be fulfilled wearing those cumbersome clothes at the turn of the century! Talk about the mood going…

Keep romance alive!!

"Acting is not very hard. The most important things are to be able to laugh and cry. If I have to cry, I think of my sex life. And if I have to laugh, well, I think of my sex life." - Glenda Jackson

Alone by Choice

"I ONLY GO OUT TO get me a fresh appetite for being alone." - Lord Byron

Yes, it is true some people like and actually choose to be alone.

Who are these people and why this choice?

The reasons are varied and can be understood in the context of human relationships.

Some people have been so scarred in childhood they cannot relate effectively or positively with any other person. Some have been so emotionally damaged that they believe themselves unworthy of connection and totally unlovable. There are, of course, the mentally ill. None of these are what we are dealing with here.

We are talking now only about those adults who for one reason or another do not wish to engage in any long term or close relationship with another.

These people usually have come to their position after being hurt, and attempting intimacy that did not work.

There is a whole long list of such people. Some interesting ones include Betsy Bonaparte, from Baltimore, who was married to Napoleon's youngest brother, Jerome. Napoleon had the marriage dissolved and although the two cared for one another Jerome followed his powerful brother's command and left Betsy.

She spent the rest of her life trying to have him involved with her and acknowledging their son. No other man was 'allowed' into her life.

It appears that women do better at this than men. Men seem to need to have someone around. One example that defies that is Joe DiMaggio.

His love for Marilyn Monroe lasted his entire life and he remained alone, by choice.

We could look at any number of characters in literature, history, or film that exemplify this subject.

At times the pattern is one in which a love affair has ended and one of the parties has numerous encounters with others, only to find them all dissatisfying. Then they choose to 'give up' and remain alone.

Some people end a relationship and decide the whole world of men, or women, is like the one they ended and refuse to give their heart away again.

Some just take a breather and regroup, if you will, and then enter the fray again.

If there are too many bad experiences, being alone may become the choice and easier way to live.

Being alone means you have no one to answer to, no one trying to control you, no one getting angry at you for whatever, and doing things 'your' way.

Once the pattern is set it is difficult to break, especially after time goes on.

Being alone also means you have no one to share life with, the mundane and profound, no one to be emotional with, no one to express feelings to, and no one to really love intimately. That is fine for some people and it is always a choice.

Better to be alone than to be in a relationship that is 'indifferent' or 'brittle.' That is more pain than benefit.

Some people live rather full lives alone. Some choose not to have children and do not miss that aspect of life.

Some people find satisfaction in doing their work, being involved in activities, or connecting with a wide group of people without intimacy. Some people are passionate about a cause.

Some people have strangers or other family live with them for company and doing shared tasks or activities.

Some people have pets that they care for and give their feelings to. In those cases, they are always appreciated and get no flak back. Easier than a relationship that will always have expectations, demands, and disappointments.

We are all different with levels of capacity for connection. I am the first to say you have to find what suits you.

If you can have a full love that is great, but if not, find an alternative. Being alone may be your answer. Then you can pick and choose with whom and when to connect and at what level.

There is a difference is being alone and being lonely. If lonely you will need to find a way to be around people and keep busy.

Interestingly, I have known people who were alone most of their lives for one reason or another and at ages over sixty, married. It happens!

"You cannot be lonely if you like the person you're alone with." - Wayne W. Dyer

Are You Too Smart for Real Love?

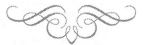

"SOME PEOPLE THINK ONLY INTELLECT counts: knowing how to solve problems, knowing how to get by, knowing how to identify an advantage and seize it. But the functions of intellect are insufficient without courage, love, friendship, compassion, and empathy." - Dean Koontz

This is the question… is your brain keeping you from what matters in this life; true love?

As a therapist and world traveler I have met many people who are very well educated, some with genius I.Q's and many very what we would call accomplished, successful people.

I am also involved with many just ordinary lovely or not so lovely other people; I run the gamut.

Now from all these decades of experience I have met a minority who have known full love, (and you know me, coupled with passion), and been able to act on it for many years.

How come I ask?

Are the really smart ones worse off than the ones less endowed with brain power?

Testing before jumping in and thinking is not a bad thing but it can be excessive.

The journey to love is not easy and the predicaments in life are real.

When you think, and think logically, and live by your wits, and analyze, you are not so ready to just go with your feelings. You are scared out of your mind about being taken advantage of, hurt to the core, giving your heart away where it is not well cared for, and being so vulnerable that you almost cease to exist without the love of that person.

This precious and rare intelligence takes time, trial and error, and heartache. Only the brave can do it!

Total surrender and getting in too deep too fast have to be part of the equation.

People who are not 'thinking' all the time may have a thinner defense system and may be more trusting.

They too come with 'baggage' like all of us, but theirs may indeed be a bit easier to cut through. Maybe not, but it is a question.

Then there are the others who never even think about any of this at all; that proverbial 'unexamined' life that just goes through the motions. Some 'wake up' at a later point. Once 'awakened' they can never be Rip Van Winkle again!

There are all sorts of values and things that make people happy or content. They can include enjoying nature, liking music, having a good meal, sharing friendship, raising children, loving parents, learning, travel, new experiences, doing a job well, progressing and being 'successful' at what they do, buying things, living graciously, or the height of it all; being creative. NONE of this matters when it comes to what this life should offer... you know; REAL LOVE! If you look at the professions people choose it can give you a clue to all of this.

How many lose themselves in minutia or specific intricate skills? Who deals directly with people in caring fashion? Now that is some criteria but that is the outside, not the intimate part.

When we measure things like I.Q. or look at SAT scores we get an answer about what some others have considered potential for learning or what is considered smart. That is never the answer, and no one measures or teaches what being really intelligent is about. That does not mean those people do not offer good things to the world as they often do but that is not what we are dealing with here.

Doing a fine job, no matter what, making money, (and that will be another blog soon), or performing a task is not what makes a human being smart. Competence is fine but living and loving are in a different category.

Now the super humans in my book, are the ones who possess both aspects; and that is rare and not easily attained. That includes competence, accomplishment, and knowledge in a number of areas,

WITH knowing how to give and receive love. Passion will lead the way but only as a door opener. Then it takes doing.

Yes, you can think along the way. You can evaluate the situation, and you can learn, and change various aspects of the relationship as it develops, but to be smart and not know what love is about in its' full bloom, is to be a FOOL!!

"Neither a lofty degree of intelligence nor imagination nor both together go to the making of genius.
Love, love, love, that is the soul of genius." - Wolfgang Amadeus Mozart

Beauty Matters

"ANYONE WHO KEEPS THE ABILITY to see beauty in every age of life really never grows old." - Franz Kafka

God made women beautiful so man would love her, and He made her foolish so that she would love him...

A seventy-year-old man with a young wife asks, "Would you still love me if I didn't give you money, jewels, and a yacht?" She replied, "Yes, and I'd miss you too!"

How important are looks?

The facts remain that they do matter in both men and women, but in different ways… naturally.

For men height is important. Look at most U.S. presidents. They are usually over six feet tall.

They usually have hair too! But men can trade looks for power and money to get attention, and the women they desire. The old rule of who will be a good provider for any children born from the union persists.

Now for women, it's looks, looks, and looks.

The first attraction is always how we are drawn to one another with a visceral response. We like people often who look like us.

That first initial response is automatic and we have no control over it. If we are attracted physically we want to go on. If not, we reject any further advances. No matter what they say, a good personality and a lovely person don't get us 'there.' Without that first pull, forget it, it never comes… not in the same form; with passion.

What about those arranged marriages? They work, but I believe they do not have 'juice' except by accident. You can only talk yourself into so much.

While the usual full passion, in the best of circumstances, usually lasts from two to seven years what can you expect when it's not there to begin with?

The findings show that attractive children receive different attention in school and they are responded to differently by the entire outside world, let alone within the family.

True, we have different criteria of what we deem beautiful, and it changes with different times, but we always have a standard.

What is it today?

Females are thought to be beautiful if their faces are symmetrical and they have full lips, and full heads of hair. Their bodies are thought beautiful if they are close to 34, 24, 34. Men like that distribution.

Some men prefer large breasts and others like shapely legs. They are usually attracted to the same type, over and over again.

Women like firm bodies and some prefer rugged good looks while others prefer 'pretty boy' types.

Look at who is selected as the sexiest man or woman each year.

Years ago women with wide hips, for example, were thought the ideal by painters. The reason was perhaps for breeding purposes when childbirth was often fraught with problems.

At any rate good looking people do have an advantage in life, generally.

When they say beauty is only skin deep, but ugly goes clear through they know of what they speak. Some people can have beautiful natures and many are loved and sought after for other qualities, and I don't mean to say that beauty alone is enough, but it is a good start.

Problems can occur when beauty fades as with aging.

Another issue is being sure one is truly loved, not just for the sake of beauty. With men it can be the question of whether they are really loved for who they are as opposed to their status or bank account.

Just look at what people spend on products to enhance their looks, and what they do to improve how they look. Cosmetics, plastic surgery, hair transplants, diets, and clothing… all for the sake of looking good, and attracting someone.

If you start out beautiful, you can certainly save money!!

"Nature gives you the face you have at twenty; it's up to you to merit the face you have at fifty." - Coco Chanel

Choose Me

"A MAN LOVES HIS SWEETHEART the best, his wife the most, but his mother the longest." - Irish Proverb

If you learn, nothing else ever from my book learn this; THERE IS ALWAYS CHOICE!!

From day one, we learn whether or not we were wanted.

We then learn, if there are others in the family, whether we are the favorite.

We go on to schools where we feel chosen, or not, by peers, or by teachers.

We begin to exert our own choices in whom we like, what we do with our time, how we display our talents and so on.

It makes no difference as we move on whether it is a dessert, a dress, an occupation, or how we spend our money; we have choices.

The things we decide upon are not out of thin air.

Most of our decisions are based on our culture, our logic, our information, and those whose opinions we trust.

The most important choices we make however are usually based on our FEELINGS. Whether we like it or not. Whether these choices work for us or not, our hearts, not our minds, does drive them.

What is especially precarious is that when it comes to our relationships our choices may seem valid but often turn out to be not in our best interests.

The good news here is that again you have CHOICE.

Some of today's choices were not available in years past. You do not have to marry. You do not have to have children. You do not have to stay in one job or profession. Women can be independent. Life expectancy makes for many more choices than ever before. That's all good news.

The news that does not change is that as human beings, when it comes to that all elusive thing called LOVE, we sometimes have an extremely difficult time in making a good choice.

Now there are some things that seem like we have NO choice, but I am here to say there is ALWAYS choice.

True, things happen that we have no control over; illness, deaths, losses, accidents, even catastrophes, but within all of that there is still choice. The choice is how to handle it.

By that rule of thumb, you stay in control.

The really hard part is that with LOVE you are not in control. That's the real nature of true love.

You have choice but the emotional pulls are so powerful you give up control, and you must!!

If, however the love turns out to be unfulfilling over time you then have the choice to give it up. The good news here is that if it isn't working over time the feelings may change and make it easier to abandon. CHOICE!!

If you are secure, in who you are and what you offer, you never have to worry about being the chosen one.

If you are competitive you have to be number one, and you will be. It becomes a foregone conclusion based on a wide variety of experience and reaction of others to you.

No, we cannot be chosen as number one in every facet of our being but we can be in the areas in which we excel. Choose your area…s.

When it comes to love a recent example from China is rather unique.

A man in Ningbo, China was faced with a really tough choice.

His new girlfriend and his jealous ex jumped into a river to test whom he would save. That old question!

He had arranged to meet his ex at the riverside park where he and the new girlfriend intended to tell her to stop trying to break them up.

To find out if he still loved her the ex-jumped into the river calling him to save her.

With that, the new one also jumped in and screamed to him.

This guy then went in and saved them both!!

He was then rescued by emergency workers and taken for medical care!!!

Guess that answer is not finished.

So, make your choices, and make them work for you. If not, you have only yourself to blame! "Being number two sucks." - Andre Agassi

Choose A Partner Wisely

"In olden times sacrifices were made at the altar, a custom which is still continued." - Helen Rowland

Choice is the operative word here. We ALWAYS have choice.

What used to happen no longer happens in the manner in which we choose partners, whether for short term or the more important, long term connection.

The best rule of thumb is to be mature, (not an age), and experienced enough to know what matters to you.

When people married young without much knowledge or experience, in or out of bed, it was a real crap shoot. There were restrictions that kept couples together, even when they knew they were not good for one another.

Today we have a new set of standards and expectations. We also have more open knowledge, and experience.

The problem today may be that we have TOO much experience and we do not have romance or value partners. They become expendable. Many people wait until they feel the age for having children may run past them and they then grab whomever in order to fulfill that wish. Some don't need a partner to even do that. Science has assisted in the entire process.

But if you do want a partner for a while what do you set up as criteria? Studies have been done that show people choose partners who have facial symmetry and are considered handsome or beautiful. That is an indicator of good genes. It also helps in the female being orgasmic. She is ready for pleasure, even though you may need a GPS to find that illusionary G spot! He is always ready.

Primal ecstasy is so wonderful that those few seconds, and that is all it is, seconds, have lasting memory and the need to repeat it is strong. In one study they found that only twenty-three percent of women were orgasmic from male penetration. So, women, and men have learned what to do. The various sexual behaviors have been learned and are widely practiced. Great!

The more you know the better it is and that holds people together. It is the 'glue' if you will of any really intimate relationship. The better in bed the better all around.

Now being a great lover does not make for a great relationship in and of itself but it sure helps.

Other qualities are important.

Watch how he treats waiters, cab drivers, and others not in his category. Look at his tie or lack of it to his mother, in particular. Is he kind and caring to you? Does he try to please you even when he doesn't agree? How is his frustration and anger expressed? Is he a responsible person you can trust? Does he open up and share his feelings with you? Who are his friends and what are they like? Is he controlling?

How does he show he wants and needs you? How do you spend your time together? Are your goals in life the same? Does your family like him?

Now almost the same questions for a guy to contemplate when choosing a female, but some are different.

You want to know what her expectations are in the relationship? Does she want a family? If she is annoyed or upset with you what does she do? Does she have a good relationship with her father?

Is she using her education and talents? Is the relationship the core of her being? What does she do to keep harmony? Do her parents seem happy?

Is she affectionate and earthy enough when it comes to sexuality?

Both people need to look good, feel good, and want the best for their partner, even if it means they do not get 'their way' at times.

This being together is not easy and never fifty-fifty. Many times it is a hundred to zero. In time it should even out like a see-saw. There are some couples however who have established a pattern of the same one always giving in. That can work if the partner doesn't feel taken advantage of over time.

The key is communication… talk, talk, and talk some more. About everything…

There are never guarantees and the new thinking and what I have always believed, is that relationships should have a check-up every five or so years. Then the partners decide if they want to renew the contract, so to speak. Being together when children are young is important, but once they are on their feet, the relationship needs to be assessed. It's just like getting a medical check-up regularly. You can avoid or prevent problems with this approach.

Is Compromise A Dirty Word

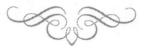

"WE MUST DEVELOP AND MAINTAIN the capacity to forgive. He who is devoid of the power to forgive is devoid of the power to love. There is some good in the worst of us and some evil in the best of us." - Martin Luther King Jr.

Yeh, yeh, yeh… try that when you're in the midst of a fit and hating that person.

It doesn't work then, and for some people it never really works.

It can feel like loss of power or control and at times the loss of pride. That's just the way it is.

Now, of course, we are also talking about those times when you are unreasonable or sure you have the answer or are right. All of it gets mushed up together to make life miserable.

It is never fifty, fifty. Being lovable is not a full time event. There are passive aggressive people who do things that are not overt but they infuriate. We all learn what buttons to push and we are who we are.

At times it truly is one hundred percent on one or the other. In some cases, there is a pattern where one person is always the one to forgive or reach out with a hug or words that move the situation along and make it better.

You can understand some things and yet not agree. For people who have to be liked all the time this whole business can be tiresome.

Sometimes you just can't explain and get our message and its' reasons across.

If you don't 'win' you can feel diminished and less a person. Compromise puts you in the position of not getting your way! If you are not used to that, compromise will be truly difficult.

I see this often in both men and women who have positions of authority and decision making in their professions. When they come home or out on a date they don't automatically turn off and become sweet demure pussy cats!

This is especially hard in today's world where there are many 'successful' women. The role of being vulnerable and giving in does not come easily. Men do not usually like bossy or crass women. They are not fragile or needing them. The soft coquette is not the lawyer or doctor or boss finding love easily. If the woman is the higher wage earner this also affects the way they relate to men and men to them.

Men want to protect and provide and please women they care about. Women want to nurture and induce love in men. When these traditional roles are not played out in the authentic self, there can be problems. If you are meeting deadlines, and aggressive at work you cannot be another person with a partner easily.

If you have to be cold and aloof and be competent meeting goals, you cannot abandon those aspects of your nature.

Anticipation, intimacy, and abandonment of self, which great love requires, needs warmth and understanding and a shared connection.

While we always have choice, our personalities sometimes don't recognize or want to choose what makes for a dynamic loving relationship.

Hench we have many perfunctory, pedantic, mundane connections; sometimes for decades.

Giving of oneself emotionally, intellectually, and indeed physically demands touch and caring expressed. Shared interests and values can make life pleasant but true romance requires something more.

Love finds you, you don't find it, and then the relationship gets going.

My theory is it should be your best friend who's sexy!!

Now you, and only you alone, know what areas you can compromise… and we all have to.

The good part about a lot of this is that sex can be the glue and healing remedy for hurt or bad feelings. It is also important to fight fairly and disagree without tearing the partner down or going over their history, or saying things like, "You always… or you never."

Many times it becomes a will struggle and then neither one will back down. That can lead to the erosion of something that might have been good.

In "Love Story," the phrase was "Love means you never have to say you're sorry." I ABSOLUTELY DISAGREE.

If you have been burned by past relationships, it can also be a factor. Risking your heart is scary every time. Putting it in a safe place takes experience and trust.

None of us is perfect or always right, (except me).

One man I know said he gets up every morning and announces, loudly, "Honey I'm sorry," and that makes his day really fine!

Sometimes it's better not to say what you think.

"Always do sober what you said you'd do drunk. That will teach you to keep your mouth shut." - Ernest Hemingway

Can You Fight Fairly?

A Chinese proverb says, "Most disease comes from things that enter the mouth, most trouble comes from words that leave it."

So, what gets you angry? Think about it. It's usually an emotional need or an unmet expectation or a lack of feeling in control.

Study when you become upset or feel unappreciated or unloved. The pattern is probably there and set from years ago.

When we 'fight' with someone, say our partner, we want to hurt or pay them back for hurting us.

It's easy to let it all hang out; to say nasty things, yell, curse, scream, and slam doors, walk out, or cry. All of it gets the sting out, BUT in the end it doesn't usually change things.

Now, I'm not suggesting we walk around with UN helmets on and sit and quietly say what we feel, or negotiate it all. Even the UN hasn't worked that out but we can be mindful of some destructive behaviors that don't work for us in the end.

The worst things a woman can say to a man relate to his sexuality and ability to please her with his performance.

The worst things to say to a woman deal with whether she is the one that is loved and also her appearance can be a sore spot.

Cutting off loving feelings is usually the first step and that's OK because we can't love the person who hurt us... at least not right away. And to try to think of the positives that they bring us won't hold water at this point.

The best thing is to be aware that fighting dirty includes the, "You always..." or bringing up the last ten years of things that they did to bother you, or to relate it back a few generations... "Oh, you are just like your father..." None of these really accomplish what you want in the end; a resolution.

Also, you cannot fight with yourself so if one of you clams up it is a maddening experience.

The most constructive way to handle these matters is to yes, let it out without saying awful things that will long be remembered. Later, sit down maybe in a restaurant with a glass of wine and say,

"You know you hurt me when you did or said such and such..." "I would prefer it if you..."

It helps to be kind and considerate like we are with others, when we know they may go away and we don't care. We take advantage when we know the partner probably will stick it out. If it is an abusive constant 'fight,' you may need professional help or a change of partner. By looking at your pattern and helping the people you are close to know what you would like from them, (and no, it is not losing face to talk about your hurts), may make change possible...

Sometimes the patterns are so ingrained they cannot change and then the difficult task is to concentrate on the positive qualities and make the pleasant outweigh the pain.

No one is immune from these things and how good it would be to be a bit more mature and handle them after the emotions have run their course.

Then, of course, make up sex can be glorious!

Fighters go ten rounds; how many are you willing to go?

Don't Be Taken for Granted

"Get a life in which you are not alone. Find people you love, and who love you. And remember that love is not leisure, it is work." - Anna Quindlen

"Everyone has an invisible sign hanging from their neck saying, 'Make me feel important.' Never forget this message when working with people." - Mary Kay Ash

Anyone who has loved has probably, at some point, felt taken for granted or that they are a matter of convenience. It is just human nature; acting out.

We all get a bit too comfortable and into habits that let us do this. It is fine for a while, BUT beware it can make you feel badly every so often. It can rear its ugly head from time to time depending on the circumstances. When a need is not met you will feel badly and go down that slippery slope. There is danger in that as the unresolved issues come bubbling to the surface they in fact may take over and in some cases, ruin a good thing.

When you feel slighted you MUST tell your partner so that they can deal with it, correct the way they behaved or just explain the situation, and reinforce their love. When you feel that you are not treated as you think you should be, be sure you are not unreasonable and that you have reviewed the facts… not suppositions. Even if the feeling is based on unrealistic expectation it has to be dealt with honestly. Only the two people in the relationship can iron out their differences and move on… or out.

If your ego is not strong and you are repeatedly feeling taken for granted the first step is to try to get your message across and don't let your partner get too comfortable and always see you smiling and meeting their needs while yours go by the wayside.

Being revengeful will only go so far and not get the change you desire in the end.

When two people truly share love they can work anything out and both will have to compromise in some areas. Loving is learning how to balance two people with different backgrounds and ideas. NEVER easy!!!

Pablo Neruda, a Nobel Laureate poet, who married three times, wrote a gorgeous poem about being bound together:

If You Forget Me

"You will never know true happiness until you have truly loved, and you will never understand what pain really is until you have lost it." - Anonymous

Do Not Listen To Your Head

"PASSION, IT LIES IN ALL of us, sleeping… waiting… and although unwanted... unbidden... it will stir… open its jaws and howl. It speaks to us… guides us… passion rules us all, and we obey. What other choice do we have? Passion is the source of our finest moments. The joy of love… the clarity of hatred… and the ecstasy of grief. It hurts sometimes more than we can bear. If we could live without passion maybe we'd know some kind of peace… but we would be hollow… Empty rooms shuttered and dank. Without passion we'd be truly dead." - Joss Whedon

I write a great deal about this subject because I want everyone to learn about their true feelings and learn, more importantly, how to deal with them in a rewarding manner. Here I will speak about passion between a male and female but it can be in any form. And, of course, there is passion for work, causes and so on but that's not the subject now.

When two people are passionately in love the world sees it. It causes a glow, an aura that is inescapable. The eyes are the giveaway… they shine. The two lovers reach through to their souls with their gaze. Words help but are not always necessary. Tokens of love help and are silent reminders but the real depth comes from the passion they feel when together or even when they merely think about one another.

So where is the head in this? It's there and it can do a lot of damage and that's why I say don't listen to it. At times you will act absolutely out of character and just plain crazy! You cannot think and have passion at the same time… no way!

Recently someone shared an experience that will help illustrate the point. The guy was away and did not call for over a week. That was unusual, so the lady began to wonder all sorts of things.

They had been together going on five years and were madly in love. Both were mature responsible accomplished people. What could have happened? Well, thought she, maybe he needed a breather, or met someone else. Maybe he decided to go back to an old relationship. Maybe he had a major health problem. In this world who knew what could have happened.

They had been through a couple of trial 'break-ups' before, but they always returned to each other pretty quickly. Maybe this time was different. Maybe… maybe… maybe…

She drove herself crazy. To help, she drank a bit more, took a pill off and on, and spoke in general terms to a friend. Nothing eased the pain, real pain, not just mental pain. Her throat and stomach had a knot and she could barely eat or be civil to others.

She told herself she was not the first nor would she be the last to go through such torture. That didn't help either. Your own hangnail can be as painful as someone else's cancer at times.

She thought of all the nice men she knew who were interested and attracted to her. She just might move on to one of them.

Anyway she then made a list of all his faults. Everyone has faults and every relationship has problems. She thought and thought and wrote down her ideas and what she didn't like in his treatment of her. She read it over a thousand times.

When romantic music came on she wanted to die! She had a very old record of Theresa Brewer's called, "Got Along Without You Before I Met You, Gonna Get Along Without You Now." That lasted two minutes.

She tore up his pictures, removed his number from her cell phone, unwrapped gifts she had ready for his birthday coming up, and deleted messages she had saved on her phone.

Her head was on overdrive.

Now the people who do not give in to passion, and there are many, save themselves from all of this frenzy. Is it worth it?

We all must decide for ourselves. The risk is great and overwhelmingly frightening. I am not talking about just sexual passion here… I'm talking about the whole nine yards… LOVE, baby!

If you have tried it and been burned you are right to be cautious, but I believe it is worth the gamble after you have done some screening about who is 'right' for you. The head does help here but it can't rule… ever!

So, what happened to my lady?

Well, after over a week she received a call and the connection was bad and he merely said he wanted to know how she was. She tried to reach him and he did not answer so she assumed it was over and that was his way of handling the matter. Coward, she thought.

She called and left him a message saying she would never call again.

An hour later he called and left a message that he had phone problems all week with no way to get through to her and he loved her and couldn't wait to see her!

How did it end?

True love will NEVER be denied or duplicated by anyone else. She had to relearn to trust that and what they had together. She did; nestled in his arms.

Feel it, don't think it!!! Love is never sweeter or deeper than after it's been tested!

Does Love Conquer All?

"In moments of great joy you know tragedy is lurking around the corner." - W.B. Yeats

"If all misfortunes were laid in one common heap whence everyone must take an equal portion, most people would be contented to take their own and depart." - Socrates

In this most difficult natural disaster that has come to our beloved America what will happen to close relationships?

When things are going well it is easy to enjoy life and a partner. It is when the going is tough that the relationship will be tested.

There are many examples of couples that have weathered storms of all sorts.

The one that I will write about today is that of Hannah Arendt and Martin Heidegger.

They met when she was his student and eighteen. He was married and thirty-five.

He was a famous philosopher and she was precocious.

They had an intense affair. She showed him how to love uninhibitedly and not to feel guilty. He wooed her with his brilliance.

He suggested she marry but still love him and she did just that.

In 1936, she separated from her husband, Gunther Stern, and lived with Heinrich Blucher whom she married four years later.

Her professional life blossomed and she became a well-respected political philosopher. Her teaching and writings were world known.

As a Jew, she worked for Jewish refugee organizations during the war.

Meanwhile Heidegger would write to her off and on and send her love poems. He always was the 'master' in the relationship telling her when she could write back to him. He also became a Nazi!!

Some of his acts included having Jewish professors fired.

While she wrote about Eichmann and his trial for the New Yorker, she knew about her lover's associations. She created the phrase," the banality of evil."

Arendt excused Heidegger's behavior and the two intellectuals shared deep feelings for one another. It proves the theory that love indeed is irrational! She called him when she left New York for a trip to Germany, after the war, and they saw one another. The passion was still there. He even had her have tea with his wife!

She was able to rationalize that his actions were caused by the despicable influence of his wife and so she excused him. It was as though his genius was enough.

So, when love is there it does conquer all!!

The moral might be that perhaps it is not evil that is banal but love!!

Hannah Arendt died in New York in 1975 at age sixty-nine.

Her famous books include, “The Human Condition,” and “The Origins of Totalitarianism.”

“If winter comes, can spring be far behind?” - Percy Shelley

“The capacity to care is the thing which gives life its’ deepest significance.” - Pablo Casals

Can You Love Two People at The Same Time?

"LOVE IS MORAL EVEN WITHOUT legal marriage but marriage is immoral without love." - Ellen Kay

"Love is only a dirty trick played on us to achieve continuation of the species." - W. Somerset Maugham

In recent surveys, forty percent of women today have never been married. Data also shows that one in two marriages break up within twenty years. People with higher education have marriages that last longer. The divorce rate for people over fifty has doubled in the past two decades. Over 600,000 in 2009. Women initiate this most of the time and cheating is not the primary reason.

Women have realized they can have a fuller life these days. Over fifty-three percent of these people have been divorced before and are using on -line dating sites!

Nearly forty percent of individuals polled by the Pew Foundation not too long ago said marriage is becoming obsolete. Cohabitation has doubled since 1990 and the majority feels it is a step toward marriage. While the majority do not feel marriage is essential they all value it.

Things are different in Europe. In France marriage is mainly a civil contract.

Stephanie Coontz wrote all about the changes over time in her book, "Marriage, A History."

Two other recent books, Pascal Brucker's, "The Paradox of Love" and "The Curious History of Love" by Jean-Claude Kaufmann review the idea of marriage and love today.

So with this backdrop is it any wonder that people have affairs?

In "Marriage Confidential," by Pamela Haag she suggests we have affairs if the need is there and maybe it is a good idea to share the information with a spouse. How much, if anything is shared depends on the relationship. Many marriages are not truly happy or able to continue the passion or even have a sex life so one or both partners long for that aspect of life and seek it. Sometimes the need is so strong another will pick it up when the individual is not even aware they are transmitting a message. The hit by lightning may pull two people together like a magnet. Instinct is not an accident, and whom you connect with is based on deep feelings.

What happens next is a conscious decision. Will a sexual union take place? An affair without sex is not what I am talking about in this article and is not what I call an affair. Affairs are different at different stages of life and different points in a marriage. In younger people, it may be because the relationship was not good to begin with and perhaps the couple was too young to know better.

In a middle aged couple, it may be boredom, children going off on their own, or out growing a partner. In older couples, it may be trying to find real happiness before it's all over; mature love.

At any rate, the issues are the same... the big ones' deal with guilt and trust.

Guilt may not be strong depending on what the relationship at home has been. If the wayward partner feels they have given their all and it is not appreciated or able to be reciprocated they rationalize they are due their fling or maybe chance at a better relationship. I am not talking about one night stands or sex for sex here. That goes on too but is just for thrills or a change of face and perhaps having sex in different ways from what is offered at home. Recreational, that's all that is. For most women however that is not easy.

The issue of honesty is important. In a good marriage that counts. Having to make or take phone calls from a lover, having assignations, and being together is all a problem. These can be worked out over time. Not being discovered or having people to share the relationship with is difficult.

Not being able to go out, travel or just doing what normal couples do is hard. Not having to deal with life's daily activities and ups and downs and being secretive can however be a plus making the affair exciting. Longing and looking forward to being together and always looking and being at one's best can also be a plus. Feeling desired can make anyone feel good and young! The dynamics are the same at sixteen or sixty.

Most married men will not leave a wife and especially when there are young children still at home. No matter what they say, it is not the norm. They are afraid of the wrath the wife will inflict, money may be an issue, or just habit or duty. They get what they deserve, a facade.

Many married women also do not want to leave.

The longer an affair goes on the more it can get to be a routine, which may make it boring and limited at times, and there is only so much that can be offered under the circumstances.

If the woman, (usually), wants marriage she will become frustrated and resentful. Whatever he does for his wife and whatever he buys or has given her will be a thorn in the relationship. These issues may be discussed or seething or cried about alone. Men may resent the time his lover spends with her spouse and want to be sure she is only sexual with him. He may also resent what her partner does and gives her. They can share what they do apart in word and deed as that is most of their lives.

They each need reassurance of the love they share, as it is purely voluntary and without formal commitment; this also makes it a true choice. There is no ideal... not marriage, nor a second love.

Sex however is such an important and driving force, and feels so good, that it is usually worth the tribulations.

It is possible to love two at the same time but usually not possible to have a rewarding sexual life with true intimacy with more than one at a time. The marriage partner serves one purpose and the lover another. It takes rare people to maintain this duality. History is replete with famous people, many creative types, that have sustained two such relationships; many for all their lives! So, now know thyself and be aware of all that is involved before you say, “I like you too.” If not, bon chance!

Can You Be Committed and Free?

"To enjoy freedom we have to control ourselves." - Virginia Woolf

What does a commitment entail? Marriage certainly has taken on a whole new look and attitude.

People are marrying later, if at all, and deciding if they even want children.

Women are able to be independent and support themselves as well as have interesting productive lives.

Both men and women can be free sexually and hopefully enjoy that wondrous aspect of life.

So who needs a commitment and what does it look like?

If there is money involved arrangements and prenuptial agreements are the norm.

As far as the 'tasks' of living go they can be negotiated.

How money is spent and how time is used is all part of any relationship.

The details of extended family goings on and friends are all part of the duo package.

So where does this thing called commitment come into play?

You guessed it… the bedroom.

If you look at many older couples when standards were different, you see lots of quietly miserable people going through the routine of make believe living. It is what they are used to... a bad habit. Comfortable in its' routines solely, brittle, and flat.

These people were cowards and never had the gumption to move on.

Then there are the ones that get out their misery in all sorts of ways; some subtle some not so.

Then there are those that never took the time to take that inner look to really see how they felt emotionally. They substituted all sorts of nonsense instead of the real thing… passion and love.

They are the gerbils running around the wheel forever. It's merely an endurance contest!

In a society like ours, where money is god, it is easy to lose sight of and maybe never learn how to develop oneself and seek true happiness.

The people who can keep one another in a basically happy overall state are the smart ones. Smart where it counts... in the bedroom ultimately.

There is no true love that is held through control. The freer the partner the better.

The partner who has a life apart from the relationship brings something to it.

The partner that keeps expanding and growing holds on to their mate.

The partner that is curious about the world and delights in exploring other people different from themselves is fascinating.

The partner that tries new things, in and out of bed, is a delight.

Then you are both free and come at one another willingly, and joyfully, with anticipation of what love and romance is about.

Yes, feeling loved and cherished and knowing you offer what no one else can allows a real commitment to take place.

There is no need to check up on one another, distrust one another, or even feel threatened in any way. You are all that is needed.

Can there be down times? You bet. Can there be breaches… sometimes. But, in the end if you are confident of what you deliver you will always be the chosen one.

Some relationships can tolerate a lot of freedom; some not so much. As a couple that should be talked about.

Can you flirt? Sure, as long as you bring the body home to your bed.

Can you fantasize? Sure. It can even help in your own bed. The only danger here is if the fantasy is not someone you will never meet but someone who may be available.

Watch out for that.

Talking about any and all feelings is the key and in a real relationship that goes on.

Do you want a guarantee that this will go on forever? Forget it. No piece of paper can do that. Do you want a certain continual proof of commitment? Sure. You decide what that should be together.

Without freedom, there is no real love.

Ironclad commitment is prison… not what anyone human wants.

Total freedom also doesn't work. Being human includes jealousy and worry.

Somewhere in between is ideal and that will differ from couple to couple.

When it doesn't work look at it, talk about it, renegotiate, then hug, and kiss!!! And afterwards…

"The best way to hold a man is in your arms." - Mae West

Is It Better to Remember or to Forget?

"LOVE WILL MAKE YOU FORGET time and time will make you forget love." - Gordon Livingston

There are many forms of meeting people and dating these days and as a result there are many ways to get to know one another, break up with one another, and maybe, just maybe stay together for some, maybe forever, time.

In counseling, I have heard it all, and the stories of lost love are often the saddest. No matter who ends it, and relationships ALWAYS end, the problem is whether to forget or to remember.

The new ways of meeting include the internet and that includes a whole string of new formats.

Some of them are:

The manicorn hunt, as it has been dubbed. This is the hunt for the next guy who may be 'perfect.' It is non- ending.

The breadwinner issue.

Today many women earn more than their dates. Watch who or how the bill is paid in restaurants, for example. Males still have a hard time and women come to resent it when they are the ones carrying the load.

Churning relationships. This happens when you break up and get back together a million times. It prevents you from moving on and finding someone more suited to your needs.

Ghosting is a new phenomenon in some ways. This occurs when the guy disappears after a few or more dates, and you have no reason why. How frustrating!

Nexting is when you hear from him the obligatory one, or two days, after a date. This is really nice.

The MWH, (men with headaches), is the male version of what women used as excuses to not engage in sex. It is difficult for women to acknowledge that men can be tired or stressed, and it has nothing to do with them not being desirable et cetera, as women.

And then there is meeting not on the internet but through someone or through an activity that you enjoy.

All of it is fine once you are in the game, as it were.

Now the hard part is when the relationship is over. All relationships end; some quickly, and some after a lifetime; with death. Endings are never easy even if you are the one who ended it.

Now you can go two ways; remembering or forgetting. Remembering can often become obsessive and ruminating about every detail and what might have been different. This can make you crazy and prevent you from moving on. Even meeting a new person can go sour as you review it all with them. They don't really care past the first story.

Forgetting should be like the Greek story of souls crossing the river of Lethe where drinking the water washed away all the memories and pain. This however left them like stone so they were trained to resist thirst and then drink from the river of Mnemosyne. This allowed them to remember everything that had happened to them, suffering the sorrows and joys of life; turning grief into wisdom. Wisdom is impossible without reviewing a past!

So in the end Socrates was right. The unexamined life is not worth living.

It doesn't mean many people live without really looking at their lives and feel they are happy; it just means that thinking can offer so much more to your life. Those that do this cannot imagine living any other way. By exploring the past and remembering, and looking at today, we can improve ourselves and our relationships.

Self-awareness is better than therapy!

Sadly, our US society keeps us busy with work, consumption, and other mostly empty pursuits so that contemplation is not a high priority. New 'stuff' will NEVER fill the void of living loveless!!!

"There is not any memory with less satisfaction than the memory of some temptation we resisted." - James Branch Cabell

Ask Each Other Questions

"It is better to ask some of the questions than to know all the answers." - James Thurber

When it comes to this life, there is much we don't know about and things we will never know.

One way to discover anything is to ask questions and to be questioning. The most interesting people are the curious ones. The smartest, ask questions all the time. The not so smart hide that fact by not asking and showing their ignorance.

The way to discover another is to explore them and that is done through questions as well as behavior.

Life is never, 'solved.' We have many perceptions and often they are not accurate. The way to test them is to unravel the answers.

Now, I suppose there can be too many questions and that then becomes a way of life not just a part of it. It's the right mix that makes all the difference.

Marcel Proust did a good job.

He lived from 1871 to 1922 and was a French novelist, critic, and essayist.

His monumental work, a novel is "In Search of Time Lost" or the English translation, "Remembrance of Things Past." This was made into a movie.

It is a work in seven volumes with more than two thousand characters!

As a closeted homosexual, (not unusual for the times), he was one of the first to feature homosexuality openly and at length in his work.

He gave us a questionnaire that I really like and recommend couples to do it together.

Here it is:

What is your idea of perfect happiness?

What is your greatest fear?

Which living person do you most admire?

What is the trait you most deplore in yourself?

What is the trait you most deplore in others?

What is your greatest extravagance?

What is your favorite journey?

What do you consider the most over-rated virtue?

On what occasion do you lie?

What do you most dislike about your appearance?

Which living person do you most despise?

Which words or phrases do you most overuse?

What is your greatest regret?

What or who is the greatest love of your life?

Which talent would you most like to have?

What is your current state of mind?

If you could change one thing about yourself, what would it be?

If you were to die and come back as a person or thing, what do you think it would be?

Where would you like to live?

What is your favorite occupation?

What is the quality you most like in a man?

What is the quality you most like in a woman?

What do you most value in your friends?

Who are your favorite writers?

Who is your favorite hero of fiction?

Who are your heroes in real life?

What are your favorite names?

How would you like to die?

There you have it. Did you discover anything new about yourself? Your partner? I hope so.

"Learn from yesterday, live for today, hope for tomorrow. The ımportant thing is not to stop questioning. "- Albert Einstein

Auditioning For A New Lover

"Tis better to have loved and lost than never to have loved at all." - Alfred, Lord Tennyson

A love affair can be a beautiful experience, and it should be. That can be if the lovers are single or not. It affords a couple a relationship not possible under other circumstances. The attraction is strong and when given in to, it is ignited in a unique fashion.

The passion will be lit each time the lovers are together. It will light them up if they are in the same room together and it will grow and continue and become even stronger with each assignation. Just thinking about the other person will afford extreme happiness and pleasure.

That will exude to everyone.

Dressing to please the other party, wearing special perfume, and doing a million things to delight the beloved will all flow.

Now if one or both parties are involved or married to other people a whole other set of circumstances occurs.

There have to be means for communication, ways to see one another, and dealing with the feelings for two people at the same time.

There will be no competition for the drive that lovers feel and display toward one another and can never be equaled; especially in a stale, old, or never intense relationship before.

Lovers share what they bring to the situation and their former experiences will be there out in front.

There will always be comparisons with what went before. That is true in every aspect; the sex part is particularly vulnerable here. But even in this area the drive to be close will tolerate much.

There may be shared learning and that too is not bad.

Pledging love and eternity in feelings will usually occur.

Feeling so special is what happens.

Now, comes the hard part; time.

Over time, as in all relationships the things that 'bother' come to the fore. With lovers it has to do with time spent, how love is shown, what does the lover do for the 'other' person or family members. How does he or she make sure to SHOW their love? Is it enough?

How do the differences come out? What happens when they do?

The bottom line becomes, how satisfying is the relationship over time?

Sex is not just for fun and games here. What I am referring to are long term really loving affairs. They are all around. History has some fabulous examples. People have killed themselves over some of these. The depth of feelings is enormous.

Lots of times troubles arise when one or the other does not feel appreciated enough, or they are not equaled in what they feel they deliver, so it becomes one-sided. Sometimes it gets to be a Pygmalion, teacher relationship, especially if age and experience are different.

At times it is that one shows up to be emotionally limited at some point. One may develop, as in any relationship, and the other may lag behind. It is not different from any other on- going pair in these respects.

The difference is they have chosen and re- choose one another totally at will. They do not have the… 'ties that bind.'

The thrill of it all may be unrealistic without the tedium of daily life as the best has been distilled and is indeed exciting. Pure wanting one another for all the right reasons. That is in a mature good relationship, naturally. None of this is about short only sexual release getting together or revenge affairs.

By being careful the other partners need never find out or be hurt in a significant way. If something important wasn't missing there, none of it would have happened in the first place, and it should not be used as a payback for anything.

So now what happens when one of these miraculous situations ends?

The reasons are varied and who causes it is again a factor BUT some may in fact end. Too bad because the lucky ones have enjoyed one of life's pleasures that is indeed rare.

Here again, relationships are never easy and always meeting the needs of those involved.

If it ends the best is to know what led you into it, what you gave and received, and most important what you learned.

That is the key.

You have to keep reminding yourself of the negatives about the person or situation to help the heart's feelings diminish. One day those feelings will go, and the 'sting' will be gone. If you have been really hurt, do not let anger take over. Consider the source and that person's limitations.

They might be pitied instead.

If you are ever to want to enter into another situation, and most of us who know how to love do, use the knowledge well. There is never any perfect and we humans keep trying. The best part is to not be afraid to love again.

The 'auditioning' for a new lover should then include all the information gathered from the last one. It will help reduce the risk of repeating the same mistakes. Just be authentic and share and once you have had intimacy you will never want to live without it.

There are a whole array of people just waiting for what you have to offer.

"A person is only as good as what they love." - Saul Bellow

Are You Assertive... Shy? What?

"We do not attach ourselves lastingly to anything that has not cost us care, labor, or longing." - Honore' De Balzac

My contention has always been and is, that we are born with a certain predisposition to our personality. While there can be some modifications and maybe a lot of work to alter or change what we are born with, I still believe that the core 'you' is basically well imprinted for life.

Now where we are in the birth order; only, eldest, middle, or baby, of the family has a role to play. We are assigned, if you will, a role in the family. Clown, peacemaker, intelligent one, leader, and so on also plays a part. BUT, and it's a big BUT, what we are at birth seems to seep through.

It is especially interesting to see different members of the same family, or even twins, and notice the differences in the kind of people they are from birth on to adulthood.

Some of us are 'naturally' assertive and can push our way to the front of the line from early childhood. Others are shy or retiring and let things just happen to us. Either way it is no rosy path.

Can you be both under different circumstances? Maybe.

What you are comes shining through no matter what. You can push and be assertive sometimes if you have to, but if you are basically shy it's hard. The other way around holds true too. If you are pushy it will be hard to sit back under certain circumstances.

So, deal with it, accept it and make your life work for you.

When it comes to intimate relationships again the pattern will be there and mesh with one another... or not.

Opposites can admire and enjoy what they don't have in their own nature. That can wear off in time in many cases and become a detriment.

While we all 'use' people for our emotional purposes the patterns of shyness or assertiveness cause challenges.

Maybe you were assertive enough to get him to commit, for example, but now he wants a more acquiescent lover.

Perhaps you liked his take control attitude but living with a really controlling man may not be such fun after all.

We should have emotional goals that lead us into 'safe' territory.

What are our goals? What are the ulterior motives? Are they compatible? Are they shared? What did we assume and what are the facts?

What 'games' are played to get what we want and need? Are we passively aggressive?

All good questions. Hopefully good answers as well; that's answers that keep the relationship fresh and loving and 'juicy.'

What we are does not fluctuate all that much so like 'buyer beware'; what you see is pretty much what you get.

The danger is that this wonderful thing called love, ignited with passion, can cloud or gloss over the personality that will rear its head before too long. Then what?

Well, then you need to evaluate. Is this the way you want to live your life? Communication is always crucial but here it is essential.

Can you accept and shut up about what you don't like? Can you not make yourself unhappy by dwelling on the negative?

Can you love one another IN SPITE OF...?

Two people with the same temperament can be fine, as well, as that opposite pattern. Love takes place under all sorts of conditions. It's up to you to keep it alive!

What is fun to observe sometimes is what people do under the influence of alcohol, for example. The shy one becomes free to assert themselves, and the assertive one is able to relax and turn off. I am not suggesting becoming an alcoholic but it can be helpful to release oneself from the yoke so to speak, from time to time. Amusing at the very least!

Just be who you are, share it, and be appreciated for YOU. That includes appreciating your partner for who they are. Remember why you chose one another to begin with.

Not being true to oneself never works in the end.

If one or both have developed and changed dramatically that needs a new evaluation. The assertive one and the shy one can smile and love one another and they should!!

"Other people are very like ourselves. They are shy and well meaning. They wish to be liked in spite of their failings. They want to please and be pleased." - Frank Swinnnerton

"We deceive ourselves when we fancy that only weakness needs support. Strength needs it far more." - Madame Swetchine

Absence

"FAILING TO BE THERE WHEN a man wants her is a woman's greatest sin, except to be there when he doesn't want her." - Helen Rowland

So, which is it? Absence makes the heart grow fonder. Out of sight, out of mind. When the cat's away the mice will play.

Maybe all of the above.

When lovers are separated there is first of all the question of, why?

If the reason has merit and they both understand and agree about it… no problem. If, however it is a one-sided decision or one that the other feels is not justified… problem!

When couples are apart they are able to see their situation more clearly. They can harp on the positive or enlarge the negatives. They can do some of both.

What happens during the separation can take a variety of forms.

They can keep busy and not dwell on missing one another. They can stay in touch through other means, especially today.

They can look around to see what else is out there, or again all of the above.

Love is not static. It moves and takes on a life of its' own when people are apart.

It is a true test of what they share.

I have counseled individuals who were glad for the separation and were able to see they needed to move on.

On the other hand, I have also worked with people who found that what they shared was so unique and special that nothing could replace it and when they were reunited they were even happier.

One answer does not fit all and each relationship will be tested with a whole slew of things, let alone separation.

The couples who are glued at the hip are worse. They do not have an individuality and life apart that can enrich and be shared when together. Often these are very emotionally 'needy' people.

While we all know there is no perfect relationship and love lives go up and down, the truly great ones can stand anything, including long separations.

It is like the rest of the deal; the feelings have to be shared and dealt with.

Things can happen and special events cannot be shared in the same way when people are apart but they can be talked about or written about. Being sensitive to a partner's feelings is the base line.

How the love is expressed will determine if the distance can be withstood.

If anger or rejection is felt it will take extra work to keep the flame burning.

Feelings can change and people can drift apart without reinforcement.

If there is deep hurt or feelings of rejection, there can be consequences that are negative to the duration or continuation of the love that used to be.

If deeply hurt there will be sadness, and scar tissue over the heart, and the one hurt may close off emotionally for the future or forever.

Most survive and either get back together on an even deeper level having withstood the separation or they can decide to move on and learn from the experience.

You can look at couples throughout history who have been separated and gotten back together in fantastic ways. You can do the same with history or novels where the party hurt or not able to tolerate the separation, short or long, has ended it, or themselves!!

Some people who used to believe in love give up on it… too bad.

The partner who cannot bear separation or becomes super controlling is a dangerous one. He or she can become irrational and act out in terrible ways.

It is good to have experiences in love matters and see what you have survived. It helps to reflect on that.

If it is a new experience, consider it a part of your life education.

Being angry, saying awful things, withholding sex, or just withdrawing are not good responses.

If it is used as an ending, go out there and hold auditions for a new partner!!!

"Absence abates a moderate passion and intensifies a great one—as the wind blows out a candle but fans fire into flame." - La Rochefoucauld

Are You a Saint On Valentine's Day?

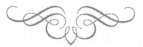

"TRUE LOVE BEGINS WHEN NOTHING is looked for in return." Antoine de Saint-Exupery

Try that on your piano... lots of luck, especially on the day set aside for lovers. There are lovers and then there are lovers.

How does one become a good one you ask? It doesn't come naturally to most. True love is expressed in a thousand different ways.... every day.

It is touching, doing considerate things that a partner enjoys, apologizing when you are wrong, or even if not, making life happy, remembering important occasions, sharing time and having experiences to cherish, being there for the 'bad' times, and best of all giving of each other's bodies for sexual pleasure.

Talking about everything and working through issues is high on the list. Just looking into each other's eyes and knowing you are at the core of their happiness makes a good lover.

Doing special loving things as a surprise works.

We all know who does not or who does love us no matter what they say or do. We FEEL it. Here you can trust your instincts.

What people do to display their caring differs according to culture and custom. It also depends on their learning about love, their talents, and their resources.

The history is rather fascinating.

It began as a religious celebration for one or more Christian saints named Valentinus.

A popular story states that one of these saints in Roman times was imprisoned for performing weddings for soldiers who were forbidden to marry and for ministering to Christians.

During his imprisonment he healed Asterius, the daughter of his jailer. Before his execution he sent her a letter signed, "Your Valentine."

The day is celebrated in many parts of the world and it became associated with romantic love in the high Middle Ages with Chaucer when courtly love flourished.

In the 18th century, lovers expressed their love with flowers, candy, and cards. Hooray for commercialism.

Nothing wrong with taking that step back and thinking how to show you love him or her. It's mostly him showing her.... but can go both ways which I happen to like.

Send him flowers. Why not?

The main thing is to DO something.

I have known many females who have taken that proverbial 'fit' because a man they thought loved them fell short not thinking the day important. Think again you guys.

Love... American Style

"When people are free to do as they please, they usually imitate each other." - Eric Hoffer

We who live here and love our country know how special it is. It is when you travel to other parts of the world that you truly appreciate what America offers. The freedom in so many respects allows us to develop ourselves and offer unique things in many areas to the entire world.

HOWEVER, when it comes to that wonder called 'love' we would do well to work on our values.

There is a new film, "Where Do We Invade Next" by Michael Moore that causes a pause for reflection.

It deals with the values we Americans have come to live by as opposed to many other parts of the world; primarily Europe.

While we have benefitted from our 'me first' attitude and independence it really does not foster true love. While we have accomplished wonderful things with our competitiveness, it too does not foster love.

With our 'goal' orientation attitude; that certainly does not allow for love and especially sexual glory to occur easily.

The idea of winners and losers gets in the way of it all.

Our society is youth oriented, and worships material success. We like action and getting ahead. That certainly does not work in the area of the heart or bedroom.

Our emphasis might do better if we looked at what real pleasure and enjoyment come from. It sure as hell ain't money!! That is very short lived and never enough.

Being famous has its' rewards too but listen to those that are there. They mostly feel their lives are not fulfilled. How many take drugs? How many are alcoholic? And suicides? Think about it. Where does true joy and happiness come from?

Interestingly, women have now figured into the mix. They now want to be accomplished. They want to be free sexually. They have learned about sexual fulfillment and are not shy about stating what they would like in bed. Hooray!

All of this has caused the relationships between men and women to shift. The men who are secure in themselves welcome the change and enjoy the rewards. The insecure have a bit of work to do to relax and become a real partner in every sense of the word. They learn it can be glorious in the end.

The Europeans, for the most part, have allowed their people to play, have fun, enjoy what is important in life; being with those you love and sharing good times. It can be around the table with a wonderful meal, taking a walk and enjoying the sunset, playing in bed, and being seductive, and whatever else you do together.

When in love the simplest activity in the most unlikely places takes on a glow and meaningfulness.

You don't need anything but being together and showing your feelings of connection. It is a shame, I believe, that we cannot incorporate some of this in our system of doing things. It is unfortunate that our values are not stressed in different ways.

The question is, can we combine the old ways of thinking with new ways?

I believe we can incorporate at least some of it jointly.

We can achieve our individual potential along with our ability to value what real love brings.

Being happy should be the goal not dollars in the bank!!

Do not think I am unaware of what necessity money is and how that has to be there for you to have the time and freedom to love. I am well aware. The thing is how much do you need, and for what purpose?

Capitalism breeds greed and that's too bad. What you see in the end is the wealthiest giving their money away to causes. Why not let that money come from the government for worthy causes?

Who needs a billion dollars? Why? What is the purpose?

Why should children born into poverty be doomed at birth? That talent should be fostered to its' utmost. The world needs it.

If we are not all in the same boat it doesn't matter; we will all sink or swim together, no matter if it is the Titanic or a raft!

So, my hope is that we can take a look at our beloved country and what we are teaching outright or subtlety.

Greatness in human beings or countries will only occur through love.

For my money I'd have every political candidate measured for their capacity and ability to love. Then they would be content and be able to work together for the benefit of all!

Utopia here we come!!!

"A thousand years hence, perhaps in less, America may be what Europe is now.... The noblest work of human wisdom, the grand scene of human glory, the fair cause of freedom that rose and fell." - Thomas Paine (1737-1809)

Love Is Not for the Weak

"PERFECT LOVE IS RARE INDEED- for to be a lover will require that you continually have the subtlety of the very wise, the flexibility of the child, the sensitivity of the artist, the understanding of the philosopher, the acceptance of the saint, the tolerance of the scholar and the fortitude of the certain." - Leo Buscaglia

Try that on your piano!

Perfect love? Lots of luck!!

However, there can be a CLOSE to perfect love. How?

Easy actually.

Well, first of all, you have to know what the f... love is. Then you have to be WILLING to give it what it needs to grow and flourish.

This is where it gets tricky. Love DEMANDS vulnerability and complete surrender. That is not for the weak. That is for the really, really strong. Now you can be strong in any variety of ways; not physical here, but mentally, and emotionally, and getting through tough times. All of that is fine but it is not what love requires. Love requires that your strength is in your ability to withstand disappointment, anguish, hurt, not having your needs met at times, having someone who does what they want, not what you prefer, and being at the mercy, so to speak of another.

To be WEAK in this way means a loss of face to some, a loss of control for others, and a giving in where you don't want to. I am here to tell you; there is NO real love without that!!

Can anyone be that strong?

Good question.

Over time, every relationship works out a pattern. The two people involved share themselves in intimacy and tell each other so much about themselves that they are in tune so to speak. They know who they are and they know who their partner is. They know what to expect. They say what they feel and say what they need.

There are always compromises along the way. No problem. If the compromises are too great, the relationship may not be a lasting one.

If the needs are not listened to and dealt with and changes cannot be made the relationship may also end.

The STRONG ones are those that survive the slings and arrows and go on. The strong ones are those that can compromise and change, and the strong ones cannot be pulled asunder. The two people will not allow it. They won't allow it because the relationship is like iron and they do not want to live this life without one another.

He didn't call when you wanted him to; she didn't show her appreciation for... the friends disapprove; the in-laws do not like him/her; there are money problems; work issues, children; differences of interests… you name it.

All this is bombarding the duo. Do they withstand it? Alone? Together?

One of the real problems is when the couple ignore or mask the differences. The worst cases I ever encountered in therapy are those that say, "We don't care," or "It's no problem." Watch out for denial or repression. Hurts do not disappear. They just go underground. They will rear their ugly heads in another form; health, alcohol, drugs, avoidance, severe exercise and so on. Real feelings DO NOT DISAPPEAR!!!

Being strong is not easy. Being able to withstand all the crap that any relationship deals out is never easy. Only if it is that important and meaningful can it withstand all the junk and survive. Not just survive but also become stronger, more united, and more fabulous.

Then and only then is it rewarded with what a deep emotional connection offers… pure love, and affection, and physical unity.

Nothing better!!

There is NO better return on any investment in life… try it!

Be Superman and Superwoman in life for real!!

True love in all its' manifestations is not for the weak.

"Have the courage to live. Anyone can die." - Robert Cody

Let the Games Begin

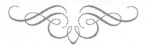

"HUMANITY IS A PIGSTY, WHERE liars, hypocrites, and the obscene in spirit congregate." - George Moore

Sound pessimistic and jaundiced? You bet!

Is it true? Often… BUT not always.

The problem is we all try to put on our best show and when we feel we cannot, we resort to playing games.

Sometimes with ourselves, even.

Some really believe their own lies and deceptions. Others make excuses to justify their behavior, and some do buy their own deceit. There are many good actors in all of this and even the best of us succumb to gilding the lily, if you will, at times. When, how often, under what circumstances, and most important with whom, will tell the true story.

No, we cannot or even do not want to be completely honest with who we are and how we deal with one another at all times. Sometimes it is easier to skirt, or avoid an issue, or make it so that we do not really hurt or wound another. Some are merely scarred and 'chicken.'

When we care about someone, we should try to be 'mostly' honest. The truth will out by what we DO, not just by what we say.

When our needs emotionally are not met we can cook up all sorts of games to attempt to have them fulfilled or just understood.

The game is ON when we knowingly do something not direct or talked about.

Some usual examples are sort of fun if not amusing to look at.

The not answering phone calls. Pretending to be out or busy when it is not the case. Telling stories about made-up people or adventures.

Purposely avoiding a contact or confrontation.

Using others to get a message across... a la Cyrano de Bergerac.

Sending anonymous messages... easy today with all the resources available.

Rationalizing or philosophizing to make it sound, 'right' and both believable, and justifiable.

Being unable to be contacted.

All games!

Useful, to be sure, at times to get the message across. But, can a truly loving intimate relationship have games too?

Yes, indeed. Sometimes they help move a process along.

There are some that have worked wonders.

Leona Helmsley is said to have sent herself a big bouquet of roses pretending a suitor sent them to get Harry jealous and have him propose to her rather than procrastinate.

An elderly fabulous woman, Maggie Kuhn, the founder of the Grey Panthers, spoke at Harvard and announced she had a lover thirty years her junior, to which the students stood and applauded. It got her such a lover.

A woman whose husband was in the public eye, and liked attention, arranged for him to meet a fan only to discover his wife was there dressed to kill, waiting to greet him. Messages delivered… Game Over!

It is always just a matter of time before relationships get dull, ho hum, boring or dead. Games can liven them up, or make a new beginning.

Now, I am not suggesting this as a way of life but maybe just a bit of spice to keep us all on our toes and so that 'taken for granted' is diminished.

Feeling special and having it demonstrated is what loving is about.

Promises are only good when signed at the bank!!

In the end a bit of game playing may be in order but only a strong real relationship will take it in stride.

"This business of learning how to love is probably the most important lesson anyone ever learns in life, if he is fortunate enough to learn it." - William Menninger M.D.

Listen To The Deeds - Not The Words

"Do not say things. What you are stands over you the while and thunders so that I cannot hear what you say to the contrary." - Emerson

We receive many messages in any relationship; verbal, non-verbal or body language, and behavior.

Whenever the messages are not the same ALWAYS trust the behavior not the words!

I would teach that to all young people.

It is wonderful to hear many words like," I love you," or "You are beautiful," and so on BUT when they are the primary means of showing caring and consideration with little else or small somewhat 'easy' gestures BEWARE!!!

The real message is what that person is truly willing to DO to show their love. If they are inconsiderate and not thoughtful in a number of ways, watch out!

Yes, all the words are nice and indeed necessary but they have to be coupled with other ways of showing the beloved they really matter.

I for one have always counseled that the sex act in and of itself is a means of showing deep connection when it is coupled with loving feelings, but again that is not enough either.

Spending time, doing caring things, putting the other person's feelings and needs above your own takes real devotion. Buying things shows appreciation, and doing cute little things for the other shows thoughtfulness, and demonstrates how you feel.

When it comes to being loved you know if you are or not. It's sometimes a sacrifice of some part of oneself that speaks louder than anything. The effort to keep a loved one happy should flow, and come naturally and be given willingly.

No, it cannot be all the time but enough to keep that flame burning and the desire to be close strong.

When you feel badly it is usually because some need is not being met. The best thing is to share the feelings and hope the partner can understand, even if they don't agree, and then DO something about it.

If the pattern or stubbornness is too strong the issue will come up again and again.

Men fear domination and control and being with one woman. Women fear loss of love and abandonment. Hench many women put up with things they really do not like. Some men do too, but the reasons are different.

In love it's the person you can live with and can't live without!

When you are turned off by behavior that does not make you feel cherished and valuable you cannot be close in any way with that person. Sometimes you see couples where the woman, (usually), goes along with all sorts of 'junk' even to having sex when she doesn't want it, just to keep the relationship. Bad idea and will only erode the relationship or make it a sham, or cause depression in the end.

You can NEVER fool your heart.

Now, it is true that when you talk things out and your head hears what the partner says you can be turned around, but again, the behavior will be the test.

What you settle for is up to you and what makes you feel loved can differ from person to person. What men need is definitely different from what women need to feel important to another. However, in the final analysis they both need the security of knowing they are valued for what they are and what they deliver.

If it gets to the point where you keep thinking of the slights and hurts, it will get in the way of having closeness in any form. If you have to keep reminding yourself of positive things, that's too much to do. It has to be there or it isn't.

Time will give the answer.

There may be different expectations on both parts.

He may think a card is sufficient while she knows he is capable of buying a nice gift and doesn't. He may think a brief call is fine while she wants to talk at length about something. It is all a matter of discussing and trying to understand what the partner would like and then trying to deliver it.

One man's gift of a Mercedes may not satisfy his lady while another's dozen roses is pure delight for his woman. It's also nice to send your man flowers!

What value do you put on yourself and the relationship?

What do you want from your love? Do you give each other enough or make up for what you don't give in other ways? Be honest or it won't work!

This is probably the most difficult part of any relationship, especially over time. Just giving things is never enough and mostly words won't do the trick either. It's both, and they should be in harmony with a single message… I really love and want to make you happy in order for you to love me. My joy is in showing I love you….in all its forms!

"Faults shared are as comfortable as bedroom slippers and as easy to slip into." - Phyllis McGinley

Love is a Competition

"IF AT FIRST YOU DON'T succeed, find out if the loser gets anything." - Bill Lyon

Who wins and who loses when it comes to love depends on the criteria used. If you think you like someone enough to love them and go 'after' them, the competition is on. If there is NO competition maybe you are already dealing with a loser!

When it comes to females the list certainly includes how that person looks, and that is face and form.

The same holds true for males.

After that initial attraction there are a number of forces and qualities that come into play. Many of them based on the values you were subjected to growing up.

These can include religion, class background, and then naturally the aspects dealing with personality, and intelligence and education. Yes, you can overcome the 'looks' part but not easily. It would have to be a VERY dark room. And, of course, many people change with time in any number of aspects… and not for the better usually. SO, on with the chase.

It is like everything else in life; the more experience the better. Learning about love is not a course in our lives although it ought to be.

Many people try to win the race to the heart through a variety of means. The old adage that the way to a man's heart is through his stomach never won the race in my decades of counseling.

And those that become involved with a man because of a great car or money usually end up with what they deserve… hollow hearts.

Can the situation change… yes indeed.

What was 'adorable' before you got together, over time, often is exactly what you come to really dislike!

The real issue is that after a short time any relationship is tested and in order to keep the juices flowing things have to be DONE!

It is usually the woman who teaches and keeps romance going. It is up to her, not exclusively, but a lot, to keep him connected emotionally, which includes physically. He also needs to know how to satisfy her in bed.

For a while his and her natural drive and need for sex will hold BUT not forever. So, be prepared. Getting 'noticed' originally takes thought and preparation afterwards.

You need to look good, smell good, be interesting, plan things together. Have a project, learn something new and so on. Just buying a house, taking a trip, going out with friends, and raising children are all part of it but not the heart of love.

The heart of love is being totally open emotionally, which means being vulnerable and able to be hurt to the core. When you truly love you only want to make that person happy. That does not mean being a martyr or the only one to give in either.

It is never a fifty-fifty proposition. It can be a hundred and nothing at times but over time that should balance.

If his or her initials are really carved into your heart you will know it. It will flow and you cannot get enough of her or him.

True, over time the extreme passion may wane but it does not go away when you enjoy a good intimacy. Intimacy means talking about everything, especially feelings. You need to stoke the fire. It is learned!!

I have always taught that if a man is wise he learns how to bring her to orgasm and she will never want another. She will also learn how to pleasure him as no one else can and he also will never want another.

Variety and flirtatious friendships should exist if we are alive and vibrant but they do not have to be acted on sexually if we are satisfied and love and are loved elsewhere.

We can develop at different rates and in different areas but that can make a relationship more alive by sharing new thoughts or interests. Pillow talk can include the feelings aroused by others and then the good part; acting out with our beloved.

When the 'magic' is there you never have to worry about you or your partner yielding to temptation. Being emotionally and physically satisfied is what it is about.

Love is saying it, and showing it in a thousand different ways. The best part is giving your body over totally to another. Talk about magic!!

In the end it means taking the juicy part and building on it. If it gets brittle and the starch goes out of it, it may be over. Your heart will tell you… LISTEN TO IT!!! Ecstasy needs attention to be achieved. That would be what I would have all students learn before any graduation!!!

"Tell me who admires and loves you, and I will tell you who you are." - Charles Augustin Sainte-Beuve

Keep Your Illusions

"Do not let too strong a light come into your bedroom. There are a great many things which are enhanced by being seen only in a half-light." - Ovid

Should you go into a relationship with illusions? Yes, and no. Confusing? Indeed!

When in love you idealize the lover and when you are in a relationship over any period of time you see the real person and many of the illusions disappear or become downright annoying. It ain't cute any more.

When it gets too comfortable people let their hair down, so to speak, and they take one another for granted.

Ever hear the tone of voice when she talks on the phone? Ever hear that addressed to you? Probably not. She's all cutesy- putsy with the outside world but snaggletoothed with you!

Ever see him so attentive with another woman and just going through the motions or half listening to you? You bet! Many make no effort to put on or deliver what you need.

The first marriage or relationship of time is always the parent of the opposite sex… emotionally. Like it or not there is little escape as that is what we have lived, and learned and are comfortable with and believe is right.

When it doesn't fulfill us we drink, smoke, kick the cat, yell at employees, eat, shop, take drugs or find other sources of comfort, or substitute emotion for work. Most of these solutions don't fill the void, and some are downright destructive.

It takes a lot of hard work and insight to change the pattern, so many just keep it going. Often even when a mate is changed the pattern persists, just the name changes.

You really have to go through the process of emotionally 'killing' the parent of the opposite sex to grow up and be a person in your own right. Then and only then can you move on. It is not easy to have that important person angry with you but it MUST be done. For those that haven't done the job they are still looking to the parent for approval and you have all seen them calling the parent or being with them TOO much. If you have completed the task, it will later help you live with other people of authority especially, not 'liking' you.

Every male in a relationship includes aspects at given periods of being a son, father and lover. Every woman is a daughter, mother, and lover. In the really good relationships it's more lover to lover over time. And sex will get you over many a bad day and unhappiness.

The old saying of look at the mother if you want to see what your spouse will be like in later life and vice versa for the males is usually true. They are the role models. And the relationship will mirror what went before UNLESS you want to change it. Today there is also the factor of women and men's roles changing and that enters into it… not always for good. If you did not like what you saw growing up, you may go to an extreme to be different and that can happen but not fast or easily, or sometimes not for the better.

If you have made the beloved what your illusion was before really knowing them, you may be very disappointed later. The cute slob before is the mess now, and the way she flits around is no longer desirable as a trait on a steady diet.

He wants to be alone or out with friends, while she wants to shop and spend money. Sex after a baby is not what it used to be and the different ideas about child rearing raise their ugly heads, just to name a few disillusionments.

So, what's the last nice thing you did for your partner? Could you think about that regularly or do you become too angry, hurt, or disappointed? Do you fret and have to be right?

Where is the fire, passion, fun, playfulness and so on? Have you become someone just going through the motions and accepting a ho hum life thinking that's all there is and all you deserve? Peggy Lee sang that song.

We are walking this planet for a very limited time and yes everyone closer to the finish line says it is a short life. Well, maybe not if you have LIVED!

Only those who have not been fulfilled fear death; those that have, accept it. We are the only species that knows what the end will be and it's just a matter of how and when. Hard to live with at times but live it we must… My hope is to have you look at it NOW, and regret little at that finish line!!!

Make your illusions a reality and revel in them and share the joy with that special one and it will spread in many forms to all those around you. You can spot the people who have, 'it.' Dead people have NO illusions.

"Understanding is a lot like sex: it's got a practical purpose, but that's not why people do it normally" - Frank Oppenheimer

Lovers Are Made Not Born

"ANYONE CAN BE PASSIONATE, BUT it takes real lovers to be silly." - Rose Franken

You see, we are born with certain capacities I believe. What gets nurtured and learned then makes us who we become.

If wanted and loved at birth, we are off to a good start. If we are fondled and touched, we are off to an even better start. Love includes all of this in the end, BUT it must be coupled with knowledge and experience and intense connection, which has to include talking about it all. Sharing a body is not enough. Just having, 'sex' is not what makes a 'lover.'

Since we are all different with varied backgrounds the real connection has to be worked on. In America sex is still a difficult subject to talk about; our Puritan history did that.

When it comes to real lovers it is always fascinating to see couples who on the surface appear vastly different from one another. That may be age, race, culture, looks, or education. Those things are not what gets it going when it comes to being lovers. It's the attraction and ability to satisfy one another in and out of bed. The two areas have to be there for real love and love making.

Now what complicates it is the fact that, like it or not, agree, or disagree, I believe men and women are so basically different that to not understand that puts you at an immediate disadvantage.

For women a man is her core of life. How he talks to her, treats her, and most importantly how he lets her know he is attracted to only her and loves her is what gets her 'juices' flowing; literally. The caresses, words of endearment, the physical response he has that she feels, all contribute to making him a lover for her.

For men they are busy with their work, conquering dragons, and making their mark in the world. A woman is a PART of their lives. True that women are accomplished today but still that man and his phone call come first!

For a man to be in love she has to treat him and his body as though it were the best in the world. She must NEVER criticize his genitals or sexual performance. She can discuss things about their sex life together at a later point but it is a most sensitive subject for men.

In the act of lovemaking a woman needs at least fifteen minutes of direct clitoral stimulation. She can tell you where and how to touch that area and with what body part that she prefers; penis, tongue, finger.

A man can do the same about how and where he enjoys being handled. If he is too quick to respond she can learn the squeeze technique. As he gets close to orgasm she can hold the top or shaft of the penis and squeeze it to slow him down. He can work on it himself with thoughts; maybe think of his mother? That might put a damper on things for a bit!

I have written about setting the stage for love with a quiet dark room, candles, music, perfume, using feathers, rose petals, an ice cube in the mouth to slowly move down the body of your partner, chocolate sauce, whipped cream, etc. You can experiment. One thing is important and that is to put everything out of your mind except feeling the pleasure of your and your partner's body. Think about the sex, not the day's activities or what to do tomorrow!

The overt body of the male's is really wonderful, while the female is internal and not seen. However, the female orgasm also releases fluid which he can feel.

Never worry about spontaneous together, although with time and practice he will learn to speed her up and she will learn to slow him down and then maybe…

With aging it is a fringe benefit that males slow down and that makes it more compatible for the pair.

Being a lover also means that females need to tell their partners what they enjoy about them, about their bodies, about their lovemaking. The brain and ears are good sex organs!!!

This life is not long, and it is filled with difficulties, problems, crises, and boring times. The best and worst is never planned. We cope. We use all sorts of coping mechanisms. For my money, great sex, with a really good lover, makes this life the best that can be offered. It will get you through the 'bad' parts.

Learning to be a lover is not fast, or easy. It takes time and practice. There are many road blocks along the way. There are false starts. There are hurts. There are rejections, and disappointments. All part of the package. Do not be thwarted. In history people have died for love and everything in between. It is worth every minute of true love and when you are a lover and find 'that' special person you will cherish it more than all the gold on earth! AND you need to keep at it, never take it for granted!! Trust me!!

"Among the first-rate, man's life is fame, woman's life is love. Woman is man's equal only when she makes her life a perpetual offering, as that of a man is perpetual action." - Balzac

Petty Is Not Missing The 'R'

"GOOD SENSE ABOUT TRIVIALITIES IS better than nonsense about things that matter." - Max Beerbohm

What do we spend our time with and about? Most of it is little daily nonsensical stuff.

Few are great minds, or creative people, or philosophers. Most of us are just trying to get through this life the best way we can. We buy into the value system we were taught and see all around us.

The pity is that the real joy in this life is not taught or shown. You know what I'm talking about… LOVE!!

The majority of people live in that biggest state of all; the state of denial. They just can't get out of their own way and in fact make themselves quite unhappy.

The petty things that annoy or occupy our time are really silly when seen at a later point if they are examined at all. It is not pretty; it is without the 'r' and petty!

Being petty creates an atmosphere; narrow, withholding, and constipating. Literally!

The prurient person, (lustful), is the salubrious, (healthy), one. Learn new words; it's fun!

Those that think and act big in spontaneous, generous ways, enjoy a different and for my money, a better life.

They are not ever envious because they have the best of life; giving and sharing.

Now pettiness can take many forms. It can be about money, information, advice, dancing on those proverbial pin heads, or anything else.

Being caught up in nonsense is easy. Having the ability to grow emotionally and think beyond one's self takes learning. Not book learning either. Some of those 'educated' ones are the most stupid when it comes to living large and joyously.

It seems to me men who are the 'thrusters' are usually broader.

Women, on the other hand, who are the receivers internally, so to speak, seem to be the ones to nag, complain, show annoyance and find fault in the little things that make up life.

Think about what you get upset about? It is usually that the other person is not doing or reacting the way you would.

You don't like… Fill in the blank.

Ever hear the mantra about the mess, the driving, the way the child is treated, the way money is spent…

Most of the pettiness is seen as important, at least at the time. Most of it can be done away with and things would be just fine. You don't think so? Why not?

If we all just took a step back and realized that we are truly here as specks of sand, and for a short time, we might decide that what we think is important really isn't.

It would make life less tedious, and certainly leave time for a richer connection between us.

Young people today have different issues. They spend so much time disconnected except by technology that they may be caught up in a different form of minutia.

They don't read, write, or have gracious manners. They want instant everything. Their world is filled with a different sort of pettiness.

What we all need is to learn how to LET IT GO; in our emotional as well as our sexual lives.

Dwelling on anything too long or taking things apart and examining them too closely takes the fun away, and the happiness of discovery is lost.

If we concentrate on the bigger picture, and stay with the positive, we can lead happier days, and years, and decades.

Picky and petty doesn't get you there.

I cannot tell you how many distressed and downright unhappy people I have counselled who could have had wonderful times if they could have gotten beyond their small self-serving selves. We are always our own worst enemies.

The trick is to see it, want it changed, and then go about retraining yourself.

It is all a matter of habit and with time and persistence it is possible. Do not be one of those 'strongly mediocre' ones who think and act like the other lemmings and think that makes it okay.

Grow and blossom and you will not be disappointed.

"The one serious conviction that a man should have is that nothing is to be taken too seriously." - Samuel Butler

When Forever... Isn't

"Love never dies a natural death. It dies because we don't know how to replenish its source. It dies of blindness and errors and betrayals. It dies of illness and wounds; it dies of weariness, of withering, of tarnishing" - Anais Nin

So, I've been accused of being somewhat cynical when it comes to love and especially marriage. That's okay, but I am here to tell you the reality and what it takes to prevent some problems and how to make love last. Like it or not, most relationships will end in some form or other. The trick is to work on keeping 'it' alive.

The first kiss is magic, and the second intimate, and the third is routine, according to Raymond Chandler.

Well, what we have learned is that love and passionate love is unlikely to last a long time otherwise no work would get done!!

We are also hard wired to crave variety which triggers dopamine in the brain causing the similar high that drugs elicit.

Once we have a mate, after about two years, we cease to be sexually attracted as we were in the beginning of the relationship. And that doesn't change until maybe after the children have left and we still want to be intimate.

Now many women lose their desire before men and then they need novelty more than men do!!! The surprise is that women don't seek more variety for whatever reason. Martha Stewart not withstanding!

Most marriages settle for a companionship form and for many that's all they want or are capable of, or get used to.

Pity! Many were never 'juicy' from the beginning. Sex is a tricky business.

The saving grace would be to have learned how to put 'surprise' into the situation…. from day one. Listen to me, it's fun; and it works!!!

If a relationship is to thrive and change in a positive way that is definitely what it takes. Who teaches you that? ME!

Don't get TOO comfy is the message.

Some say that the secret to a happy marriage is delusion. Interesting.

Delusion that your partner is all that you want him/her to be. Keep on those rose colored glasses.

When they come off and you see objectively and some basic needs are not met or correctable you may want to end it and move on.

Then that promise of 'forever' or 'eternally' may not hold.

It's over when your heart does not respond to the sight of the beloved any more or when orgasm has to be faked or sex avoided. You will know it. You will feel it and then the fish hook has to be taken out of your mouth and painful and scary though it may be it will heal.

Friends, family, vodka, or whatever, will help. No, I'm not suggesting you become an alcoholic but whatever it takes to ease the pain and it is pain, use it. In time you will get over it. You will. Even Cher sings that there is love after love.

We usually only fall really in love maybe twice in a lifetime.

My feeling is that you should wait for marriage closer to thirty years old, have children, and then re-evaluate the relationship as the children grow. An unexamined life is NO life! Once they are on their own a new focus comes on the relationship and it may have to be renegotiated. Some get better then.

There are many divorces these days of fifty-year old's plus and that will be a topic for another day.

At any rate 'forever' needs to be taken with a BIG grain of salt and forewarned is indeed forearmed in this case. One day you will tell me so.

"Love means to commit oneself without guarantee, to give oneself completely in the hope that our love will produce love in the beloved person. Love is an act of faith, and whoever is of little faith is also of little love:" - Erich Fromm

You'll Never Change Him

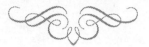

"No woman ever falls in love with a man unless she has a better opinion of him than he deserves." - Edgar Watson Howe

How many times have you seen a couple and thought, "How can she be with him?" Or vice versa.

It happens a lot. You get only so much just by looking. The other part is the way people relate to one another. And if you really get to know them you have a hunch what the relationship is about.

The truth is, only the two people involved know what they feel and how they behave in private.

When we meet someone we are all on our best behavior. It is only over time that we expose our true selves and maybe not completely ever.

If you are involved with someone for reasons like; how he looks, what he gives you, sex, his intelligence, success, and so on that's all fine. The way he treats you and your attraction is the best part of it all. BUT, when you see things you do not like and feel are so against your grain you had better take notice, because the likelihood of changing him is next to impossible. With your head in the clouds you can't see clearly that a storm is brewing.

Now as a therapist you know I believe in change and helping couples compromise, learn new avenues for communication, educating them about sex, and so on... however the basics can rarely be altered in significant ways, once we are past adolescence. Some professionals think after age seven it's a done deal.

The major ways people change are through therapy, (only if they want to), crisis, or through a real love relationship.

People who are self-centered, narcissistic, insensitive to others, or their opinions, or live superficially without insight, are very difficult to begin with let alone in a real relationship.

If his anger is out of proportion at times, if he is controlling or depressed, lazy, lives for power, and social image, he is probably not going to become a different person with you in his life. Red flags are flying, and they don't sell insurance for this.

Some people should come with warning labels!

DO NOT delude yourself that you will be the ONE that will alter him and he will give up what he IS!!

I would have a Romance Academy and give diplomas for life to the people who have tried this and won.

The relationship for many of these couples becomes a domestic battleground. They try and try and fight and fight but nothing really changes.

I speak of women wanting to change men which is more often the case. Most men just want their women to leave them alone and have sex with them. My bias!

Things can change over time, especially with aging or health issues. Some couples just resign themselves to 'what is' and live out 'dead' lives. Others have 'conditional' love and only have sex for example, or give money, when the partner performs the way they desire. It's sort of how we train children and animals like Pavlov's dog. We do respond in those ways, like it or not. Reward good behavior or punish bad behavior.

Of course you can go too far such as Lorena Bobbitt!! She cut off his penis when she didn't like the way he behaved! That's a message!!!

At times it's good to reflect and ask, "What am I doing with YOU?"

Self-discovery is always good and difficult. Being honest about YOUR rotten parts ain't easy.

Of course there are major changes in society and that affects what happens down the line.

Just look at the role of women today. Yet with it all only nineteen women are CEO's of the Fortune 500 and there are still men making up eighty-two percent of our Congress. It's a slow process.

Now how do we get him to change anything besides what I've already mentioned?

You DON'T, so relax and enjoy the good parts and tell them to yourself and soft pedal the ones you don't like. You can train yourself to make your thoughts go the way you want. Try it!

Put your energy if you want to keep him, into showing your love and take pleasure in that OR you will erode the whole thing… you will.

Know as much as possible before you give your heart away, (it needs a safe place), so there are few surprises and see him in all his glory…. happy, sad, angry, disappointed and so on. Look at the way he relates to his mother. Trust me that will soon be YOU!! Temptation will always be out there if you don't do your homework beforehand and your head work after the fact. It's worth it if the scale tips to the positive. Otherwise find another!!!

"You cannot teach a man anything, you can only help him find it within himself." - Galileo Galilei

A Broken Heart Is Absolutely Necessary

"Have you ever been in love? Horrible isn't it? It makes you so vulnerable. It opens your chest and it opens up your heart and it means that someone can get inside you and mess you up." - Neil Gaiman

Mess you up is the least of it! It can make you wish you weren't alive! Some people do end their lives when love has broken their hearts.

The phrase itself says it… a broken heart.

When you have given your heart to someone and you have entrusted it to them you are taking a chance no matter how carefully you have screened them. It is also true that feelings can change and one or both partners fall out of love with one another.

You know it when it happens. You drift apart or you have an eruption.

Now no one… no… not anyone can escape this process in life when you really have learned how to love. Most of us love this way, maybe twice in a lifetime. It is a process of experience. Some people are in love with love and fall in and out or so they think a lot, but real intimacy happens rarely.

You do give up a part of yourself in this kind of a relationship.

You idealize the masculinity or femininity of the partner based on your ideals and values.

When you start to fall away from those feelings and see him or her in living color, so to speak, you may see things that truly make you want to run in another direction.

Now for some the feelings may be rekindled. Maybe through time and communication the hearts are reunited. Maybe by withdrawing a little or a lot, or through bad communication, the feelings are exasperated and you know you need to get away from this person emotionally. They are not good for you. If you linger on, the truth will eventually out and you will know it. There's that song about never getting 'that' feeling back again. 'That' feeling never lies or betrays itself. You cannot fool your heart.

So, if you have not had a broken heart at some time you haven't loved!!

That's the good news! To love is to be able to be hurt… almost mortally.

I am not talking wounded; I am talking 'killed.'

The next phase is to either stay with the broken heart, vow never to try again, or to mend it.

How to mend it you ask?

A number of ways.

First know who you are, why you loved this person and look at what you now want and need.

If you are to love again then that will help because that message will be picked up and indeed in time you will love again. Maybe not in the same way, maybe even better.

I believe in doing whatever it takes to move along. Have a glass or two of wine, take a Xanax occasionally, talk to friends or whomever and get a message in your head that helps you rid yourself of that person! Get involved in whatever activities please you and keep busy.

Of course if you were the one, 'done to' that needs different repair work. You have to know your strong points and get confidence back. How you feel about how you look; your face, body, et cetera, may need a bit of work. Maybe that was just what you needed to be secure in yourself. See it as a fringe benefit!

Get a newer than new you and get a dream…

Love is never planned; it happens!

If you look at history and what people have done who have had many different kinds of losses, you will see the will to survive and find happiness. One of the strongest messages came from Claude Lanzmann who did the film, "Shoah" about the Holocaust and the people involved; perpetrators and survivors.

Even in concentration camps people fell in love and had babies!

There is currently a museum being formed in Los Angeles devoted to Broken Relationships.

It will show mementos from these relationships. There will be jewelry, letters, pictures, and all sorts of memories from a past relationship. You can donate to it!!

The stories that will accompany the tangible items will be from all sorts of broken hearts. How creative!!

You might do the same in your own way. How many wedding rings have been thrown in the ocean?

Emotional heaviness is part of life and a broken heart can be mended. The scar tissue will make it stronger!!!

"The heart is the only broken instrument that works." - T.E. Kalem

Tinder-ellas Ain't Cinderellas

"THE DEEPEST NEED OF MAN is the need to overcome his separateness, to leave the prison of his aloneness." - Erich Fromm

Ain't it the truth?

Of course, it is and the journey to get THERE is slow, painful, and difficult. It is also not accomplished by many.

My goal has always been to help you get there. My whole professional life has been lecturing, writing and counseling to educate people about how to connect completely emotionally. It is a glorious task when it happens and the younger the better although it takes a certain amount of experience and living and indeed maturity with insight to accomplish the end result successfully.

Today many, usually older people, are concerned about the use of technology, mainly the internet for a way to expand your possible mate base.

It is a fabulous resource and makes the world of connection open up, as it never has before.

The negatives involve people lying, perverts using it, and just the cautions that are out there. All that is true, HOWEVER, it is a great resource to meet a whole wide range of people never before possible.

Now many, including professional counselors, are concerned that it causes people to become very promiscuous about sex.

I may be in the minority, but that does not bother me so much.

True; people can be hurt, mainly females, who crave to be desired AND loved, perhaps more than guys, but it may be good experience.

There have been any number of famous stories about promiscuous women when it was a real negative, who have gone on to live full, productive loving lives with a partner.

I am not so sure that meeting new partners for long or short, for sex, or companionship is a bad thing.

Actually, it is the release Oxytocin which occurs with orgasm that creates the need for bonding!

One big problem is that many guys don't know how to bring their lady to that point! Read one of my blogs about that issue.

Holding out on sex may be fine for some and only the individuals involved can determine what works for them.

If sex is used as a tease or bartering point, it may not work in the end. If sex is too freely given that too may not foster a durable relationship. If it is used to hold on to someone that never works for the long haul.

How much you are attracted, share, and how you resolve differences, are all part of this package.

Meeting through on-line sites offers you an opportunity to explore one another before meeting to test the waters, so to speak.

It may mean that by the time you are face to face you have a basic connection and being close physically will be a natural next phase.

The problem today is that there is a plethora of people out there and many are just looking for the next one that may be 'better.'

Cinderella found her Prince Charming and he responded to her... slipper and all.

With Tinder etc. there are many feet that fit that slipper.

How to know when enough is enough and you can be satisfied with 'this' one? Good question. There is ALWAYS choice.

For my money I still believe in love with its' strong desire to be together. To miss that specialness about him or her, and to be free to be spontaneous and show caring in all its forms, tells you what you need to know. Your FEELINGS will let you know.

Experience may numb you, or you can have bad ones that sour you, but the real thing is possible if you allow it to happen. That, of course, means being vulnerable, and that is scary!!

Time does give us answers and the first step is to meet. So, go meet....

"...it seemed to me that I had known her for a long time, and that before her I had known nothing and had not lived... And here I am sitting opposite her, I was thinking 'I have met her, I know her, God, what happiness!' I almost leapt from my chair in ecstasy..." - Ivan Turgenev

What Do You Say

"Do not say things. What you are stands over you the whole and thunders so that I cannot hear what you say to the contrary." – Ralph Waldo Emerson

We are all sending out messages all the time; verbal and the more important, non-verbal ones.

What I want you to do is examine what you say, to whom, and under what conditions. Then it will be easy to observe others and what they are communicating.

There are many categories for interaction and many are common.

There is the superficial stuff, reflecting of course, the superficial person or the non-interested message. These can include; the weather, current events, where you have been, and talking about other people. All of it, BORING, BORING, BORING. Necessary at times but of no value.

Then there are the interesting conversations from and with, naturally, interesting people. These categories include, insight, deep examination of feelings, new ideas, philosophy, and life experience and learning.

Now some people are only able to reinforce their own ideas with people like them. Others can take in difference both in people and ideas. They are the fun ones who continually expand, both as individuals, and mentally. They are electric and exciting and keep you on your toes.

Then there is the connection under the influence, of alcohol, for example, when the barriers come down and the real you comes out.

When you have to 'protect' yourself and your image you are not so ready to share or trust that you will be well thought of if you share what you really feel and think. It is not easy.

We all have defenses that protect us but some have armor that is a foot thick and some have tissue paper.

It depends on what you learned growing up and how you feel about yourself. Those people that are insecure, do not bare themselves and like to 'grade' others as a way of taking the spotlight off them. Easy to spot.

The fact of the matter is that whatever your real feelings are the other person knows them no matter what you say! You know who likes you and who doesn't!

Children and the mentally ill have the sensitivity to say what they think and feel outright.

What is fun to think about is how you relate to males, females, and older people and so on.

The people you were close to and loved or feared as a child are represented all throughout your life with the same emotional reaction.

People who are curious, especially about other people, are wonderful to be around. Oscar Wilde said it well," Questions are never indiscreet. Answers sometimes are."

We can never be complete unless other aspects of our lives are fulfilled.

Abraham Maslow, the psychologist, had a hierarchy of needs.

The lowest is the physiological one including the need for food and drink.

This is followed by the need for safety and then the need for belonging and love.

Next comes esteem, and finally self-actualization.

Many never get to that last one and remain stuck at lower levels.

To be self-actualized can take a lifetime but boy, do you know it and recognize it when it's there!! You can recognize it immediately in others.

What do self-actualized people talk about and what do they transmit? All the things mentioned earlier; mainly feelings, and new ideas.

Things that can help get you there include, reading, studying, learning of all sorts, expanding horizons outside of known and comfort zones, travel, and just plain taking a step back and thinking.

It is Socrates and the examined life. You do not just have to bungle through and never look at what you are doing, or most importantly, FEELING!!!

The truly smart ones are the ones that are fulfilled emotionally and demonstrate that, especially to their children.

Many people mouth the words that life is short and we only go around once BUT how many of them really live joyfully, and juicy?

Lots of stuff can and will get in the way; life is not easy, and values are not always helpful in our society, but once you have experienced that level of contentment you want to share it and spread it to everyone. Being FREE is the goal. The meek do NOT inherit the earth, or live fully.

So, the message is, connect and do so with those you care about or want to know, and say what you have to. You won't be sorry and you will be surprised on many levels.

"They will forget what you said. They will forget what you did but they will never forget the way you made them feel." - Maya Angelou

Who Needs Whom And Why

"I HAVE ALWAYS THOUGHT THAT every woman should marry, and no man." - Benjamin Disraeli

Not necessarily, and not so these days.

For those of you who like statistics it turns out that women function quite well on their own especially as they age while men do better and live longer when married. Makes sense… They need order and a 'mommy' looking after them at home.

Men seem to choose a complacent existence much more than women. Women, however, will put up with a lot of 'junk' if they need or want the material things some men offer. Women on the whole will walk out of a marriage sooner than a man, unless he has someone waiting, and she will go with children and often with reduced income. Why, you ask?

It is the nature of women to live in the realm of feelings and emotion and romance, easier than men.

Many times the guy will stay to provide for his family, but there is no emotion in the primary relationship. These are the ones who are miserable or make do, or get sick. Look around. They are everywhere.

The women if they work, or are retired, go on with what their lives have always been; nurturing and emotional.

So who does need whom?

Adam Grant a professor at the Wharton School at the University of Pennsylvania wrote a book, "Give and Take; A Revolutionary Approach to Success." He contends that women help men treat employees more generously, and share knowledge, and help people with motivation, cooperation, and innovation. They do this as women and as supportive women to men. How lovely! Weaker sex, my foot!!

The story is that it was Melinda Gates who was behind Bill's idea of a foundation giving money away for causes.

Okay, so that's some thoughts, but what else do men and women need from one another?

It can be a whole plethora of things depending on the personalities and their maturity, (not an age), and their emotional needs.

There are some basics so see where you fit in. And remember none of this is static and for all time.

When young we test out our attractiveness and see who wants us and whom we like. Good start and sets the stage for later on. We don't forget the good and certainly the hurts.

As we age we may want a partner. You may think it's for life… I have my doubts!!

How many of you stop and really assess the qualities that might be important? Not many. Sex drive and passion rule and they should but if you plan to have a family or want stable support, financial and emotional, there are things to evaluate. Who does? Not many. Okay, human nature rules. As a marriage counselor I have tried to have couples look at their areas of sensitivity but they always only want to talk about wedding details. Better shot in second marriages.

Recent studies, again, show men like to spread their 'seed' but some also want to be sure their partner isn't straying so that the offspring have the best chance of survival. I think monogamy is risky at best. It can go on for decades and be wonderful and when passion ebbs fun and sharing can be enough, but most of us have at least two real loves in life. A later blog will deal with older lovers. That's really fun!!

Today living apart for some of the time with other means of communicating makes the longing last. The missing of one another can deepen the relationship. Skyping, e-mailing, texting, sexting, eliminate a lot of negative interaction. Not all bad. When together it's like Christmas. While not real and dealing with the nitty-gritty of life it can be pleasant. Living apart has advantages… until it doesn't.

Most couples in love want all the time they can have together.

She needs to be adored and told so, and knows that she turns him on.

He needs to feel she appreciates his contributions, physical, and material, and intellectual. OR they can compromise on some areas and still want to be together and love one another. Sex is important and the glue that makes it all worthwhile. There will soon be a blog with the details about pleasuring one another. IT MATTERS!!!

We are not dealing with raising children or the other intrusions between couples but all that will be down the line. Right now it's he and she.

Love and romance include suffering. No one will ever be or do all that you would like… nor are you perfect. No, you are not. Being demanding doesn't do it. Being in control messes it up, and guilt ruins the whole thing. So, women use your given talents to nurture and be a sexy goddess, and men flex your muscles, and go out and slay dragons. That will NEVER change.

"I'd the upbringing a nun would envy… Until I was fifteen I was more familiar with Africa than my own body." - Joe Orton

When Love Makes You... Nuts

"Love is of all the passions the strongest, for all it attacks simultaneously the head, the heart and the senses." - Lao Tzu

"We are not the same persons this year as last, nor are those we love. It is a happy chance if we, changing, continue to love a changed person." - W. Somerset Maugham

So why doesn't he call? Why doesn't he call, when we want him to? Why doesn't he say what we want him to… when we want to? Why, why and why?

And from a man's point of view why doesn't she understand I'm busy? Why doesn't she like what I say? Why doesn't she like whatever I do? Why, why and why?

The flame of love causes the best to go 'nuts,' (a scientific term), at times.

I don't care who you are, how accomplished you are, how smart you are, guaranteed there will be times when you are completely crazy over your beloved and what they are NOT doing for your emotional needs.

The reason we all want someone who is US!! Think like me, be sensitive to my needs, say what I want to hear, when I want to hear it and do what I want you to do.

Now the ways in which we handle disappointment is different for each of us.

You can get angry, cry it out, drink or take drugs, exercise or kick the cat. There are always issues to be worked through. In working relationships that go on, these areas can be resolved over time. If not, you have to decide if there is enough positive in the relationship to move and not get caught up in the particular unhappiness. It is never easy and never, ever, automatic.

Many couples do not really discuss the nitty gritty of what bothers them and certainly not in constructive ways after the feelings are put out. The worse marriage counseling cases were always the ones coming in holding hands telling me they never fight! Then there are the long term marriages that pride themselves on the many years lived together but they are just often bad habits and two housemates living together... no real "juice" going on between them.

Desire is what makes us want to be close to someone and that desire is almost never verbalized even between the two people involved. Sex can mask it and it can be shown in that form but usually it is a taboo subject. It is that desire that drives us and makes us out of control and vulnerable. True intimacy has no defenses and to be accepted in the raw so to speak is what we long for and not many achieve. People will tell you almost anything but not what they feel and share in bed. They can't ask their partner what they like or prefer sexually and they cannot talk together about their deepest feelings, fearing they will no longer be respected or loved if their partner knew this or that. Sad!

Buddhist teaching and Freud understood that desire is the cause of all suffering and we are never so defenseless against suffering as when we love.

The fear of loss of the beloved for whatever reason is strong and can cause much unhappiness and indeed in the insecure person it can become a self- fulfilling prophecy.

Revenge is an area of concern here because when we are hurt, real or imagined, we want to hurt back; the old adage of a woman scorned. Becoming depressed is anger turned inward toward oneself.

So, many people choose not to truly love because of all of this. Again… sad.

Water finds its level… emotionally. Those who know how to love find others who can, or they know who is teachable and ready to jump in. When changes occur after maturity it can be risky business; that is why marrying young is not a good idea, even though maturity is not an age it can help with the years lived.

My own theory is to pitch to the positive and remember what you really love about the person before going completely, "nuts." And if you do get crazy, hopefully, it is short lived and you get it out, share it, and go on. Women want to be adored and men want to be appreciated. And don't forget, sex is a great healer here.

Dale Carnegie had a phase I like: "When dealing with people, let us remember we are not dealing with creatures of logic. We are dealing with creatures of emotion, creatures bristling with prejudices and motivated by pride and vanity."

Women Who Beguile

"She walks in beauty,
Like the night of cloudless climes and starry skies;
And all that's best of dark and bright
Meet in her aspect and her eyes." - Lord Byron

From the beginning of time there have been women who over the years have learned that they possess the power to inspire love in men. It is almost part of their DNA. They always know who they are, sometimes from childhood on, and they use it all their lives.

The Kinsey group recently came out with a new study about sexuality and they showed that men are drawn to attractive women and the perfect proportions are 36, 24, 36, while women look for status and security to protect them and any children they may have. Thus we have two very different reactions leading us to one another. In a later blog I will be discussing this at length but for now suffice it to say we have some women who make men fall madly in love with them. They are not all beautiful, by the way.

Some examples throughout history will illustrate what I'm talking about. From biblical times we have Bathsheba, whom King David saw bathing and later seduced her. She held on to him leaving a husband and after marrying David gave birth to his son who later became King Solomon.

Moving up in history we all know the story of Cleopatra, who was not thought to be beautiful, but she had, "It!"

Josephine was no slouch for Napoleon, and of course there was the Marquise de Pompadour who delighted the French king, Louis XV.

We have the Duchess of Windsor, who I'm not sure loved her spouse but that's for another story another time, as are many other women. More recently we have Marilyn Monroe, and lately Kate Middleton.

The list is long and varied. You get the idea....

So what's going on now?

Well, we can name just one as a recent example. John Edwards who wanted to be president and then... wham! He was besotted and look what happened.

And today we have the general and his lady.

Can we blame them? Are they bad people? Is the world ending?

NO, NO, and NO!

As far as I'm concerned they were struggling with the human dilemma that ALL healthy men struggle with... spreading the seed of the alpha male as often as possible to insure the quality of the next generation. It's Genetics 101.

Those of you who follow my blog know what I think about long term marriage and how rare it is to keep both love AND passion alive. Marriage never ends from the person on the outside, it erodes from the inside when needs are unmet.

Now, yes, many men suffer in silence and do their "duty" or protect their assets or young children, but what a waste!!!

It is only when one is in love that one can be joyous, giving, and productive to the highest degree. We probably only experience it once or perhaps twice in a lifetime. Doesn't that tell you something? And then, of course, there are the poor creatures who never truly love intensely. Again the reason for my blog is to help with that.

So, what do we do about all this?

Yes, discretion could have helped save feelings in Petraeus's family, and if national security is at risk that is a problem, but short of that, let the general and his," lady" rejoice in the fact that they found one another and have shared what this life's deepest joy is all about. If it's long term and love it cannot be fought! Like it or not those that are so curious or punitive probably have a very sad and empty life without intimacy and live a hypocritical life as well!

"One is very crazy when in love." - Sigmund Freud

Who Pursues Whom

I HAVE ALWAYS BELIEVED THAT men and women are not just genetically different, but wired differently emotionally.

When it comes to the question of who should do the pursuing, the biology tells the answer. Men have built in advertising that can light up at any time while women can only do promotional work behind the scenes!

Shakespeare said it well. "Love looks not with the eyes, but with the mind; and therefore is winged Cupid painted blind."

"Death ends a life, not a relationship." - Jack Lemmon

My favorite story is about Apollo and Daphne.

After killing the giant snake, Python, Apollo encounters Cupid and teases him about his archery skills.

Cupid is not pleased and shoots a golden arrow inciting love into Apollo and then he shoots a lead tipped arrow into the beautiful nymph, Daphne.

Apollo becomes overcome with love for her while she wishes to repel love.

He chases her through the woodland and she runs like the wind.

She had told her father Peneus, the river god, that she wanted to always remain a virgin and loved sports. Her father agreed, after pleading for grandchildren, but said her face would make it difficult for her to remain unmarried.

After being pursued for a long distance by Apollo, she tired and he caught up to her.

He imagined her even more beautiful than what he saw in her eyes and lips, and hair flung over her shoulders. He entreated her to come to him, but she fled in terror.

She called out to her father for help and he changed her into a tree. She became encased in bark, rooted to the ground, and began to sprout leaves.

Apollo was overcome with grief and stated that Jupiter was his father, and he himself is the god of song, and knows all things, but an arrow more fatal than his has pierced his heart. While he is also the god of medicine no balm can cure his malady.

He embraced the beautiful tree before him and said, “Since you cannot be my wife, you shall assuredly be my tree. I will wear you for my crown and when great Roman conquerors lead up triumphal pomp to the Capitol you shall be woven into wreaths for their brows. As eternal youth is mine, you shall always be green.”

The Laurel tree bowed its head in grateful acknowledgment.

If you have seen the most beautiful marble sculpture in the world, according to me, you will know what this story is about. It is Bernini’s Apollo and Daphne in the Borghese Gallery in Rome. See it!!

Let the man pursue and if you wish, let him ‘catch’ you!

Who Ends It... Matters

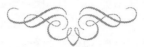

"If you marry, you will regret it; if you do not marry, you will also regret it." - Soren Kierkegaard

When a relationship is over it's over. Hopefully the two people involved mutually decide, but if one of them has had it, it can be very painful for the person still in love.

Who makes the decision determines the outcome and the feelings.

If you are the one who ends it the feelings will be relief and you will move on, but if you are the one 'done to' the feelings involved will be a mixture of love and hate in some form.

How nice it would be if we had contractual marriages where the two parties review the relationship and determine whether or not to continue. This could be every year or every ten years. The reasons for marriage have changed and the ways in which we relate to one another have changed and so too must marriage.

My own professional and personal experience has shown me that two people should only be together if they desire one another. Relationships vary and change over time and as people mature the ways in which they want one another are different.

In America we all read Cinderella and we want a wedding in a white dress with our Prince Charming and vow to be together 'til death do us part. Ridiculous! Fairy tales for children.

Let's teach people what it's really all about.

One of the big problems as I see it is how long to tolerate the things we don't like and have we tried to work things out? If resentment doesn't get resolved; only the cowardly stay. I am always amused by the older couples who proudly announce how long they have been together. Years mean nothing! Many live like roommates with no emotional attachment and certainly no sex.

What a waste. Dead people walking.

Without love and PASSION, you might as well be dead!

Now my formula is not for everyone. Many cannot tolerate the vulnerability that true connection demands and that's OK for those people. Then there are the "parasites,", as I call them. The old ladies, who never worked, are just there in name only to enjoy the fruits of their husband's labor.

He's the nice guy who is doing what he was taught to do and maybe never even thinks about his emotional needs, let alone his physical ones. Just look at the workaholics and alcoholics Poor substitutes!

Today women demand more and they too engage in romantic affairs. We're talking about love not infatuation.

Younger women have changed and want to be fulfilled emotionally and sexually so hooray for that. The problem as I see it here is that they often don't connect for a period of time and the business of longing and seduction is often missing. It's too instant.

Love and great sex take time and knowledge and practice… all fun.

So, when one decides to end it; get a new puppy to replace the dead one or think of all the negatives about that person and relationship and then know there is someone out there waiting to meet YOU and move on!!

So how will all this change the world? Maybe we end up with happier more contented people, which can't be bad.

"For a male and female to live continuously together is… biologically speaking, an extremely unnatural condition." - Robert Briffault

Winding Down

"When a love comes to an end, weaklings cry, efficient ones instantly find another love, and the wise already have one in reserve." - Oscar Wilde

This 'love' business is the most fascinating topic on earth. Not just to write about but to experience.

It is fraught with every conceivable human emotion.

We all know the beginnings. They are magical and you are in a euphoric state. The loved one is 'perfect.' All faults are overlooked, ignored, or rationalized away. That basic drive to unite physically supersedes all else. The goal is to be one; to be close in body and mind. Whatever you do is wonderful. Wherever you go is fine, and whatever is shared or said is enjoyable and fun.

Just hearing the voice sets you in motion for wanting to see one another, touch and be intimate.

Hugging, kissing, and body contact is desired all the time and it is never enough. When apart there is a longing and missing of one another. All great… until it isn't.

After time and 'togetherness' feelings can change.

Now there is no specific time on this aspect. It can be soon after the initial euphoria or it can be after months or years. You will sense it and feel it.

Naturally after time there is a familiarity and comfort together BUT it is when that 'fire' no longer gets lit and when being close, especially physically, changes, that it is winding down.

There is a long list of things that can cause this to occur.

It can be a general lessening of the core sex drive for that person. It can happen as a result of communication diminishing. It can be a lack of real understanding. It can be changed goals or values. One of the main reasons is a realization that this person does not meet your emotional needs. He or she is not attentive, caring, or doing what you think they should be doing for you.

They are not considerate.

Being interested in someone else only lets you know things are changing.

When the 'rose colored glasses' come off you may see the real person. You may also see what they mean to you. Why you cared about them and what role the sexual part played in all of it.

Sometimes it comes as a shock to you but often others who care about you saw it all along. They may even have tried or talked to you about it. You were deaf… then.

When parents do this the reverse happens and the young person, especially, will hold on to prove their independence or to thumb their nose at the parent. When friends warn about the relationship they are told they just don't know the real person the way you do. All in all, it is a lost cause to tell anyone what they want or need romantically. We all have to make our own choices and often mistakes. Sometimes the mistakes are big ones and stay with us for life.

Bad marriages, hurt children, and a life of 'un' love is no way to live.

When the winding down first rears its' ugly head you have a choice. Be aware or ignore it. Talk about it, try to make it better… or end it.

It is usually the case that when one person feels the relationship isn't working the way it used to the other person is well aware as well. A real relationship is never one- sided and we do not live in a vacuum when it comes to this thing called, love.

While it is true many relationships go on and last a long time even when the feelings have changed not everyone wants to settle for that limited, puny life. We are here for only so long, and vital for only so long and to not use ourselves well in this most important aspect of our life is foolish.

Ending a relationship that we thought was love is never easy and often not quick or painless.

Who ends it and how is crucial.

Acknowledging the wind down should be the start.

If two people are mature and caring, then it is a mutual decision and one that both can agree upon and accept. If not there will be a see-saw back and forth, up and down, and it can become very hurtful.

Winding down happens. The sizzle changes in every relationship. In the real LOVE ones they can rekindle; move to a deeper level, and get better. If not the wind down goes way down and there is no longer anything to wind.

The thing to bear in mind is that if one person can't appreciate you the way you need to be appreciated another will. Once you know how to love you will never have to be without love or alone!

"Real loneliness consists not in being alone, but in being with the wrong person, in the suffocating darkness of a room in which no deep communication is possible." - Sydney J. Harris

Want to Be Smart or in Love

"It is only intellect that keeps me sane; perhaps this makes me overvalue intellect against feeling." - Bertrand Russell

Is this a dichotomy? I think it can be.

If you are a smart, logical, analytical person you spend a good bit of time reasoning, thinking and reviewing. That can preclude addressing or even acknowledging your FEELINGS.

Now I know feelings can overwhelm and get us caught up so that we become 'crazed.'

It's true. And of course, too much feeling without thought can cause other immense damage. So, where is the right mix, Goldilocks?

There is no precise answer and one size does not fit all, and we change over time with experience as well.

Let's take a look at the love life of a really smart guy - Albert Einstein.

A great deal has been uncovered since his personal letters were found.

He was married in 1903. She was three and a half years older than he.

He and Mileva had two sons and a daughter who died young. The marriage was not good after a bit, and in 1912 he asked for a divorce. They had a long rancorous divorce which ended in 1919.

His second son Eduard had schizophrenia and was in and out of asylums.

He drew up a list of expectations that were to be followed in case of divorce which showed him to be quite set on his views of women, even educated ones. Some of it may be attributed to the times. He had also agreed to give her the money should he win a Noble prize, which he later did.

In 1912, he was besotted by Elsa who was his maternal first cousin and his paternal second cousin!

He was in love signing one of his letters to her with," Kisses from your Albert."

We don't see him that way but there it was in black and white. Genius with FEELINGS and in love! How great is that?

He also had a number of mistresses along with her after four years, just proving he was human and gave way to his drives. He combined passion and intellect. How many do?

The problem is that one can override the other. Then we have to be aware and decide which path to take. It is a choice, and it is only when we are in touch with our feelings that we can look at the issue at all.

Many smart people spend their lives being just that; smart. They have feelings but do not address them.

They can be extremely successful and even somewhat happy but never really fulfilled.

They do what is expected; they marry, have children, do well at their professions, and live a busy social life. They however are skirting on the surface of life. They can do it forever. You see them as they are everywhere, all around us.

BUT, when you see the people who can also be smart, but FEEL, you know it immediately. They have crossed over into heaven on earth.

Now that doesn't mean it is just honky-dory. No indeed it is not.

As a matter of fact, any of you who follow my blog know I am the first to tell you, there is no pain on this earth like that which is and has to be associated with real love.

You are totally vulnerable; your bare self, (in all its forms), is totally exposed. You can be mortally hurt emotionally. Who chooses that?

Well, you do if you are really smart… because there is no good life without it.

How did Einstein get there? How does anyone get there?

It is by taking that leap, that risk, that willingness to connect in a full sense of the word.

You can bite your tongue, grip your fingers into a fist, close your eyes, whatever, BUT jump in.

You probably won't die if rejected at any point, although you might wish to.

You will however experience what this life is about. And better to try it early in life to know what it's all about in time.

This is a holiday season where we spend time expressing and being with those we care about and love. Make sure your heart is joined with that someone who gives YOU joy, just by loving THEM and showing it in a thousand ways. If you want to ask Santa for anything put that on the top of your list!

"Love looks not with the eyes, but with the mind; And therefore is winged Cupid painted blind." - William Shakespeare

What's Your Role in Your Relationship?

"THE FAMILY YOU COME FROM isn't as important as the family you're going to have." - Ring Lardner

As holidays approach we are usually with family. This can be any assortment of individuals these days. Step whatever's, same sex partners, in-laws, (that's always fun!), and those mixes of the generations. Whatever the composite is there will no doubt be a variety of mixed feelings.

Many of these will be revisits from past times and years. The feeling parts do not disappear. In some cases, they get worse. If fueled with alcohol the real junk comes out earlier and easier.

Now that doesn't mean that family times are bad or uncomfortable but it does mean that being aware of your feelings and how you deal with them can make all the difference in a happy or horrific holiday get together.

Parents can like or not like the way their grown children have developed. They may like or not like the in-law partner. Competitive siblings go at it subtlety or not. There may be disagreements with the way the grandchildren are being raised... and so on.

What can happen is that your personal intimate relationship may be torn apart as a result. The 'taking of sides' is not uncommon. The allegiances and protective gear come out This is where the real differences between you and your partner become crystal clear. If you get it out it can cause disruption. If you, 'suck it up' you can end up with a gall bladder full of bile in later years!

Sitting around the holiday table you can see it and hear it.

The real feelings of who likes or loves one another is evident no matter what is said or done.

You FEEL it!

We all learn how to *BE* from our growing up. We learn a role and we usually keep it for life.

Your order of birth sets a tone. Whether you were a wanted child and a preferred male or female also factors in here.

Then your personality comes into play and you have a role in your family.

Now that can be, the intelligent one, the clown, the peacemaker and so on. You know what it is.

In the family you make you continue to act it out. How secure you are as a person and how comfortable you are with allowing and respecting differences will all show your maturation. In every close relationship you can observe the dynamics of whether the male is more father, son, or lover. In the females she is also mother, daughter and lover.

When people are not fully developed the relationships are more parent and child.

In the real intimate ones the pair are mainly lover to lover. It is not easy to get there and to have it for a long time.

If you get two only or first born children, there are familiar patterns with a lot of competition.

With middle children they have learned how to compromise and negotiate, usually. They are easy to get along with and not as 'successful' as the first group.

With babies of families they can just be and are the delight and spoiled members of families.

When babies choose a 'baby' partner there can be big problems. Both are needy.

Now that all doesn't mean that in every relationship there aren't times when we need to be parented, or childlike. It also means at times we need to be the 'strong' one. It merely means that for the most part in the grown up version the lover to lover is the dominant theme. In that relationship the respect and willingness to 'do' just because you 'love' is paramount. What fun it is too!!

Sex, of course, is another big factor here and only adds to the pleasure.

The trick at these family holidays is to be on guard for your role and do not let anything, said or unsaid, get in the way of fusing you and the people you love together; mainly your partner. If anyone can cause that you are in trouble. And yes there are people in families that want to cause just that result... separating you for their own reasons. BEWARE!!

Having a meaningful and joyous family time lives on in memories as well as the uncomfortable memories. Make yours work for you!

"The successful mother sets her children free and becomes more free herself in the process" - Robert J. Havighurst

When a Man Loves a Woman

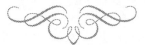

"MAN HAS BOUGHT BRAINS, BUT all the millions in the world have failed to buy love. Man has subdued bodies, but all the power on earth has been unable to subdue love. Man has conquered whole nations, but all his armies could not conquer love. Man has chained and fettered the spirit, but he has been utterly helpless before love. Thus love has the magic power to make of a beggar a king." - Emma Goldman

I dare any woman to listen to Percy Sledge's rendition of the song, 'When a man loves a woman' and not understand what she is after.

Men who truly know how to love are at a premium and sad to say somewhat rare. It is not easy to 'slay dragons' most of your life and then give in to feelings, and passion with a woman.

The two qualities are not easily compatible. Maybe that's why so many men settle for such limited relationships at home and have short term furtive release of their sexual energy elsewhere.

What seems to be the case, more often than not, is that a man will take over part of his life for a woman, while a woman will take over the whole of her emotional life for a man. He can be fulfilled for a time with that proverbial slaying of dragons, (i.e. being 'successful), here in America.

Men define love with sex especially when they are young. They have to learn about love and that when coupled with sex only then are they really in heaven on earth!

It is not easy.

When a man is really totally in love and willing to be vulnerable to the core he is a different human being. He can NEVER go back to what he was before. He will suffer for a lifetime without that feeling.

For a man to be a real man and be loved for who he is coupled with his sexual ability is what we are after.

He knows how to give his woman what she needs to love him in return. It is a two-way street.

She needs to hear his words of endearment, BUT he needs to show it in any number of ways as well. Only then do his eyes light up at seeing her, his body responds wanting to touch and be close and he wants to sexually unite with her. He shows it in every way. Small and large gestures are the icing on the cake and exemplify his feelings and appreciation of what she does for him.

He shares himself openly and honestly and cares about her needs. The chores or intellectual parts are the everyday doings that surround the core. They are NOT the core. When all of this is there people are healthier and only then truly happy.

Look at the men in love throughout and in current history, and what they have done for the women they loved, both when they were married or had lovers. That is not the issue, although that needs to be addressed in some form. Men only have lovers when they are dissatisfied with another woman.

The list of some of the most fascinating is long and varied;

Romeo

Napoleon

Kings of France

Kings of England

Marc Antony

Picasso

Salvador Dali

Charles Dickens

William Randolph Hearst

Nelson Rockefeller

Richard Burton

Woody Allen

George Balanchine

Grover Cleveland

Woodrow Wilson

Alexander Hamilton

Franklin Roosevelt

Lyndon Johnson

Jack Kennedy

The list could go on ad infinitum. The message is that men who 'risk' it for love are rarely sorry.

They experience a depth of emotional connection that is not available without that leap.

How long love lasts is up to the partners and what they bring to keep it alive… like any relationship.

The intensity and longing, (different from today's generation with instant gratification), makes the feelings raw and the yearning never ceases.

While there are many categories of 'love' there is only one real one that counts; the one with passion at the root.

Those that 'settle' for dull, ordered, dependable, familiar, are short changed or limited as individuals, if that is the basis.

Be responsible, be creative, be accomplished, BUT… be in love and you will be the man you want to be and dream of being!!!

It can only happen when a real man loves a real woman!!!

"To be in love is merely to be in a state of perpetual anesthesia. To mistake an ordinary young man for a Greek god or an ordinary young woman for a goddess." - H. L. Mencken

Some of The Best Are Gay

"BISEXUALITY IMMEDIATELY DOUBLES YOUR CHANCES for a date on Saturday night." - Rodney Dangerfield

While waiting for a table at a trendy brunch restaurant I sat next to a very handsome guy. Being friendly, he began talking to me and I also being friendly went on talking with him. He was bright and interesting and with his male partner. There was no doubt he was gay.

Looking at people all the time, I am quite aware that there are few good-looking men around, of any age. I am married to a handsome man so the looking is just that… looking.

At any rate, we had a delightful conversation and then our respective tables were ready.

The years I have spent as a relationship counselor and sex educator have included a great deal of time and attention paid to both transsexuals, (whom I wrote a book about), and gay people.

First of all, I am not sure of the origin of some of the terms used for a whole group of people. Today it's 'gender queer' meaning not necessarily man or woman; trigender, pangender, bigender, and ruby rose.

I really love the term, 'gay.' It just sounds positive and fun!

The term goes back to at least the 1920's and was a slang word among homosexuals. It entered the mainstream about the late 1960's.

The term 'gaycats' was used among older hobos who travelled with younger men who exchanged sexual favors for protection and instruction. Another plausible explanation is that it meant people who were addicted to pleasure, self-indulgent, or immoral.

Whatever the root I like the word, and who can deny that having a rainbow for a symbol is wonderful!

Anyway. There are flamboyant homosexuals and there are those like the 'lipstick lesbians' that would be totally unnoticed as 'gay.' That's how Rosie O'Donnell was surprised when she saw her beautiful second marriage partner for the first time.

Even though the Stonewall riots in 1969 brought gays out fighting there is still anti-gay behavior in America.

Our America with rights and voices for all has many places and people, important people, saying or doing anti-gayantics. Listen to some politicians about sex in a variety of forms: abortion, the church on pre-marital sex, and politicians with gay marriage. Then take a look at how we are bombarded with sexuality in all forms morning, noon, and night.

We are either schizophrenic or just plain hypocritical!

So many of the gay people I know or have counseled have fabulous creative jobs, are law abiding and in long- term loving relationships. The issues are NO different from my heterosexual clients.

They are human with the same needs, desires, fights, and solutions to problems. Many raise children who are NO different than other families. Maybe even a bit more sensitive, worldly, and accepting of differences. How nice that would be for a worldview.

I am so sick of the small- minded, living 'safe' people that I could throw up. What a narrow, simple, BORING life they lead.

They need scapegoats for what they don't allow themselves to understand and appreciate. This just doesn't apply to gays; it applies to all minorities and those that are not like them. Heaven help us if they rule the world!

At any rate, the thing is to get to know individuals as individuals, not as a lumped in-group where, 'all' of those people fall into a category. Accept people as unique and see what they are truly made of and what they offer you and others.

We should not care what anyone does with their body. Taking care of our own is a full time job and most screw, (no pun intended), that up quite nicely themselves.

Sex is wonderful in ALL its' forms. Relax and enjoy it… all of you!!

We are all a composite of good and bad, lovely, and not so lovely. Only by being truly human can we accept others and ourselves.

You cannot change what your heart gives you. The struggle with being gay starts in childhood and it is fought alone at first and then often brutally with others. The shame and embarrassment is difficult for many. Coming out to parents, siblings, friends is murder. Living the life takes courage and pain.

Being in a group helps, but does not solve all problems.

Learning to trust and love is not easy for any of us and especially hard when you are 'different.'

So, whoever you are out there I loved meeting and talking and looking at you. As I once said to the famous gorgeous Catholic Father Hesburgh, for heterosexual me, "What a waste!"

"Understanding is a lot like sex; it's got a practical purpose, but that's not why people do it normally." - Frank Oppenheimer

Give Up and You Win

"THE WHOLE WORLD IS A comedy to those that think, a tragedy for those that feel." - Horace Walpole

This life is tough, and this world is not easy. In order to survive you have to be 'tough.'

Getting strong and being able to stand on your own two feet, and being independent takes work. Taking care of others requires even more.

Because of all of this many people decide not to 'share' themselves completely emotionally. With enough practice it becomes easier and a habit. That makes a person responsible only to themselves.

They don't have to care about doing anyone else's bidding, pleasing anyone but themselves, and certainly not being vulnerable. Their routines are like that gerbil on the wheel… going through the motions.

They can be busy, involved with work, and any number of activities; some even doing good for the broader world. But, in the end they do not have the experience of opening up, and baring their heart, to a shared experience. Rationalizing or not even looking at their lives they believe that this is all that life offers, and to be sure, many others look exactly the same so maybe that's it.

Perhaps that is it for the majority of people. Not everyone is able to 'give' in all its' forms.

Can that be learned or changed? I think so. Hence this blog and all my years of counseling and family life education.

To share oneself intimately happens with someone you are connected to; in all its' forms! The steps may be slow or maybe fast and it usually works in tandem. I tell you how I feel and you share your deep thoughts and feelings and in tandem we learn to trust one another. We move along and it gets us closer and closer.

Attraction and lust starts the ball rolling but real love takes time along with that.

We test one another and we have areas of independence and then dependence… emotionally.

Sometimes a really self-contained successful person views giving up oneself to another as 'weakness.'

Self-protection is necessary but to get to be totally vulnerable we have to jump in and take that leap of faith. Testing before will help us bite the bullet.

Intense feelings, needing someone to love, desiring, and being desired are all part of this package. Frightening to be sure. Losing oneself is never easy. Once lost there is no turning back.

If you have chosen well it will be the most fabulous experience on earth. If not, you will retreat and not jump in so fast again… maybe not ever. It can feel like a win or lose situation. Keeping control can prevent you from doing what will bring you true happiness.

Now none of this is constant but a little goes a long way.

Knowing you are loved and loving manifests itself in thousands of ways; some small, some large.

Time will test it all, and love will always win out if it is genuine. Sex is the glue for it all.

If a relationship has outlasted its' usefulness there will be no real love; just that gerbil thing.

When a relationship is deteriorating it takes work to alter it, move it along, bring it to new depths, or end it. All of this is hard, hard work, and can only be accomplished if there is a connection that goes to the two hearts involved. It has to be acknowledged and then talked about, cried about, laughed about, and fought about. All good raw emotions.

This can only happen when each one is ready and able to 'fight' for the end result… continued connection… in every way.

Now not every relationship can withstand this, and maybe this kind of closeness was never there. Again, the gerbil. There are couples that live this way all of their lives, and think they are fine. So be it. Some of us have higher standards, and do not settle. Some of us are capable of the best that life offers. My hope is that you are one of those. You don't know until you 'give up' and connect in that special way.

It will not diminish you, you will not be seen as, 'weak' and you will not disintegrate…. You won't.

What you will do, is be a winner in this life because you will have won the greatest prize of all… LOVE!

Ending It Takes Courage

"SOMETIMES OUR LIGHT GOES OUT but it is blown into flame by another human being. Each of us owes deepest thanks to those who have rekindled this light." - Albert Schweitzer

For a therapist like myself the greatest reward is knowing that you have helped people live better fuller, satisfying lives.

This week I had a call that was as rewarding as it gets.

Over thirty-five years ago a doctor and his wife came to me for counseling. He was mid-forties and a gentleman from the word go. She was pretty and vivacious. They had three daughters.

The marriage was exhibiting problems and they were both willing to work on them. Good start.

I saw them together, took histories of their growing up, former relationships, and the marriage.

From the start I had the feeling he was the more sensitive one and the one more capable of giving and receiving love.

She seemed more shallow and self-centered and materialistic. Her ideas of happiness were superficial.

I asked to see them separately and after a month or so it became clear he was becoming more aware of what his needs were and that she could not deliver emotionally.

While we therapists can guide, and present the options and have people look at and explore and test out all areas we NEVER give an opinion as to what a client should do.

Being a mature and intelligent insightful man, he decided he wanted to end the marriage.

Now that decision is one of the bravest any person makes. Especially when there are children involved. In this case the children were in their twenties, not infants.

Making a decision to end a marriage or intense relationship takes all the courage in the world.

This is true no matter what; children, money, job, moving, family, friends and so on all make it hard or easier.

The riskiest thing any of us do is to give our heart away. Not everyone wants to or can do it either.

However, when the pain outweighs the pleasure and you see that this may be for the rest of your life, you should listen to your heart.

It is good if you have family to discuss the issues, or a good friend can help, and a professional will be unbiased and present the options. This decision should never be done in haste or anger but only after time and thoughtful consideration. The new life may not be what you thought it would be. Caution is the word!

Once the decision is made there is a new opportunity for a relationship that will better meet your needs. Love will find you, I promise!!!

Do not waste your life or live it without passion. It takes learning and a relationship that ends is a fine teacher if you pay attention. None of us are perfect or the best partners all the time BUT we can be the best overall for the ONE we truly love and have the desire for. It's whose feet you want next to you in that bed every night that counts in the long run.

So back to my doctor.

He met a woman a bit older than he and they married. She had been widowed for a while and had two children.

While she was a bit of a plain Jane she had what he needed.

What he called to tell me was that now, at about eighty, he had a terminal illness but he did not want to leave this earth without telling me how grateful he was for my helping him decide and giving him the confidence and hope for something better. He is married thirty years and so very happy. I had met her after they married and they were truly bound together and joyful. His illness will be dealt with in a beautiful way as a result of the intimacy that they share.

What a lovely ending, sad in some way that it is an ending, but as we both said together, not everyone is brave to do what he did and live so lovingly for all those years. I was deeply touched.

Unhappiness and stress are the killers in this life and only love really matters in the end.

"If you cry because the sun has gone out of your life, your tears will prevent you from seeing the stars." - Rabindranath Tagore

The Perfect Woman... Madonna AND Whore

"I DID NOT COME HERE to talk" - Mark Antony to Cleopatra

"Women have a much better time than men in this world; there are far more things forbidden to them." - Oscar Wilde

What's all this commotion lately about Sheryl Sandberg's book, "Lean In"

She sorts of says women need to be like men to get ahead. NO, NO, and NO!

Women need to be what they are; WOMEN!!

It took four million years for humans to stand erect, and then many more years until they had sex face to face and we are here primarily for reproducing.

Before you start screaming; I believe in women being educated, and using their backgrounds. As a matter of fact, male college enrollment is going down 43%. Girls are now valedictorians 70% of the time, and 66% of the girls value high paying jobs compared to 59% of the males. Girls are still paid only .82 cents to every dollar a male earns.

Some things are changing and boys find it hard to sit still in class and view school as less manly, while girls excel in communication skills. There are gender differences.

The role of men is also changing as women enter and move up the ladder to that glass ceiling, (whatever that means).

Men are staying home and helping with the house and children. I don't care what they say there is nothing like a good mother. Ever watch a guy looking after his young child? They are oblivious!

At any rate here we have it; talented women in the work world. Let's not discuss what happens when she earns more than he does.

Now if these ladies are attractive there is exposure to other men and the whole business. If the marriage or relationship is waning that presents other variables. Very different from the older generation who stayed at home.

I think women want to be beautiful and be inspiring love; in the end. So how does it all get played out and how can women be that Madonna who is accomplished and be that sexy, whore where that counts?

Is it possible?

Not for many. Why?

Well, to be in love it takes surrender, not a good quality in getting ahead in a profession. To be in love you have to be playful. Not a quality to possess in running a business.

To be in love you have to go crazy at times. Not a bonus in the real tough world. To be in love you have to be vulnerable. Not what CEO's are listing on their resumes. To be in love your brain becomes like an addict's brain. Not a plus in the world of work. Some of this is true for men as well but different for a truly feminine woman.

Can you turn it off while at work? Perhaps but not at the root, in your heart. What matters?

In my view, it takes an extraordinary woman to possess the dual qualities of accomplishment at high levels and the femininity to have an intense intimate relationship!

Go find her.

There are some rare ones out there but few and far between.

There is one theory on the horizon that can help and that is expounded by the CEO of Business Talent Group. She says there should be top positions that are available on less than a full time basis. That would give those women at the top the opportunity to perhaps work three days a week or so. The job would still be done and taken in shorter bites.

Time for love, children, and other activities. Great idea!!

Whatever the outcome, over time, top people will make their world and hopefully not have to suffer the job taking over their lives… because...

Life with love and a relationship with intensity is the ONLY pure joy in this life. Accomplishment and using one's talents and remaining female to the core is not easy today. No one has it all and there is no rose covered path for anyone… men, or women. My belief is that the best will still be what nature gave them and centuries of evolution cannot be wiped away… nor should they.

The 1960's and birth control, along with books like, "The Joy of Sex" helped liberate women in those areas. Now we need to address this issue. This is all about being at the top but there are millions struggling as well, who are not in those lofty arenas. Get on with it for all women, (and men too).

Those that can't incorporate the Madonna with the whore are usually just limited and jealous.

"Moral indignation is jealousy with a halo" - H. G. Wells

Get Touched in 20XX

"You've got to accentuate the positive, eliminate the negative, latch on to the affirmative, but don't mess with mister in between." - Sam Cooke Lyrics

This is good practice and it takes practice! I am speaking about all kinds of closeness; including that essential one, physical closeness.

We feel shy, shame, fear, and all sorts of bogey men. Look at the ways in which you prevent closeness. With emotional issues we fear being rejected or thought silly, or not worthy of being loved. With the physical side we don't like parts of our bodies, or know little or nothing about our parts, let alone the partner's.

The end result is that we 'cover up' literally. We do not expose our genuine self with all its yucky sides, and we do not share our physical self with another, with all its flaws. Ain't none of us perfect! Too bad.

There is nothing that will ever replace being connected with both mind, heart and body.

Now I know this is not easy. Some people can jump in and out of bed with any number of partners and think nothing of it. That is what it is… nothing but mere physical release.

Sometimes it is a substitute for real feeling and later it becomes clear it was all a masquerade.

You are not alone if you have difficulty 'baring' it all. It is a frightening business this thing called love. We see so much non-closeness around us, and we probably grew up in homes where it was never what it could or should be.

We had few if any role models. The media, especially movies, present unreal situations for the most part and they don't show how to get close. That school has yet to come into existence and give diplomas.

But all of this is how much of yourself you reveal and under what conditions and to whom.

It is sort of like peeling an onion a layer at a time.

With the emotional side it is sort of a see-saw working in tandem. You tell something and he or she tells something. As each layer comes off it gets deeper and more close to the heart. The phrase 'I am touched' when said about a gesture tells it.

With real touching it is also in stages.

We can touch a hand, we can hug, we can kiss, and we can have total flesh on flesh and mingle our bodies.

What is nice to do is to really touch many body areas and talk about how you like to be touched and how your partner enjoys touch. It is the human connection that is most meaningful.

Some people like soft gentle touches, others prefer strong sometimes almost painful touching.

There are a variety of fun ways to touch the human body.

You can stroke with a feather while having your or your partner's eyes closed. You can run an ice cube slowly over a naked body. You can shower together or share a bubble bath and wash one another… all over.

You can put whipped cream or chocolate sauce on specific parts of a body and lick it off. Use your imagination!

The thing is to not be inhibited and communicate your desires. Let your hair down, so to speak.

Go with your impulses.

You can play games, but don't be manipulated or manipulating. It has to be direct and open. You will find what is enjoyable and what are the turn-ons.

Candles and wine can also help get you going. Music is pleasant as well. Whatever works! Just touch with words and with body… Make 20XX a touching year.

The more you practice the easier it becomes and you will have patterns that you will really like.

It will never be boring. The possibilities are infinite. Couples who are intimate in every way have learned what to do. It is like everything else in life; you need knowledge, risk, communication and practice.

You can learn together which is the best! There is nothing more positive, and less negative than human caring shown by touching.

ENJOY TOUCHING!!

"Your body needs to be held and to hold, to be touched and to touch. None of these needs is to be despised, denied, or repressed. But you have to keep searching for your body's deeper need, the need for genuine love. Every time you are able to go beyond the body's superficial desires for love, you are bringing your body home and moving toward integration and unity." - Henri Nouwen

Free at Last... YIPPEE!

"OF COURSE THERE IS SUCH a thing as love, or there wouldn't be so many divorces." - Ed Howe

There was an interesting statistic reported recently; that conservative Protestant Christians, mainly from the Bible Belt, had the highest divorce rates in the U.S. Atheists had a much lower rate!

This Christian group is also the group that vociferously raises alarm about the state of marriage being very important and they oppose gay marriage… go figure. Maybe they should all be Hindu where there is the lowest divorce rate! Better-educated people also have a lower rate.

This business about divorce is a delicate one as it involves people at their very base.

What they are, what they feel about a partner, how they react, and the fall out for any children is all important. Practical issues, not withstanding, there is disruption of a lifestyle.

The main area to be addressed is what was the relationship for from the start; what evolved, and how did it change and what feelings are there?

I myself have a bumper sticker I'd like to see on cars; 'Stamp out first marriages!'

All of life is learning and hopefully growing emotionally and otherwise, and then sharing oneself. To learn and it is learning, to be intimate, and fully realized sexually, takes time and communication.

Any 'first' is a beginning of that process. Some people are able to educate themselves and learn from others; others are not and remain what they always were. Many remain emotional teenagers, for example, for life. The pattern does not change, and the needs do not develop. They are never able to offer much in the arena of relationship to anyone. They just keep reinforcing old patterns of behavior.

Divorce or also just ending any meaningful relationship means you are moving on and out and then 'free.'

Now emotional freedom means you really are not tied or attached with feelings for that other person. Not in any way including anything that keeps you like stepping on chewing gum and bouncing back.

When the heart is 'free', it feels different.

If you have to keep reminding yourself of the reasons to move on or the bad stuff to keep the process going that's fine. If you stay stuck in the fantasy, that it will be better or that the good times were enough or wonderful that prevents movement.

If the reasons for staying are superficial but none the less real; money, not being alone, the children etc. that will only eventually cause resentment, anger, and a hollow existence. You do no one a favor, mainly yourself, by staying for reasons that do not include wanting your feet next to theirs in bed!

If you have tried to correct the things that aren't working and they just don't get corrected or you are not able or willing to make the changes yourself, you might try professional help. Maybe what is there can be accepted as sufficient? Sometimes the best help gets you to the point where you can end constructively as opposed to a destructive bitter ending.

Compromise is in every relationship and issues of disagreement are always there, but when enough is enough, it will erode you in the end unless you GO!

What gets reinforced are bad habits that will be repeated in another relationship unless you see it for what it was and know what to look for or change in yourself. You can excuse or forgive a lot for love but real love is reciprocal and meets needs maturely.

Divorce when children are involved means that the best outcome is to be civil enough to be in contact and act in the interests of the children; not payback for your wounds. Shared time is usually worked through. Badmouthing a former partner serves a negative purpose for the child.

If money is the key that is hopefully negotiable in the end. It need not be the "War of the Roses."

An interesting divorce was the first society one by Alva Vanderbilt Belmont. She turned out to develop into a suffragette and doing much good, which never would have been possible without her 'freedom.' One of her quotes I really like is she said she didn't want to be around, "Women with sawdust brains and wax faces." There's a lot of them out there, then and now. She was a brave lady and withstood a great deal of scorn as a result of her action. Today we are not dealing with the shame of divorce. If anything, we may be jumping into it too fast without really trying to salvage the situation.

Being 'free' at last is scary. It is a new life. It can be like having a burden lifted or if you were the one 'done to' it can cripple you if you are not strong.

Family and friends are important here. Being and doing positive things is crucial. You are now able to answer just to you.

If another love is in the picture that will help and you can look at that relationship more closely.

It's sort of like when your beloved dog dies, a new puppy helps.

Your raison d'etre or reason for living should now be addressed in new ways. It is absolutely an opportunity for a new and better life. Embrace it!!

"It's a toss-up between marriage and divorce. They're both right and wrong now and then, but mostly right." - Nat Goodwin

How to Impress Her or Him

"If rich people could hire other people to die for them, the poor could make a wonderful living." - Yiddish Proverb

Does money mean success and is that all it takes to impress someone?

According to some studies, that statement is true. In my book, part of that is true but often any horse's ass can have money and be totally superficial and shallow. Substance and a real human being requires much more.

In one study they did indeed find that, money, not intelligence, helped men to have more sex but it was also true that it was intelligence that helped them make money!

Another study found that anytime you bought something beautiful that you really loved and fully enjoyed without guilt, you were definitely improving your mental health.

What it takes to be successful and have money today takes a toll on us and what we can give emotionally in relationships. Wealth and concrete achievement are only one piece of the 'good' life.

Few of our presidents, for example, have been successful businessmen. Warren G. Harding was one. Most of those we revere have suffered and conquered adversity.

We pay attention to the wrong values and set limited goals for our children.

Being worldly and curious, knowing people from varied cultures, and being capable of true intimacy, makes us genuine.

Whom do we pay huge sums of money to, and who are our children's role models?

Where is any of this explored or taught?

The apostle Paul wrote that the love of money is the root of all evil, and Dante reserved his Fourth Circle of Hell for those guilty of avarice and prodigality. This is obviously not a new subject for review!

Now… if you have some money and want to impress, here are some ideas:

Jewelry: JAR in Paris

Handmade shoes: Gaziano & Girling in England

Men's shoes: John Lobb, Pierre Hardy, Louis Leeman

Ladies shoes: Christian Louboutin, Manola Blahnik, Jimmy Choo, Chanel

Men's clothes: Savile Row in London, Nino Corvato, custom made suits in New York

Women's clothes: Too many to list, Special mention: Alaia, and Vionnet

Lingerie: Sabia Rosa and Chantel Thomass in Paris

Restaurants; Zomato.com to discover the best reviewed in your neighborhood.

Personal perfume: Lyn Harris in England, Nova Studio in Brooklyn, Yosh Han in San Francisco, Francis Kurkdjian in Paris, and Roja Dove the most expensive (40,000! In a crystal bottle!)

Wine and Champagne

The finest champagnes are produced by Krug and Jacques Selosse. Large Champagne houses are mostly pricey due to marketing costs.

Caviar: Sevruga, should be eaten off the back of hand near thumb!

Burgundy: Romanee Conti

Bordeaux: Château Lafite Rothschild, Mouton Rothschild, Petrus, Le Pin

Sauterne: Chateau d'Yquem

You can have all these great wines and more delivered to you from Canada's most prestigious wine site: WineOnline.ca

Premium Resort: Amanresorts.com ($43,000 a couple for seven nights)

Luxury Yachts: Burgessyachts.com

Skiing: JohnFalkiner.com

Travel to your roots: ancesrtalfootsteps.com

Portraits: lehmannmaupin.com

There it is… a list for fun and pleasure and to impress others. All it takes is money!!!

"Money is human happiness in the abstract; he, then who is no longer capable of enjoying human happiness in the concrete devotes himself utterly to money." - Arthur Schopenhauer

Have A BIG Fight... Please

"Once the realization is accepted that even between the closest human beings' infinite distances continue, a wonderful living side by side can grow, if they succeed in loving the distance between them which makes it possible for each to see the other whole against the sky." - Rainer Maria Rilke

As a marriage counselor, I have often said the worst cases are the ones coming in saying they never fight. Of course not because they are not intimately and emotionally connected. There is no passion.

Now there are all levels of disagreement; and there better be because no two people have the identical background, personality, life experience, or values. So what gets you angry? What is the pattern? If you know it, it can help but believe me it will not change it necessarily, because all of this is based on FEELINGS.

The worst thing that can happen is that your partner says you shouldn't feel that way!! Oh, really? Well you do.

It's that feeling part that gets us every time.

Most of the time it's based on old sore spots and over time it gets to be a part of you.

The needs that are emotional and not met in the way you would like sets the stage.

Why can't your partner see that? Why can't they think like you? Why can't they understand?

Why, why, and why.

Well, it's simple… they are not you!

Many times, it's petty stuff but it represents a larger issue. He didn't pick up his mess, translation… I am not in control and he is not doing what I expect and want.

Now you can fight dirty or constructively.

Dirty says,' you and your mother and'… taking it a few generations and compounding it. You can go for the jugular or Achilles' heel and we all have it and know it in our partners. Or you can really get nasty and say terrible things that are never forgotten and will sabotage the whole relationship in the end.

But if you want to continue with this person, the best thing to do is yes, get it out with all the emotion, and then later think it through. TALK about it, and ask your partner to work with you to remedy the pattern and recognize danger signals before they get overblown.

Many marriages, for example, end or become dead inside, because they never really got it together.

Now the bottom line is that if it is a really strong emotional relationship, the drive to love one another and SEX will get you through and improve what goes on.

You have to really and truly care how the 'other' one feels, and care about what they think.

You can have a life like a Misery Festival or you can work on Love Muscles, just like any other exercise.

Clearing the air and getting out honest to god feelings is what this life is about. Sharing it is okay when the bond is strong. This is a bit tricky in early relationships and some never get off the ground and go around the same merry-go-round all their lives together. Others bury their true feelings and try to compensate with other things… which never fill the void in the heart.

When you really care, that person is the only one you want to hate… temporarily!

I once had a client who came in saying that anyone who met her husband didn't like him, but when they got to know him, they hated him. Turns out, she was in the same boat.

One of my favorite comedians, Bobby Collins, says there are things you say on the 'outside' while the 'inside' says something very different. He has been married and in love a long time.

When someone is ill, famous, or insecure, it becomes more difficult to risk letting them know how you feel. The thought of losing them can overcome the issue. That again, in the end, does not work.

So, get it out, evaluate the relationship over and over again, or if you are not cared for the way you need to be, move on. There are many, many people out there, longing for a genuine, and real loving connection. We are mainly FEELINGS.

"Man is a rational animal, so at least I have been told. Throughout a long life, I have looked diligently for evidence in favor of this statement, but so far I have not had the good fortune to come across it." - Bertrand Russell

Prove That You Love Me

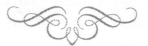

"LOVE IS ALWAYS BESTOWED AS a gift- freely, willingly, and without expectation. We don't love to be loved; we love to love." - Leo Buscaglia

There are so many stories showing 'proof' of love that we could never exhaust the list. Famous ones are there from the bible, mythology, history, and contemporary lives. There is your very own way of showing and exhibiting what you feel when you truly love someone.

Now it all depends on your abilities, capacities, and knowledge.

The Romeo and Juliette story is known to us all and few of us would want to kill ourselves for love but some do. Cleopatra is in that list. The beautiful story of Eurydice and Orpheus is a great one. She is bitten by a snake and dies and goes to Hades. He is so overwrought that he begs Hades to let him bring her back to earth. His music is so sweet and moving that she was released with the provision that he not look back as she followed him back to earth. As he approached earth he wanted to be sure she was there and as he turned to look she was swept back to Hades.

Whenever you hear music that mourns lost love it is his!

Then there are the talented people who use their lovers as muses.

There are many in this list as well.

Some of them include Billy Joel who wrote wonderful music inspired by his love.

Picasso who painted the women he loved who gave him inspiration.

Hemmingway whose four wives helped us have great stories.

Balanchine whose ballets were often choreographed for his muse.

Then there is the long list of those who gave something according to their resources. When you love there is nothing that is too much to do or give.

Randolph Hearst had a castle built in America. Elizabeth Taylor collected jewelry, and she also gave to her loves. Pamela Harriman was given rare paintings. Angelina Jolie has children. President Harding wrote love letters. President Roosevelt left money in his will. Nelson Rockefeller gave money for property.

Jackie Onassis endured hurt with dignity and grace.

Julia Child whose husband's love gave us great recipes.

This list goes on forever.

The other proofs of love can come from many sources depending on your position, and resources.

Samson cut his hair and lost his strength. The Duke of Windsor gave up the throne of England.

Napoleon made Josephine his Empress. Tsar Nicholas had Faberge design fabulous jewels.

Ralph Lauren designs gorgeous clothes.

Again think of what you do for your love to prove it. What does your love do for you to prove it?

The proof of loving someone should flow. It is not calculated. There is no price tag on it.

Although the reality is that you know what you are capable of and what you can spend. That is in the mix, but the wanting to do and give should be there in full force; just as it is in the physical side of things. There can be no limit to the touching, hugging, kissing and intimate moments which include full abandoned sex that is shared. There's a real proof!!

So in the end there are many ways to prove this thing called love. It includes the little things; the compromises, maybe even sacrifices, fighting for love, paying attention, doing the big things like changing in certain areas, doing what you don't want to, not being hurtful, putting up with things you don't like, protecting your loved one in every way, keeping love alive no matter the time spent together or even distance, and bringing things the partner will enjoy.

The story of Camelot is a good one. It goes back to King Arthur's day.

His wife Guinevere falls madly in love with his faithful knight, Lancelot. He declares his love for her and they have a passionate affair for years.

When Arthur finally learned about it, it became a catalyst for events that ultimately destroyed the Knights of the Round Table. She ends up in a convent and Lancelot leaves the kingdom. "Tant pis" as the French say… too bad!

Proof is in the pudding… make it a good one!!

"You can't put a price tag on love, but you can on all its accessories." - Melanie Clark

Shit, I Still Love Him

"Love is like the truth, sometimes it prevails, sometimes it hurts." - Victor M. Garcia, Jr.

So, now you think it's over. You have done all the hard work of being angry, hurt, frustrated, for the millionth time… over the same crap.

You have told yourself all the bad things about him, (can also apply to guys about her), and gone over the situation again and again.

You have done what should work; making a list of all his bad points. You have remembered every nuance of his behavior that you didn't like, and have told yourself you deserve better.

You have called old boyfriends, flirted with new people, and regarded every eligible man that walks.

You really have gotten yourself to the point that you don't give a damn about him and are ready to move on.

All the 'what ifs' are played and replayed.

All the 'if onlys' have been chewed over and over again.

You really don't care about him anymore!

Well, HA, he creeps back into you.

You try wine, you try being busy, and you try being so social you have no time to think.

Guess what? He creeps back in.

Now if the relationship has been going on for some time, maybe years or if it was wonderful at different points, creeping back in is easy. If it was mainly a struggle all the way, it should be easier to abandon hope.

When you have a true love affair, the heart is bound and the thoughts and memories seep through the cracks.

Chances are if you are feeling that way, so is he.

The next threshold to cross is who makes a move?

When one is too proud or stubborn, or stupid, the wait can be long. The agony horrible and the fighting off of the feelings a real task.

We are taught that independence is best and other values are more important, but guess what… nothing, and I mean NOTHING, competes with LOVE.

Now the real test.

If it is LOVE, it doesn't go away.

No matter how hard you try, and no matter what, you will come back to wanting him; emotionally, physically, and intellectually. You cannot escape.

You will come to, 'Shit, I still love him!'

When you get there, you have choices. There are ALWAYS choices.

If he has not called or come back to you with some gesture, it is up to you to act.

The tricky part is whether you both arrive at the same point at the same time.

No matter; if it is LOVE, it will happen.

Call him; send a note, an e-mail, flowers… anything. Just let him know you still care and want him.

If he is ready… great. If not, you may have a wait. Or if it is unrequited, you may suffer a long time.

You can then spend a lifetime sometimes, with the going over the past and replaying it all. That will do no good, and then finally, you may have to accept the outcome and find someone else to use what you learned.

I recently met a darling, down to earth guy, about twenty-seven, who announced to me that every girl is a bit, "nuts." He goes into relationships just waiting to find out the manner and degree of this premise. When asked if he had ever been really in love he thought that maybe for short periods of time.

That prevents him from a full falling into what love requires, total abandonment and acceptance of the total person; craziness and all. I predicted it would happen. And good to wait until a bit later to settle on one after lots of experience. Problem today is the young people may only want short relationships and everyone becomes expendable and for immediate gratification. We will see. Communication and commitment seem to need help lately.

At any rate, if you keep coming back to wanting him and he is feeling the same it WILL happen.

No rainbows until after the rain!

"True love cannot be found where it truly does not exist, nor can it be hidden where it truly does." - Anonymous

In Sickness and...

"Could there be anything worse", an ailing friend once wrote complainingly to Mark Twain, "than having a toothache and an earache at the same time?" - Mark Twain wrote back; "Rheumatism and St. Vitus' Dance."

We all feel our own pain and illness whether brief and curable or chronic or terminal and we handle it differently; each one of us.

The mere fact that we all know we don't get out of here alive can be an unsettling idea to begin with.

When young and in good health most people don't think about such matters, however with age things begin to happen.

Our bodies are not geared for remaining the same forever.

While it is true that we all react differently and someone with a hangnail can be miserable while someone with terminal cancer is stoic; pain and suffering is universal for all of us at some point. The best and worst of life is never planned!

So, if we are dealing with sickness while in a relationship the crucial questions are how long is the relationship and what are the dynamics?

If it is a fairly new relationship the illness, depending on its' nature may drive the partner right out the door.

If it is a long standing one the pattern may continue, become exaggerated or in fact change drastically.

The roles that have been played will become the focus to observe.

The 'sick' one may be the one that has always and now really uses the sickness to get attention.

The strong one that becomes ill may fight the dependent role and get nastier and in fact act in ways that are detrimental to getting better. These are the people that nurses and doctors hate in the hospital.

The 'know it all' may become challenging and question everything recommended. The Internet has helped to foster this behavior. Sometimes for the better and often with lots of wrong information.

The severe diagnosis can sometimes force people to really change. I have seen, having worked in hospitals, some real SOB's become 'pussycats' when handed a life threatening diagnosis.

Physical illness is different from mental illness but in many cases one feeds upon the other. Crisis can force major change in some people.

So, in a really loving relationship what happens? If it is truly a caring intimate duo the relationship will only become deeper as it does with all emotional challenges.

If it has been rocky or a 'dutiful' one, it will continue with that flavor.

If it has been without true emotional connection, it may continue in name only or in some cases it can be the excuse to move on. Does Newt Gingrich or John Edwards come to mind?

Being there 'in sickness' is never easy for the patient and especially difficult for the people who care about them.

In many situations there are secrets about the diagnosis and while we never want to give up hope there are situations where responsible dialogue and planning should take place. Not everyone can do it.

In many cases people should be helped to end it. We are kinder to animals!

I have not spoken about the people who make themselves the 'sick' ones and may or may not be truly ill but like that role and play it to the hilt for life.

The really chronic illnesses can be handled in a variety of ways depending on the person. Some yield to it, others fight it, and some make the best of it and don't become burdens to their loved ones.

So, when we promise to love' in sickness', do we really know what we may do? Probably not. The real test is yet to come. Then, of course, what if WE are the one who needs the patience and love???

"Fifty percent or more of the people who go to doctors to be healed of their sickness are suffering from neuroses. Most of them can be helped, many of them cured. Many others would not under any circumstances dare to permit themselves to be cured. They live only by the grace of their symptoms." - Karl Menninger

Styles of Marriage

MARRIAGE IS LIKE A BESIEGED city. Those that are outside want to get in and those on the inside want to get out! If you think marriage is going to be perfect, you probably have not left the alter yet! At any rate, there are many ways to relate to one another in marriage and there are a few common styles. Most of them are between people who are unequal.

These include:

The Mother-Son Relationship

Here the woman takes care of the partner much as she would a male child. The emotional aspect is easy to see and can be in many forms, emotional, care of the spouse, talking baby talk, earning more of the income, and making most of the major decisions.

The Opposite is the Father-Daughter Role

This is very common with men marrying younger women and really taking care of them in most significant ways. The daughter bride plays the role, as she has never truly grown up. She may be a pretty arm piece and that is all he wants. She does his bidding, and looks up to him as a child would with a parent. This type is often called the *Doll-Daddy* relationship.

The Bitch and the Nice Guy

This is clearly a common role today with so many young people being brought up in indulged households and feeling entitled and becoming very narcissistic. The groom is brought up by a "bitch" of a mother so he is used to that style of life. Many of these marriages are fraught with anger; some of it expressed and much of it not.

The Master-Slave Type

This again is another unequal relationship that is all too common. Usually the male is the master and is often a 'macho' male or in a job where he is the boss and expects everyone to follow his orders. Sometimes these partners can be abused mentally or even physically.

The Teacher-Pupil Marriage

This is the old Pygmalion story. I know more and I will mold you and teach you what you need to know. In these relationships, the pupil is eager to please and learn and the teacher likes being looked up to.

Now any of these styles can be satisfying and go on forever and will only end if one or both of the partners change and their emotional needs change. No one on the outside ever really knows what goes on in a marriage; only those who live it know.

The Final Type is the Equalitarian Marriage

This style is between mature equal partners who are emotionally not so needy and only want to make their partner happy by loving them. It doesn't mean it's better or will last forever; it just means the style is different. Many of these couples have huge differences and argue and so on, but they are usually able to work out their differences and come back together. Compromise is easier here.

The mother- son is a nurturing marriage, the father daughter is primarily a protective one, the bitch- nice guy is a challenging one, the master- slave an almost sado- masochistic one, and the teacher- pupil an educative one, while the equalitarian is a rhythmic style.

Much else goes on in choosing a mate and living a marriage and all of this will be discussed in the future.

Torn Between Two Women

"THE CHILDHOOD SHOWS THE MAN, as morning shows the day." - John Milton

Whenever Mother's Day comes up, we are all driven to contemplate from whence we came.

We can celebrate with good or not so good remembrances and feelings BUT be aware the past affects today!

There are all variety of mothers. And do not forget many people have others in their lives who were not their birth mother but who gave them the nurturing and support, mainly emotional, that prepared them for life.

There are any number of mothers who never should have been; fortunately, today that is a choice.

The women who are unfulfilled, narcissistic, not sexually complete, controlling and so on make poor mothers. They have to fill themselves up emotionally and until someone has their own cup filled, they cannot give to another.

It doesn't mean that there are not 'down' times or periods where you didn't receive what you needed from that mother; it just means that part of life includes some bad times. It is on the final scale that your mother is measured.

Now for mothers with sons the task is huge. The reason is that old Oedipal story. The first and strongest love is love of mother. Then as an adult you have to 'emotionally kill' her in order to transfer the primary feelings of love to another woman. That can be a threat to a mother who still 'needs' you in a significant fashion. Then trouble is on the horizon.

It can be shown in many forms. Anger toward the son; hate toward his woman, and so on. It can be subtle or overt.

The man who is 'caught' between these two opposing forces is in a quandary. He can love both but differently. In all likelihood, he has chosen a mate just like his mother emotionally.

These two woman will battle it out for his heart.

He tries to please them both and it is a Herculean task.

For daughters they have an easier time, although there are some girls who stay too attached to their 'daddies' and that also is not a good scene.

More often though it is the mother-son relationship that is fraught with turmoil.

If they are smart people, they can learn how to handle the situation constructively. The head will help the heart in this scenario.

For the mother the son can express his love for her and recount the positive in his growing up and past. He can be there for her and let her know he wants her included in his life; easier if there are grandchildren.

The partner can remember she is the one he goes to bed with! She can also realize that she is younger, probably prettier, and lives with him. She can make sure she is super affectionate to him in front of his mother and doesn't allow her to see any dissatisfaction or disagreement between them in front of her. He can assist in this.

The mother has to realize that their relationship is iron clad and they do not need her; only each other. It is not easy and that is why every mother should have a life of her own and not be dependent on children for her emotional well-being.

It is more difficult if the mother is divorced, widowed or sickly. Then there is another wrinkle added. Sometimes the mother can feign illness or need where none actually exists. Sometimes money is used to hold the son hostage.

All of this will build resentment at some point or the son will remain a child attached to the whims of his mother and used for her purposes. He can have a partner and fear her disapproval; just like with his mother.

The other aspect is that the partner should recognize that a man who is kind and caring to his mother will also be that way with her. A son-of-a-bitch is that way clear through.

In counseling over decades, I have seen and heard of the most bizarre things that can go on in these relationships. You really need to be careful and aware. The son, especially if he is young without insight is in jeopardy of losing a good relationship with a woman of his own if he is not careful.

There are many situations where a man is caught between two women but the one with mother and sex partner is one of the most common and most dangerous to him in the end.

The lesson is to be smart and aware, and know the past and like all of life; the more you know the better!!

"The first recipe for happiness is; Avoid too lengthy meditation on the past." - Andre' Maurois

Talk to Me

"DO NOT SAY THINGS. WHAT you are, stands over you the while and thunders so that I cannot hear what you say to the contrary." - Emerson

How true is that quote?

We are who we are and what we are, gets across to others, no matter what.

The fascinating part is that when we communicate sometimes we give out messages that may fool others and maybe at times, even ourselves.

If you listen to people or your own conversations you can hear the two main categories they fall into; the mundane, necessary, boring or superficial, and the 'real' stuff.

In the list of the 'regular' talk include:

The weather

Daily activity

Politics

Sports

Buying or selling things

Places visited or planned

Other people

The children

Fixing up (yourself, the house, the car, etc.)

Money

Family

Things you saw or heard

In the list of 'real' talk that brings intimacy include:

How you FEEL (both now and in the past)

Asking questions about the other person with true interest

Telling your hopes, dreams, and desires

Sharing bad thoughts and experiences

Laughing about funny things

Saying what displeases you and what pleases you in the relationship

Saying how you care about this person

We need both types of talk but many only have that first list for most of their lives. A waste!

When we talk we get messages across. When we act we also get messages across. If they are not in harmony; trust the ACT, not the talk!

We deliver our messages; unless we are Cyrano.

A great pair of exercises is to have a couple just look silently in each other's eyes for five minutes and then ask what the message was. Then have them give a verbal message and have the partner repeat the words and ask what was meant by those words.

The problem is usually that we do not share ourselves in this way with intimacy because we are afraid the other person will use the information to hurt us, or maybe not like or respect us if they know whatever about us. We can be ashamed or insecure or just not trusting.

Intimacy is a two-way street; in or out of bed.

Saying what you really FEEL is not easy. Withholding or deluding ourselves may feel safer but in the end we pay a price. We cannot escape who we are and what we feel. The truth will out.

You know who cares about you no matter what they say.

Another pitfall is thinking a partner can 'read your mind.' Wrong!

Thinking you know what another is doing or thinking is faulty usually.

No matter how well you know someone you should not assume you know at any given time what they are feeling. Some people are quite expert at hiding feelings or even lying. Ever have a relationship with a sociopath?

The rule is to move slowly and each one shares a bit of themselves until the core is there. Then being naked, so to speak, will be great, and not just in bed!!!

"You'll never really know what I mean and I'll never know exactly what you mean." - Mike Nichols

Disappointed... Get Used to It

"Disappointments should be cremated, not embalmed." - Anonymous (Henry S. Haskins)

I guess that means we should forget about our disappointments. Can we? I don't think that is an easy task.

How long we fret, dwell on them or get furious about them is the true issue.

Then again, it depends on where we are in life and what the disappointment is.

As children we begin to learn to cope with what we don't like and what needs are not met.

Have you watched a child scream for candy or to go where he or she wanted to go? It all starts there. Do they get what they want? How does the caretaker respond? Of course, the infant learns early on how to cry for what it wants. With language the whole business changes.

For parents it is often easier and less embarrassing to just shut them up. But, what are you teaching that way?

It is much more difficult to set limits and have children learn early on that there are unmet needs in this life and they are not always in control.

As we progress, the areas change. We can be disappointed in how we look, friends who are not friends, dating situations, parents, schoolwork, and so on. The list is endless and depends on each of our values. What matters?

With young adults, it can be around a career or job situation. You name it and someone has been disappointed about it.

Now you can fret or even be stymied over some disappointments… It's up to YOU!

At times if there are several areas at the same time, you can be on overload. If the same type of situation keeps repeating itself, you really should take a look at it more closely.

Some people get into wishful thinking or it is always the other guy's fault. At times it's that phrase, 'If only….' None of that gets the job done and you get 'stuck.'

Now with the real deal… love, of course, there are a myriad of disappointments, both small and large.

Here is where the heart gets involved and it is no longer merely a mental exercise. It is a visceral, feeling business. This is never easy.

It can be, and I will present it from a female's point of view, any number of things. The male version is similar.

I wish he had called… brought flowers, said what I wanted to hear, helped me out, and bought me something I wanted… and on and on.

When there is intimacy all and everything can be talked out. What happens after that is what counts.

Did anybody really listen? Did behavior change? Who is trying to please whom?

How you relate your disappointment is a key factor in all of this as well. The phrase, 'You never….' Or an attack of the person in anger does not make someone want to please you. Taking it back generations, 'You are just like your father….' also doesn't endear you.

If your requests are not demands and not unreasonable you should be able to get your message across.

It is also a two-way street. He has needs and requests too. A good method is to exchange requests, one at a time, and see if they can be met. It isn't always fifty-fifty, but it can be negotiated. Try it.

If requests are couched in words like, 'I would really appreciate it if you would'… helps.

Now we are not automatons and there are times when we are so frustrated or downright angry, or if the same request is unheeded, that we lash out. It only means we are human. Soon we may be replaced by robots and then see what happens!!

One of the 'cures' is to look at what really matters and what bothers and upsets you, and makes you feel unloved. Then if it cannot change maybe, you can change your expectations. Then you will not be setting yourself up for disappointment.

If you are mature enough and love enough it will happen and you move on.

If however, it is a major obstacle in the relationship that you cannot get over and your partner cannot change you may have to reconsider whether this is the right relationship for you. Put it on a scale with the positives on one side and the negatives on the other then weigh them and see where you come out.

True love will accept a lot of disappointment and go on. It will!!

“You will never be happier than you expect. To change your happiness, change your expectation.” - Bette Davis

Tell Me Something... About Love

"Love doesn't make the world go 'round. Love is what makes the ride worthwhile." - Franklin P. Jones

Recently I was in a lovely restaurant and noticed a table nearby with about seven thirty something attractive young women. I thought that was a great group to tell about my blog, so when it was time to leave I stopped by and spoke about it.

They were very interested and then one of them said, 'Tell us three things we should know about love.'

I thought for a brief moment and then said, 'It always ends, you should be an independent person, and give him what no one else can.' They laughed and applauded.

On the way home, I began to think about that experience and wondered if I gave the best answer, and what do any of us really know about love.

It is that amorphous thing the world has struggled to define since time immemorial.

Whatever your definition is, you only know it from how you feel and experience that other person in relationship with you. Are there some universals, or is it all just totally subjective?

Are there varieties, or levels, or is it one big bang theory?

In my view, there are any number of ways to love, and there can be levels of caring that can vacillate over time, BUT the big bang theory works when you feel it intensely and want to merge into ONE with that other person. If you have been 'there', you know what I am speaking about.

If not, you may be on the search. We have all read, heard, watched, or dreamed about this.

Once experienced you can NEVER go back and be content without it. It is magical.

Now does it last forever? I think not, although I have known couples who have kept it alive for decades.

Here are some ideas about how to do that. You must never take real love for granted.

Be interesting. There are plenty of others out there.

Put a note in his/her shoe, under his pillow, in his pocket.

Guys, buy her a shiny something, for no reason. It is a silent reminder of your caring and appreciation forever.

Get a star named for your lover. You can do this on-line.

Rent a billboard or take out an ad in a local paper.

Buy her sexy lingerie.

Greet him in just an apron when he gets home from work.

Wake up at midnight for a walk or bubble bath.

Go to a park and make love… avoid the police!

Get a gift inscribed with a message and date.

Hold hands and twist ankles at restaurants, movies, etc.

Read poetry to one another.

Play a love song on his cell phone and don't say anything.

Just be creative.

Being independent is necessary in this life, as we NEVER know what can happen.

And last of all; do give him, or her, what no one else can. That will be the real test. When you know someone from the inside out, so to speak, you can deliver in ways that are unique, special, and truly appreciated. Being appreciated is SO important; it should be in word AND deed, and regularly.

We all seek both routine and excitement, and being with a beloved has to include both. Give love power, and fantasy.

Without it, there is despair, and never worry about what anyone else thinks. Only you know what you need when it comes to love.

Sharing mind, heart, and body is what this life is about. Everything else is second best at most.

So, if you have found it, cherish it, revel in it, and do not let it go. We usually only find it no more than two or three times in a lifetime… the real thing.

Do not stand on ceremony, and do not be a doormat, but get your message out if you believe you see it. Attraction starts the ball rolling, and lust will fan the fire, but love takes talk, intimacy, and time. When your eyes connect in that deep, deep manner, you may be on to something. In addition, make sure it is honest, that differences can be resolved, and that goals are similar. Then maybe, just maybe, you are one of the few lucky ones out there. Bravo!! The message is that you do not want to live without giving your love to this person!!!

"The only abnormality is the incapacity to love." - Anais Nin

Text Me... Maybe I Could Love You

"Be still when you have nothing to say; when genuine passion moves you, say what you've got to say, and say it hot." - D.H. Lawrence

The next generation will have thumbs twice the size they are today from the new form of communication: texting.

Everyone is doing it, all the time. It's the only thing that gets immediate response, usually.

Mobile phones are the source of connecting.

A recent study showed about 764 messages per person were sent by text each month compared to 165 in 2012! Wow!

Men as usual, usually make the first move. It is less risky for him as he can move on right away from instant rejection and it's easier for the females to say 'no' without having to confront him.

It makes flirting 'safer'.

People today are used to group activities from childhood and they can move more easily, not investing time or effort into relationships that don't click right away.

It makes dating less expensive; no more dinner and a movie before sex, and it takes away any thought of further commitment, or guilt over a guy spending money for dinner on you. It can be a test to see how you feel over just a drink, for example.

Some guys send the same message to a number of women and see who takes the bait. They just want to 'hang out.'

The new technology gives you the control over where the relationship may go. Talking can take time and many don't want that today. Hearing a voice and engaging is a whole different matter. It's more 'work.'

First dates are the test for the chemistry between two people and NOTHING replaces that.

What gets me these days is seeing people at a restaurant and both texting or on cell phones. What kind of relating to one another is that?

And that's the problem as I see it. How to discover one another directly and how to really connect.

The follow up is when sex comes into the picture right away. What kind of relationship is that?

What do they talk about? What are the words spoken? For real fun, they should get those body pens and write messages on each other that would be like texting and then they could lick it off!!! My suggestion!

Sex is a bond but not a relationship to build on. That takes intimate communication and baring one's feelings. Texting doesn't teach people how to do that.

But for starters, it can break the ice and get the 'thing' going. What happens afterwards is anybody's guess.

Another very intriguing study showed that at the beginning of relationships women and men experience equal lust BUT after from one to four years later, women's interest begins to wane.

A new drug to enhance women's sex drive was recently put to the test. It definitely made the women want sex but the problem was that while dopamine giving impulse was strong they had to make the serotonin work in balance as that caused inhibition and organization. Manipulating these two components isn't easy. We need drive and thought together. Feelings cannot be texted so easily.

Instant love is never available. Pills can only do so much.

The delight and suffering that love requires is not easy to learn. Texting someone that looks good may be a first step for this generation to reach LOVE.

"Of all virtues the virtue of patience is most foreign to youth." - John Jay Chapman

When To Give Up... Hope

"IF TWO PEOPLE LOVE EACH other there can be no happy end to it." - Ernest Hemingway

Sad, but true. There is always some sort of ending… and of, course, the ultimate ending, death!

When you have been in a relationship and it has been able to withstand all the ups and downs and then at some point both participants, or usually one, reaches a dead end and says it is over the other must accept it, try to fix it, or ruminate with both hate and love.

So long as there is life, there is hope. If you go on hoping that he, or she, will realize their mistake, be miserable without you, and want you back, many emotions roll around inside you.

If you look at all the people who have withstood the loss of love, you will see that most find another person to share their love with. It's sort of like when your dog dies, you grieve, and the best solution is to get a new puppy. Transfer those feelings.

If your partner has died that is a definite end. People like Joan Rivers writes about this. Her husband committed suicide. Not only that but she lost her job and had huge financial problems. Now she is an intelligent woman with a fantastic sense of humor, and she talks about what she did to get over that loss. Mostly kept busy doing things she liked with people she liked, and went to work, and had her mind think about moving on.

When the loss is not due to the final ending it is more difficult.

Having worked with so many people in this position, I know how hard and long it takes to get over, if ever, a real love.

The good news is that there is usually another person to love along the way. The world is full of people hungry for love and if you are one of the lucky few who know how, you will be found…and appreciated.

We all want that special someone to light up for and to give our affection to. There is a new revelation just out about the love of President Harding and how he wrote long letters to her while he was married. Everyone wants it, not all will risk what it takes to get it and hold on to it. That's the education we should all have. Better than ANY diploma!

All of us are imperfect and just want to get through this life the best we can. It is love that let's the best feelings out.

So, if he, or she, has slipped away, or run away, and you still share deep true love it may take time to rekindle the fire. Pride has no place here, and it never matters who calls whom. If it is genuine, it will last.

Now, I am not talking about the ho hum lives, 'making do' or living a life 'sucking it up' style. I am talking about the real McCoy. You know it if you have experienced it. Once you have, life is joyless, empty, and hollow without it.

Most of us don't basically change but we do for love. Maybe one or both need to do some honest soul searching and try to accommodate and be sensitive to the other's feelings. Maybe the fantasy will wear off, but you still want to be connected. If you really do not want life without that person, you have love. If you do, there is always hope. We do not love in a vacuum. If you feel it, your partner probably does too.

If the breakup is due to all those possible practical reasons, maybe the feelings cannot surmount them; but just maybe they can. Talk, talk, and talk some more.

My own bias is that two people who truly love will find a way to be happy together… most of the time. Without unhappiness, how would you know you are happy??

Forgiveness is the biggy here. No matter for what… unless it is really horrendous.

Not having sex will also be an issue as people in love show it physically. You have to stay focused and know that in the end if all else fails, and there is indeed no hope to come together…know you are capable of moving on.

And yes, there are others out there.

If you stay in a glunk no one wants to be around you, but with a smile to start, and verve as you move on, you will be noticed.

Think of all you have to offer, and put that hope on the next one finding you, not on what you need to leave. Time will help…it will. The biggest help is your attitude and when you think hope is gone, you GO!!

"If you love someone, let them go. If they return to you, it was meant to be. If they don't, their love was never yours to begin with." - Anonymous

Ties That Bind... Suffocate

"REAL LONELINESS CONSISTS NOT IN being alone, but in being with the wrong person, in the suffocating darkness of a room in which no deep communication is possible." - Sydney J. Harris

Ever been there? Most of us have at some point in our lives, and many live out their entire lives in that arid land.

It is true we are born alone and die alone but it is the in- between that counts.

How do we share ourselves, and under what circumstances, and then the biggy; with whom?

One of the primary questions in all of this has to be have we even taken the time to explore ourselves and deal with our 'good' and 'bad' selves? Have we come to terms with accepting who we are and do we basically like who we are? All of this takes time, insight, and strength. Not easy, BUT necessary, before we can connect even superficially with another.

To bare oneself, beyond the physical, although that too is no cakewalk, is something that should be done in small steps to test the reactions and hopefully acceptance of who we REALLY are. There can be NO secrets in thoughts, and emotions, within a true love relationship. The immediate emotions are what matters. You can tell if it is the truth even if the words belie, because feelings are real and most are accurate. Trust the feelings, not just the words. Many can't even get out 'those' kinds of words.

So now you are emotionally bound, in some fashion and on some level.

If the pattern is shallow and superficial, the ties are negligible. The talk is about daily activity, news, other people, weather, plans, past history, or other necessary nonsense. Fine, that can take up a life and it can bind people together. Busy work!

In many instances, there is an element of control exercised because one or both parties know the hold is flimsy and not a deep emotional one. That makes the old remembered big bad parent, (usually Mama), or old schoolmarm personality, rear its' ugly head. Usually it is ugly and therefore the one partner knows they cannot hold the other partner any other way. Scared partners, or those trying to please, for whatever reason, fall into this category, and heel to the 'dictator.' Habits then take over.

Now these ties are there, and can be strong, or rationalized. Hopefully, at some point, the controlled one will look for and may find ways to break out and be free… like adolescents do.

It is healthier and won't lead to more destructive means to ameliorate the situation, and wrestle free. Duty works in the military, not in bed!

NOTHING brings happiness fully beyond being a free person able to love and thereby be loved completely….no ties. Freely chosen and freely given.

If you deliver real love, you NEVER have to worry about your partner going anywhere else.

Only YOU can bring that full complete feeling.

If you see parents asking their teens a million questions about where they are going, what they did, and so on, you immediately know they do not trust them. As teens that is appropriate until they proved themselves trustworthy over time.

So too in adult relationships. Happy people are not controlling; making partners alcoholics, drug users, and angry, embittered people looking for a way out. The long lasting sad ones get sick over their frustration and buried resentment and anger.

The prison marriage reflects this. Those ties that bind are awful. They are tight and suffocating and you can see the life being squeezed out day by day until there is nothing left but hollow emptiness; acquiescence, covering if not anger, rage! And the saddest part is that this is exactly what their children see and in 99% of the cases duplicate it in their own lives. Great education!

There are a number of professions that lead into this pattern; anyone with authority and the strong use of it brings it with them; it can't be avoided unless a lot of insight or help takes place. Find a bossy boss and I can tell you what goes on at home. We are not two different people, but some can change.

Being accountable, asking how and when to share things is no problem and it's only when that line is crossed that you have the noose around the neck. Look for it; don't let anyone do it to you, let alone slip it on yourself. Ties are lovely when you buy and use them together joyously and, loosely

Breath free!!! OR ELSE…

"The physical union of the sexes… only intensifies man's sense of solitude." - Nicolas Berdyaev

Time to End It

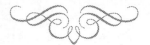

"When life looks like it is falling apart, it may just be falling in place." - Beverly Solomon

There is no such thing as a perfect relationship. The beginnings are usually magical and wonderful. We look at the beloved with those proverbial rose colored glasses. We make them our 'fantasy' love. We accept and forgive things that we formerly would not.

As a relationship progresses we all know that moment when the light goes off and we realize this is not the person I thought he or she was.

By this time a whole raft of things may be going on; responsibilities that take time and attention, perhaps children come into the picture, money issues, work related concerns, and so on. This is a test.

Is there enough to keep it going?

For many the adjustment works and they go on. The closeness, intimacy, talk, touch, and of course, sex, can work wonders and smooth over many bumps and even big upheavals.

How differences get resolved is a biggy here.

Criticizing the behavior, not the person helps. Getting the feelings of hurt or anger out is absolutely necessary. Who apologizes and is it always the same person?

Does the 'injured' party make themselves understood… really?

What are the issues? Are they always the same? Are they in fact, important?

There is no 'winning' in these cases. It is truly just deeper understanding which will move the relationship along and make it more intimate. If it is a control issue or one upmanship, or seen as a defeat or loss of face, that will not make a mature and lasting resolution. Pride has no place here.

If you have gone over the same ground a hundred times and there is no change in behavior it may be time to either take it for what it is, if there is enough other positive, forgive the partner who has a blind area, or if it is too hurtful too often, time to end it.

Life is about mostly small, daily, boring things. The fun comes from a whole mess of outside and internal behaviors that make it interesting, and joyful.

You know my theory, that without love and passion you might as well be dead. The fact is that there are huge numbers of the 'walking dead.'

Look around, watch the interaction between couples, and listen to what is said. The proof is always in the behavior, not the words.

Now you can focus on the negative or you can try to pitch to the positive but when the negative outweighs the positive and you have tried your damnedest to correct it and nothing changes. Get on with your life!!

Sometimes we expect the impossible or have unrealistic desires, or unreasonable hurts. That all has to be looked at... honestly.

Sometimes a relationship has served a purpose and outlived its' usefulness, to be blunt about it. People do change and needs do not stay static. However, after a certain age, and no one knows when, there should be a level of maturity.

The heart, however, and the feelings attached to it may not grow or expand. Acceptance and forgiveness may not be possible and then you need to move on. There are too many people out there hungry for real love to stay going around the same merry-go-round going nowhere forever.

Love means that your joy comes from loving and giving of yourself in every way possible to your partner. If you are not a martyr and there is little returned for your needs, then you should find someone else.

There are some situations or times in the course of a relationship where one or the other is limited and this should balance out over time. It is almost never a constant fifty-fifty and that's fine.

Two people from different backgrounds and experiences in childhood learn to accommodate one another; some more successfully than others however.

Growth emotionally, life experiences, and intimacy keep love alive.

If you are the one ending it you will still feel that horrible empty feeling in your stomach, wonder if you did the right thing, miss many aspects about that person and what you shared.

If the decision is a good one you have to give it a bit of time, and always remember the reasons for the ending.

I promise you, life will go on, it will not be on the six o'clock news and you will live to have another relationship that will be better because of what you learned!! I promise!!

"Resentment is one burden that is incompatible with your success. Always be the first to forgive; and forgive yourself first always." - Dan Zadra

Printed in the United States
By Bookmasters